AF654714

ACADEMIC LIBRARY AUTOMATION

ACADEMIC LIBRARY AUTOMATION

By

Dr. Ajaykumar Raval *Ph.D.*

Librarian

B.K. Mercantile Bank Law College

Palanpur

(India)

DPH

DISCOVERY PUBLISHING HOUSE PVT. LTD.

NEW DELHI-110 002

Published by:
Tilak Wasan

DISCOVERY PUBLISHING HOUSE PVT. LTD.
4383/4B, Ansari Road, Darya Ganj
New Delhi-110 002 (India)
Phone : +91-11-23279245, 43596064-65
Fax : +91-11-23253475
E-mail : discoverypublishinghouse@gmail.com
sales@discoverypublishinggroup.com
parul.wasan@gmail.com
web : www.discoverypublishinggroup.com

***First Edition:* 2013**

ISBN: 978-93-5056-363-2

Academic Library Automation

© 2013, Author

All rights reserved. No part of this publication should be reproduced, stored in a retrieval system, or transmitted in any form or by any means: electronic, mechanical, photocopying, recording or otherwise, without the prior written permission of the author and the publisher.

This book has been published in good faith that the material provided by authors is original. Every effort is made to ensure accuracy of material, but the publisher and printer will not be held responsible for any inadvertent error(s). In case of any dispute, all legal matters are to be settled under Delhi jurisdiction only.

Printed at:
Dynamic Printers
Delhi

Contents

Preface

Library automation refers to the use of computers to serve the needs of library users. The operations of a library get a quantum jump with the introductions of computers. The computers help to provide fast and reliable access to the resources available in the library as well as elsewhere. The application of computers in the library operations avoids repetitive jobs and saves lot of labour, time, speeds up operations, increases use of library resources. Computers are not only used as a tool for processing the data, but also for data storage and accessing.

Automation should always be used as a means to achieve overall better patron service. Careful planning for technology will assure that your automation project is sustainable, i.e., enhances the organization's ability to meet its service mission without disrupting the organizational stability of the institution.

—Author

1

Library Automation

AN INTRODUCTION

Since, the 1960s, libraries have used technology in general, and computers in particular, to automate a wide range of administrative, public, and technical services tasks. Designed as an overview of major facets of automation activity, this chapter surveys the current state of computer applications in six areas of library work: circulation control, descriptive cataloguing, catalogue maintenance and production, reference service, acquisitions, and serials control. For each area, the discussion briefly indicates the motives for automation and describes current dominant approaches, citing examples of representative products and services.

CIRCULATION CONTROL

Library interest in automated circulation control is, in large part, based on a long-standing awareness of the problems inherent in manual circulation systems. These problems include labour-intensive and time-consuming record keeping work routines, inaccuracy, high personnel turnover, an inability to generate statistics about circulation activity, and the lack of an interface between circulation files and other library files which contain much the same bibliographic data. Circulation control is one of the most widely automated library operations, and it is often the first and simplest activity to be automated in a given library, possibly because circulation control systems bear an obvious resemblance to inventory management, retail charge card operations, and other transaction processing activities which have been successfully automated in general business applications.

While specific circulation policies and procedures may be subject to considerable local variation, the major component of circulation control-the check-out/check-in procedure—is typically performed in a straight forward manner that is easily understood by computer application developers and systems analysts lacking formal library training. As library users, many data processing professionals have experienced the circulation activity firsthand and are at least broadly familiar with its purpose and nature. Because the bibliographic data required for automated circulation control are often less extensive and complex than those required to computerise such activities as cataloguing and acquisitions, data conversion costs, software development time, and storage requirements may be substantially reduced. Perhaps more than any other library activity, the historical development of automated circulation control has reflected changes in state- of-the-art data processing technology.

Through the mid-1970s, most automated circulation control systems were custom-developed for a single library or library system. As early as the 1930s and extending into the 1960s, a number of libraries used keypunched cards in combination with sorters, collators, and other unit record equipment as an alternative to manual record keeping. Tabulating keypunched cards with information about books, borrowers, and due dates could be sorted to select overdue items or to identify all books on loan to a given person. Such 'precomputer' data processing systems, several of which were developed for academic libraries by methods and procedures analysts and operations research specialists, were typically based on inventory control models used in business.

With the introduction of computers for business applications in the mid-1960s, a number of libraries developed computerised circulation control systems based on batch processing techniques. Such systems were usually implemented on a computer located in a data processing centre operated by a university, municipality, corporation, or government agency with which the library was affiliated. In the typical installation, keypunch or key-to-tape devices were used to convert information about individual circulation transactions to computer-processible form.

The resulting data were then hatched for processing at predetermined intervals, a computer writing individual borrower numbers into item records contained in a master circulation file maintained on magnetic tape and printing a list of all items in circulation for library reference. While some of these batch-processing circulation control systems remain in use, they are now mainly of interest for their limitations and impact on the design of subsequent systems. As a particular disadvantage, the printed lists produced by batch-processing systems necessarily reflect the status of a library's circulating collection at the time when the last batch of transaction records was processed. Part of the information contained in such lists is necessarily invalidated by circulation transactions occurring after that time. By the mid-1970s, library automation specialists had begun to concentrate on the development of online, real-time circulation control systems which process circulation transactions as they occur. Because pertinent data files are updated immediately, such real-time systems accurately reflect the status of a library's circulating collection. Printed lists are replaced by online terminal enquiries to determine the circulation status of specific items.

While real-time circulation control systems have been custom- developed for individual libraries, a number of vendors offer generalised, preformulated approaches to the computerisation of circulation control that eliminate the need for customised system development and speed the implementation process.

Such preformulated approaches, currently the dominant method of automating circulation control, can be divided into two related groups:

- Prewritten circulation control software intended for execution on a computer system operated by or for a given library; and

- Turnkey systems, consisting of preconfigured combinations of hardware and software marketed as self-contained products.

Introduced in the early 1970s, the earliest prewritten circulation control software packages and turnkey circulation systems were single-purpose products designed specifically and exclusively for library circulation activities. While such single-purpose systems remain available, library administrators, systems analysts, automation planners, and pro- duct developers are increasingly emphasising integrated, multifunctional turnkey systems and software packages which combine circulation control with other capabilities.

In addition to circulation control, the most complete integrated system implementations include interrelated application modules for cataloguing, online catalogue access by library users and/or staff, acquisitions, and serials control, a community bulletin board system, and electronic message transmission. In some cases, circulation is a standard integrated system component which may be implemented alone or in conjunction with other functions; in others, circulation control is an optional application module which must be purchased separately. Whether designed as single-purpose products or as integrated system components, prewritten circulation software packages and turnkey systems can be implemented far more quickly than customised circulation control systems which may require months or perhaps years to develop. Speed of implementation is an especially important consideration in applications where automation of the circulation activity will result in a cost reduction.

Similarly, prewritten software packages and turnkey systems minimize or eliminate requirements for local software expertise. Libraries acquiring such products usually do not need to hire programmers. In fact, customer programming is specifically prohibited by most vendors. Because the system design is predetermined, user training is limited to operational considerations. As a distinctive advantage of turnkey implementations, procurement-related tasks are greatly simplified by the availability of a preconfigured combination of hardware and software components that are specifically designed to work together. With a single source for central processing equipment and peripheral devices, the necessity of dealing with multiple hardware vendors is eliminated, as are potential problems of equipment compatibility.

While prewritten circulation control software packages are available for computers of all types and sizes, medium-sized and larger public and academic libraries have typically relied on mainframe—and minicomputer-based products. Examples for IBM mainframes include the NOTIS software package, originally developed by Northwestern University for its own use; IBM's own DOBIULIBIS programme; and the TECHLIB/STATS implementation of the BASIS software package which is marketed by the Information Dimensions subsidiary of Battelle.

Originally developed by libraries in the Minnesota State University system, the PALS software package is marketed by Unisys for use with its own mainframe computers, while the LIAS system, developed by Pennsylvania State University, operates on Honeywell computers. Examples of circulation software packages for popular minicomputer systems include Comstow's Bibliotech system for Digital Equipment's VAX product line; the Georgetown Library Information System (LIS) for Digital's PDP-11 Series models; the Washington University BACS system for Data General and other minicomputers which run under the MIIS operating environment; and the VTLS and Index systems for the Hewlett-Packard HP-3000 product line. Minicomputer- based turnkey circulation control systems are available from CLSI, Geac, Data Research Associates (DRA), Dynix, OCLC, Universal Library Systems, and other vendors.

Reasonably priced and designed for readily available hardware configurations, microcomputer-based circulation control programmes have proven particularly popular with small public, school, and special libraries. Vendors include

Follett, Gaylord, Easy Data, Data Trek, Aball Software, Nichols Advanced Technologies, Scribe Software, Winnebago Software, and Richmond Software. While the earliest circulation control programmes and turnkey systems forced libraries to accept predetermined loan periods, borrower categories, and other operating parameters, most newer products flexibly support a varied range of library requirements.

Unlike earlier systems which contained rigidly coded procedures to control charging, discharging, and related activities, all newer products are parameterised, *i.e.*, they allow libraries to specify the conditions under which items will be circulated, file enquiries made, and printed output produced. Rather than being written into programmes, particular operating parameters are selected by libraries from a range of possibilities. The resulting flexibility broadens the range of applications which a given system can address and is particularly important in installations where a single prewritten software package or turnkey system will be shared by many libraries.

AUTOMATED CATALOGUING

Descriptive cataloguing is an intellectual activity requiring considerable decision-making and one that is time-consuming. As a result, many libraries experience cataloguing backlogs which impede the flow of materials into circulating and reference collections thereby preventing library catalogues from representing those collections fully and accurately. Recognising that the cost of descriptive cataloguing can approach or even exceed the value of certain materials, many libraries do not catalogue paperbound books, low-cost government publications, or other relatively inexpensive items.

In some research libraries, materials of presumably limited interest may be placed in off-site storage facilities with only an abbreviated catalogue record created. In most libraries, conventional descriptive cataloguing is not even considered for individual titles in large microform sets, even though such materials may significantly augment a library's resources in particular subject areas, and the failure to catalogue them impairs their utility. To simplify decision-making, to save time, and to reduce costs associated with descriptive cataloguing, libraries have historically relied on cataloguing copy, *i.e.*, descriptive cataloguing information prepared by other libraries, especially the Library of Congress.

The automation of descriptive cataloguing depends on the availability of such cataloguing copy in computer-processible form. In the late 1960s, the Library of Congress developed the MARC format for the communication of bibliographic data on magnetic tape and began distributing machine- readable cataloguing copy through its MARC Distribution Service. Since, the late 1960s, MARC formats have been developed for various types of library materials, and the scope of the MARC programme-once limited to English-language monographs—has broadened steadily and significantly. The LC MARC database-the accumulation of Library of Congress cataloguing data in machine-readable form-now contains more than 2.5 million records, most of them catalogued since, the inception of the MARC programme.

Although MARC tapes can be purchased from the Library of Congress for input to local computer systems, most libraries obtain access to MARC data through products and services developed by publishers, computer system developers, time-sharing services, and other intermediaries. Among the earliest of these MARC-derivative products were computer-generated micro publications such as MARCFICHE, produced by MARC Applied Research, and Books in English produced by the British Library. Created by Computer-output Microfilm (COM) technology, both products provided more timely and varied access to LC cataloguing data than could be obtained through the conventionally printed National Union Catalogue, which was itself discontinued in favour of a COM implementation in the early 1980s.As an equally timely and flexible alternative, several search services, including DIALOG and WILSONLINE, offer online access to the LCMARC database.

A growing number of vendors supply the MARC database on CD-ROM disks or digital optical videodiscs accompanied by software which supports the retrieval of specific cataloguing records and the printing of card sets. Examples include the BIBLIOFILE system from the Library Corporation in Washington, D.C., the LASERSEARCH system from General Pesearch Corporation, and the MINI MARC II system from Library Systems and Services Incorporated. Although these products and services are important, most libraries obtain access to machine-readable cataloguing records through one of the bibliographic utilities-organisations which maintain large databases of cataloguing records and offer online access and other services to subscribing libraries.

Examples include the Online Union Catalogue implemented by the Online Computer Library Centre (OCLC), the Research Libraries Information Network (RLIN) operated by the Research Libraries Group, the cataloguing support service operated by the Western Library Network (WLN), the Cataloguing Support System (CATSS) offered by Utlas International, the LIONS system operated by the New York Public Library, the AGILE II service offered by Auto-Graphics Incorporated, and Brodart's Interactive Access System (IAS).

While they differ in database size and composition, the number and nature of their subscribers, and the specific capabilities they support, these bibliographic utilities each maintain a database of MARC records obtained from the Library of Congress and other sources, supplemented by original MARC-format cataloguing contributed by subscribing libraries. Working at local terminals, participating libraries can retrieve cataloguing copy, modify it to meet local requirements, and order printed card sets, machine-readable cataloguing records on magnetic tape, and other bibliographic products.

Local workstations are also used to input original cataloguing records for use by other subscribers. Supporting thousands of online terminals accessing millions of machine-readable records, the bibliographic utilities are among the world's largest and most intensively utilised computer-based information services.

COMPUTER-PRODUCED CATALOGUES

The automation of descriptive cataloguing addresses only one part of the cataloguing activity. In addition to using computers to facilitate access to cataloguing copy, libraries are interested in computer-based solutions to the much discussed problems of card catalogues. The most frequently cited of such problems include substantial space consumption; the purchase of expensive cabinets and supporting furniture; labour-intensive and time-consuming catalogue maintenance routines which are intensified by changes in cataloguing rules affecting the choice and form of entries; and limited convenience and retrieval capabilities.

These problems can be minimized or eliminated by the replacement of card catalogues with computer-based book-form or online catalogues. Broadly defined, a book-form catalogue contains successive bibliographic records listed in a page format on paper or microforms. Among the earliest applications of library automation, computer preparation of book-form catalogues can lower production time and costs while eliminating the labour-intensive file maintenance routines associated with card catalogues.

As an alternative to computer printed or typeset catalogues, computer-output microfilm catalogues have been widely implemented by libraries and library systems since, the early 1970s. A number of service bureaus, book jobbers, bibliographic utilities, and other vendors have developed software to produce COM catalogues from library-supplied data, thereby eliminating the need for in-house COM recorders and customised programming catalogues. Broadly defined, an online catalogue is an organised, machine-readable accumulation of bibliographic records which are maintained on disks or other direct-access computer storage media for retrieval by library users and staff members working at interactive terminals or appropriately configured microcomputer workstations. In addition to saving space and automating file maintenance, online catalogues permit remote access by authorised persons equipped with compatible terminals, and they can support information retrieval operations—such as keyword searching of titles and series names—which are not conveniently possible with card or book-form catalogues.

Online catalogues may be custom-developed for specific library installations or purchased as prewritten software packages or turnkey systems. Examples of custom-developed online catalogues include the Library of Congress Computerised Catalogue, the MELVYL system at the University of California, the LIAS system at Pennsylvania State University, the Library Computer System (LCS) at Ohio State University, and the Dartmouth College Online Catalogue. Prewritten software packages suitable for online catalogue implementations include BRS/SEARCH from BRS Information Technologies, a powerful information retrieval programme that is available in mainframe, minicomputer, and microcomputer versions; INMAGIC, a versatile data management programme for dominated by integrated library systems which combine database management and catalogue access capabilities with circulation control, acquisitions, serials control, and other operations.

Such systems may be implemented as complete turnkey configurations of hardware and software or as prewritten software packages designed to operate on a library owned mainframe, minicomputer, or microcomputer. Vendors include CLSI, Geac, Notis, Dynix, OCLC, Virginia Tech, Data Research Associates, Carlyle, Comstow Information Systems, Universal Library Systems, Sobeco, Sigma Data/Centel, George- town Medical Library, Washington University, IBM, Inlex, Sirsi, Utlas, Innovative Interfaces, Eyring Research Institute, Easy Data, Data Trek, and Unisys. Among the newest and most widely publicised approaches to online catalogue implementation, a growing number of vendors offer public access catalogue systems which employ CD-ROM storage technology. Examples include the IMPACT system from Auto-Graphics, LASERGUIDE from General Research, THE INTELLIGENT CATALOGUE from the Library Corporation, and the LEPAC system from Brodart.

In such implementations, the library provides a machine-readable version of its catalogue, typically consisting of MARC format records on magnetic tapes obtained from bibliographic utilities or other sources, to a CD-ROM system vendor who indexes and otherwise prepares it for conversion to one or more CD-ROM disks. The disks themselves are created by a mastering process in special manufacturing facilities, and the library receives a specified number of disk copies plus menu-driven software designed for public catalogue access at microcomputer-based workstations. Updated by periodic replacement in the manner of book-form catalogues, such CD-ROM catalogues are increasingly mentioned as an alternative to computer output microfilm for union catalogues and similar implementations.

AUTOMATED REFERENCE SERVICE

Since, the late 1960s, many publishers of printed bibliographies, indexing and abstracting journals, and other reference works have offered machine-readable versions of their products for use in computer assisted reference applications. Initially intended for government, corporate, and academic libraries supporting research in scientific and technical disciplines, such machine-readable reference sources have become widely available in business, the social sciences, and the humanities. In addition to databases which correspond to printed publications, a growing number of reference sources have been developed specifically for use in computer-based systems and have no printed counterparts.

While the earliest machine-readable databases were bibliographic in character, non-bibliographic numeric and directory-type databases are increasingly commonplace. During the late 1960s and early 1970s, a number of libraries purchased machine-readable bibliographic and non-bibliographic data- bases for processing on in-house computers using custom-developed information retrieval software. Most libraries, however, lacked access to the hardware and software resources required to implement such systems.

Through the early 1970s,the needs of such libraries were addressed by fee-based search services operated by the producers of machine-readable databases or other organisations such as large research libraries. Such services, which operated in the offline, batch processing mode, were replaced in the mid- 1970s by services offering online database searching on a time sharing basis to libraries equipped with conventional terminals.

Now widely utilised by libraries of all types and sizes, online search services can be divided into two broad groups:

- Multidisciplinary services—including DIALOG, BRS, ORBIT, WILSONLINE, DATA- STAR, and ESA-IRS-that provide database coverage of a varied range of subjects for a broad clientele; and
- Specialised services-such as the NLM SEARCH SERVICE, STN INTERNATIONAL, LEXIS, and WESTLAW-that provide online access to one or more databases relevant to a single subject discipline, profession, or activity, such as medicine, law, or engineering.

Various types of specialised search services provide online access to databases containing a specific type of information such as news. Examples include the NEXIS, VUITEXT, DATA TIMES, and NEWSNET search services. While they differ in the number and type of databases offered and in the specific retrieval capabilities supported, multidisciplinary and specialised search services share a common operating methodology: they purchase or otherwise obtain bibliographic and non-bibliographic data-bases in machine-readable form from their producers, convert the dataases to a form required for storage on their computers, and allow libraries or other subscribers to perform various retrieval operations on such data using prewritten data-base management software. The software features a non-procedural query language which permits a user at an online terminal to initiate litreature searches or other information retrieval operations by entering specified commands.

While their query languages are relatively easy to learn, online search services are more often providing menu-driven interfaces for novice users. Some services also offer private file capabilities which allow libraries to establish their own databases. As a recently implemented supplement or alternative to online search services, an increasing number of bibliographic and non-bibliographic databases are available on CD-ROM disks. Accompanied by information retrieval software, such CD-ROM reference products permit database searching at local microcomputer workstations (over 100 titles were available at the time of this writing). Offered on a subscription basis, they can prove less expensive than online searching for databases that are accessed frequently, although infrequent updating, slow response time for complex searches, and other performance limitations may make them unsuitable for some applications.

As a hybrid implementation with potentially attractive cost/performance characteristics, several vendors combine CD-ROM searching of back file data with online access to the most current information.

ACQUISITIONS

More informed decision-making through improved statistical analysis and reporting of procurement activity is the most frequently cited motive for automating acquisitions operations. Since, the 1960s, automated acquisitions systems have been implemented in at least four different ways: as a custom-developed programme designed to operate on a computer owned by a library or its parent organisation; as an acquisitions-specific prewritten software package or turnkey system; as an application module supported by a multifunctional integrated library system; or as a time-sharing service offered by a bibliographic utility or a book jobber.

Each method has advantages and limitations. Customised acquisitions systems, an implementation option in any automated application, can be developed to a particular library's specifications but are expensive and time-consuming to create. Prewritten acquisitions-specific software, and the acquisitions application modules supported by integrated library systems, can minimize the worst implementation problems associated with customised software development, but a library must have access to required hardware and system software components. Turnkey systems, consisting of preconfigured combinations of hardware and software, are available as both acquisitions—specific products and as integrated systems.

In the latter group, the integration of acquisitions with cataloguing and circulation in a single system offers several advantages, including the ability to establish a preliminary bibliographic record at the time an item is ordered. All of the foregoing approaches require a substantial capital investment which can be minimized if automated acquisitions capabilities are obtained on a time-sharing basis through a bibliographic utility or bookseller. Because charges are incurred as the acquisitions facility is used, this approach is especially attractive to libraries with modest annual volumes of acquisitions activity.

Use of a bibliographic utility for acquisitions offers other advantages as well. Its database can be used for bibliographic verification, and data can be transferred from cataloguing records to facilitate order preparation. In addition, the use of a single system for acquisitions and cataloguing simplifies staff training requirements, while the immediate online availability of information about the holdings of other libraries supports cooperative collection development. Acquisitions systems offered by booksellers typically feature online access to inventory data with electronic ordering capabilities.

SERIALSCONTROL

Current serials automation activities are directed towards two types of tasks-the bibliographic control of serial publications and the management of serials collections in individual libraries. The task of bibliographic control is the establishment of definitive bibliographic information about serial publications. Among automated approaches to this task, R.R. Bowker offers machine-readable versions of its various printed guides to serial publications including Ulrich's International Periodicals Directory.

The International Serials Data System (ISDS) and the International Centre for the Registration of Serials are charged with responsibility for the establishment and maintenance of a comprehensive machine-readable registry of bibliographic information about serials published through out the world. In the United States, the Library of Congress has developed a MARC format for serial publications and participates in the CONSER programme which creates and maintains a high-quality machine-readable database of cataloguing records. The CONSER data-base is maintained by OCLC, and CONSER records are disseminated through the MARC distribution service.

To manage local collections, a number of libraries and several vendors have developed systems which automate one or more aspects of serials processing, including union list production, ordering, check-in, claiming, and the routing of received issues to designated persons. Computer-based production of union lists of serials is routinely sup- ported by data management software or word processing systems. Such lists may be printed on paper or microfiche. The last option is especially useful for very long lists that will be mailed or otherwise distributed to multiple locations. As an example, microfiche is the output medium for the California Union List of Periodicals (CULP) which contains information for over 63,000 periodicals held by 700 California libraries.

The CULP database is also accessible online through BRS. As with conventional book acquisitions, computers can be used to minimize the labour-intensive sorting, filing, and other paper-handling work routines associated with manual serials processing. A number of libraries developed customised serials control systems during the 1960s and 1970s. The PHILSOM system, developed by the Washington University School of Medicine Library, is perhaps the most famous example. As an alternative to the time and expense associated with customised system development, libraries can obtain access to serials control capabilities on a time-sharing basis through subscription ser- vice companies. Examples of such time-shared serials control services include F.W. Faxon's LYNX system and the EBSCONET system offered by EBSCO Subscription Services.

Several companies and other organisations have developed pre- written software and turnkey systems designed specifically for serials control. The INNOVACQ Acquisitions and Serials Control System, for example, offers a comprehensive range of serials ordering, check-in, and claiming capabilities. It can download records from bibliographic utilities and transfer serials records to a local circulation control or public access catalogue system. Among microcomputer-based products, OCLC's SC350 Serials Control System can retrieve bibliographic information, local data, and publishers' addresses from the OCLC online union catalogue.

It facilitates the check-in of received issues, produces claims and claim cancellations, maintains binding instructions, and prints bindery slips. It can also transmit serials records to OCLC's union list component. As an alternative to single-purpose implementations, several integrated library systems support serials control modules, and others have announced such capabilities for future implementation.

PLANNING FOR LIBRARY AUTOMATION *ACADEMIC LIBRARIES*

Library Automation refers to the use of computers to serve the needs of library users. The operations of a library get a quantum jump with the introductions of computers. The computers help to provide fast and reliable access to the resources available in the library as well as elsewhere. The application of computers in the library operations avoids repetitive jobs and saves lot of labour, time, speeds up operations, increases use of library resources. Computers are not only used as a tool for processing the data, but also for data storage and accessing. Planning for an automated system, no matter how big or small, should be part of an overall long-range plan for the library. Automation should always be used as a means to achieve overall better patron service. Careful planning for technology will assure that your automation project is 'sustainable', *i.e.*, enhances the organisation's ability to meet its service mission without disrupting the organisational stability of the institution.

The present scenario of library worldwide is:

- Vastly expanded storage of indexes, statistical data bases, and document databases within the library.
- Full-text storage of documents, complete with full-text keyword searching and on-demand printing.
- Access by users to library databases from home or office, with direct downloading of information and text on demand.
- The ability to access remote databases across the country and the world, and to download information and text on demand.
- Storage of pictorial and graphic material.
- Availability of 'intelligent systems' providing transparent, one-step searching and access to various library in-house and remote databases.

These capabilities and far more have become reality. Accordingly, today's integrated system must not only provide access to the traditional cataloguing, circulation, public catalogue (OPAC) and acquisitions modules, but must be capable of connecting through the local system into the systems of other vendors, remote bibliographic databases, CD-ROM drives on a local area network (LAN), and the Internet.

Users are expecting that their library systems be capable of, among other things:

- Providing seamless integration between system gateway and OPAC modules.

- Providing access for external users on the Internet to the library's OPAC.
- Monitoring the usage of remote databases that have been accessed through the gateway.
- Accessing the Internet using a variety of graphical interfaces.

Essentially, what this means is that libraries must plan to use a local library system as a vehicle for achieving access to resources outside that system. Stimulated by the Internet, which has created universal connectivity to information resources heretofore unknown and/or inaccessible, and by Z39.50 interoperability standards and 'gateways,' users of individual local systems are expecting to access the resources of other systems—anywhere and anytime. Moreover, the traditional definition of 'publishing' has been stretched by the creation and instant availability of informational home pages and Web sites worldwide.

Given such increased complexities and heightened levels of expectation, libraries must learn all the more how to plan for the introduction of automation in an organised and systematic fashion. There is little mystery involved here: It is entirely a matter of building upon what you already know about your library, using tools that are readily at hand and, most importantly of all, involving the people—staff and users—who must live with the consequences of any automation decisions.

WHAT IS LIBRARY AUTOMATION

Traditional library work consisting of acquisitions, technical processing, serials control, circulation and reference services all entail time consuming manual work. Though these activities are essential to proper functioning of a library, they consume professional staff time that might otherwise go towards user services and library development. Library computerisation is now gaining importance necessitating the establishment of profession-wide standards. Comprehensive studies of library computer systems world over include discussions of machine-managed acquisitions, cataloguing, serials control, circulation and bibliographic service modules. The litreature in this area highlights major aspects of computer's role in the library environment. Similar to several aspects of library management, the demand for more and faster information services and the decline in library resources are compelling librarians to appreciate the role of computers within their operations.

In general, librarians are looking to maximize the benefits of automation by spreading computer use to as many aspects of library activities as possible by taking advantage of developments in computer hardware and software and telecommunications.

NEED FOR LIBRARY AUTOMATION

Even though this question seems to be very fundamental it is essential to emphasise this aspect, as the library automation is yet to take off in majority of the Indian libraries. Secondly, while justifying need for library automation more than cost-effectiveness the benefits derived by the library users become the major consideration. To appreciate the advantages it becomes necessary to highlight the different levels of library automation.

Following are considered as important factors for Library Automation:

- Information explosion.
- Increase in the collection of libraries.
- Inability of users to explore the unlimited litreature and information of their interest.
- Advances in the computer and communication technology.
- Wastage of user/ staff time in locating the information.
- Provide wide access to resources within the libraries and elsewhere.
- Better access.
- Quality in service.
- Cooperative efforts (Resource Sharing).

Out of all libraries an academic library has a difficult task of defining its mission and operating objectives. The automation programme will have to mange a wide range of litreature associated with numerous departments and educational programmes of the academic institution. Furthermore, in an academic library the collections will be diverse unlike a special research library where the collection is relatively homogeneous.

The user group will also range widely, including faculty, staff, students, scholars, administrators and the general public. The position of an academic library funded largely by the government further complicates the process of identifying and prioritising objectives. As difficult as the task might at first appear, it is nevertheless essential to the process of establishing automated systems of any type. In addition the overall health of ones library operation will benefit from a modicum of intellectual rigour in this area.

AREAS OF LIBRARY AUTOMATION

As a first step in a planning process, it is desirable to formulate a model for computerisation listing all itemised and prioritised information systems being maintained on a manual basis by the library. For this exercise it is necessary to break down these procedures into their constituent parts. When further subdividing these activities, each item is to be considered of its functional elements. The systems and subsystems listed below are only indicative and may vary with differing library system environments.

These are:

- Acquisitions:
  - — Selection
  - — Ordering
  - — Claiming/cancellation
  - — Receiving/invoice processing
  - — Extended procurements
  - — Gift tracking
  - — Fund Control

- Maintains information about all library related funds
- Ability to group funds (nesting)
- Track fund allocations and adjustments
- Fund encumbrance
- Fund expenditure
- Cash Balance
- Free Balance
- Automatic updating of fiscal information through recording of specific transactions
- Track year-to-date expenditures
- Create Purchase Orders

- Technical Services:
  - Books
  - Serials
  - Special Collections
- Cataloguing:
  - Books
  - Serials
  - Special Collections
- Circulation:
  - Charge/Renewal
  - Discharge
  - Loan Periods
  - Processing schedules
  - Holds
  - Messages
  - Blocks
  - Notices
  - Transaction Recording Devices for off-line processing
  - Member control
  - Inventory control
- Serials Control:
  - Receipt (check-in)
  - Claiming
  - Bindery control

  - Replacements
  - Monographic serials
  - Invoice processing
- Reference Services:
  - Desk services
- User tools
- Bibliographic utilisation
- Reprography
- Inter-library communications
- General Administration
- Grants Administratiuon
- Library Publications
- Bindery
- Periodical Citation Searching
- OPAC
- Bibliographic Database

PLANNING OF LIBRARY AUTOMATION

Planning for library automation has been defined as planning for 'integrated systems' that computerise an array of traditional library functions using a common database. While this is still generally true, rapid technological change is forcing a re-examination of what it means to 'automate the library.' As physical, spatial and temporal barriers to acquiring information are crumbling, libraries must plan for a broader and more comprehensive approach to providing automated services.

DEVELOPING A LIBRARY 'PROFILE'

One of the most important planning tools involves collecting basic statistical information on the library and its operations. You will find that the same basic data will be needed again and again—whether for vendors from whom you are requesting cost estimates, or for other libraries with whom you may be seeking to cooperate in implementing automation.

The following are examples of commonly needed data:

- Number of titles and volumes in the collection, current and projected.

- Number of borrowers, current and projected.
- Number of materials circulated, current and projected.
- Number of new materials acquired, current and projected.
- Interlibrary loans, lent to and borrowed from other libraries.
- Description of any cooperative arrangements involving the library.
- Library address and hours of operation.

In addition, it is important to take stock of any existing automation in the library by compiling the following data:

- Percentage of collection that has catalogue records in machine-readable form.
- Description of collection without machine-readable records, by category, (, monographs, audiovisuals).
- Description of currently-automated library functions (if any).
- Estimates of the location and number of workstations (to show where you intend to have equipment in any future system).
- Specifications for any existing equipment to be re-used with any future system (if any).

At the same time that this data is being assembled, it is important to assess user needs and set service priorities. This can be accomplished by undertaking a focused, strategic planning process designed to involve the library's 'stakeholders.'

DEVELOPING A STRATEGIC PLAN

A library planning to automate should undertake a process by which representative staff and users can identify service needs and objectives. The purpose of such an effort is to allow participants to articulate their interests and concerns, share perspectives and learn about possibilities in a collaborative setting. Group interaction is an important contributing factor in the success of the goal, which is to develop and sustain library automation in the years ahead.

Here are the basic steps involved in this process:

- Plan on a two-day, intensive planning effort.
- Ask participants to identify strengths, weaknesses, opportunities and threats in the library's environment (known as 'SWOT' factors in strategic planning) that are characteristic of or that confront the library.
- Group these factors into critical issue areas that are likely to have an impact on the libraries' future in developing and sustaining automation.
- *Ask participants to identify ideas and perceptions in relation to the question*: "How do you see the library providing user-friendly, cost-effective automated services in five years?
- Through a method of your own devising, ask participants to prioritise all of the ideas that come out of the above two 'brainstorming' exercises.
- Ask participants to shape these priorities into the draft of a strategic 'vision' for automation development consisting of a statement of purpose, goals and objectives for the library.

SETTING SERVICE PRIORITIES

Your strategic vision must now provide the framework or context for the next step in the automation process, which is to determine which library functions should be automated and in what order of priority. For example, processes that are repetitive, occupy large amounts of staff time, require retrieving information from large, unwieldy files, or are high-profile functions of the library (such as the public catalogue) are prime candidates for automation. Determining the functions that you wish to automate and their priorities relative to each other is important for all sorts of reasons.

If needs and priorities are clear, functions can be automated in phases, allowing for more effective use of frequently scarce funding. Moreover, it is a way to develop credibility with funding agencies and be able to take advantage of 'sudden' funding opportunities. Finally, evaluations of systems and options will be easier and more productive if you are able to match your highest functional priorities against the corresponding modules available in the marketplace.

A WORD ABOUT COSTS

Speaking of funding, planners need to be aware that there are certain cost elements involved in the installation and operation of any automated system.

These may be summarised as follows:

- Planning and consulting costs include direct, out-of-pocket costs, (*e.g.*, hiring a consultant) and indirect costs, (*e.g.*, training staff) associated with getting started.
- Purchase of the system includes the cost of acquiring the initial system hardware and software, as well as the cost of preparing a site for the computer system.
- Telecommunication costs are those fees paid to telephone companies for connecting remote terminals or workstations to a central computer system.
- Conversion costs are those associated with the creation of machine-readable bibliographic and, for circulation systems, patron, records.
- On-Going Operating costs include:
  - Maintenance fees
  - Utility costs
  - Bar code labels
  - Miscellaneous supply costs
  - Telecommunications costs
  - Salaries and benefits (if extra staff are hired).
- Additions to the existing system may be required to maintain performance specifications, to accommodate new users, or to allow for additional automated functions.

SYSTEM SPECIFICATIONS

At some point, you will need to re-formulate your functional priorities into 'functional specifications,' which may be defined as what you want an automated system to do for you, including things that your current manual system cannot do. 'Technical specifications' must also be established. These include standards that must be adhered to, system performance, operation, and maintenance, as well as infrastructure requirements, such as stable sources of electricity and telecommunications, and sufficient bandwidth. Developing clear and accurate functional and technical specifications that are specific to your library is one of the most important, if not THE most important, activity that you will engage in as you plan for your automated system.

These specifications will carry you through the entire procurement process, and will ensure that the system which most closely matches them will be the most useful and the most responsive to your needs.

DEVELOPING A FORMAL SPECIFICATIONS DOCUMENT

It is very difficult to compare systems sensibly and pragmatically solely by randomly looking at systems, talking to sales representatives, reading litreature or comparing broad cost quotations. For this reason, libraries use a formal document—often known as a 'Request for Proposal,' or RFP—that organises and standardises the information provided to and requested from the various system vendors. Utilising an RFP to solicit written responses from vendors makes it possible for you to systematically compare functionality, cost, maintenance, support, and all the other issues that are involved in system procurements. The process can save you money and will result in a wiser decision.

An RFP document should include these essential elements, among others:

- Background information on the library.
- A description of how the proposals should be arranged and submitted.
- Instructions on receiving vendor business and financial information.

- Criteria the library will use to evaluate vendor proposals.
- Questions regarding vendor training and documentation.
- Your functional and technical specifications.

Also, vendors should be asked to describe:

- How they will create bibliographic, item and borrower databases.
- Their system maintenance programmes and services.
- Their site preparation requirements.
- Their delivery and installation methodologies.
- Their system performance guarantees.
- Their pricing and cost strategies, in detail.

EVALUATING VENDOR PROPOSALS

Upon the receipt of vendor proposals, it will be time to begin the process of system evaluation and selection.

This process involves a number of key steps:

- If possible, form a project team of persons to assist with the evaluations and the selection who have some knowledge of automation or who work in the area(s) being automated. People involved in the strategic planning process would be a good choice.
- Try to weed out proposals that are 'fatally flawed,' *e.g.*, where the vendor fails to reply to any of the functional specifications or the system is missing a module for a high-priority function.
- Begin in-depth reading of the 'surviving' proposals, carefully noting both deviations from the requirements as defined by the RFP and any aspect that is handled unusually well. Make a list of any parts of the response that are not clear and require further clarification.
- Schedule system demonstrations. They are an important component of the evaluation process. Allow the vendors to show off the vendor's system in the most attractive light; however, be prepared

with a list of what you want to see along with questions you would like answered. Use the same list with each vendor. This permits more effective cross-comparisons.

- Consider using computerised spreadsheet software in order to compare and evaluate vendor cost proposals. Costs may not be what they seem at first glance.
- Contact some of each vendor's current clients—sites of the same library type, and of similar size, where the hardware and software modules that have been proposed to you are currently in use.
- Assign point values to the criteria listed in the RFP and assign scores to the different proposals. The system with the highest score becomes the number one finalist, the system with the second highest score number two and so on. To maintain a negotiating edge, it is better to cut to two vendors rather than one. If that is impossible, maintain the illusion anyway. Remember: The selection process is not over until the contract is signed. Until that point, never let any vendors know that they have been eliminated, including those with fatal flaws.

PUTTING SYSTEMS INTO PLACE

After the system selection process is complete, there are several important steps which must occur. You and your vendor will have to negotiate and sign a contract. You will want to test the system and make sure it suits your needs. You will want to make provisions for system maintenance. Finally, you will want to train both your staff and your users as much as possible to prepare them for when the system is up and running.

With regard to training, the following must be considered: In thinking of automation planning, there is often a tendency to focus on the hardware and software aspects of planning, and to ignore the human aspects of automation—training and public relations. Without these, however, even the most carefully designed system may not be accepted by library staff or library users. To assure the success of your hard planning work, a training and public relations plan should be part of any automation project.

Fortunately, training can begin long before the system is installed. By involving staff at all levels in the analysis of operations, the identification of needs, the setting of priorities, the development of specifications, and the evaluation of systems, staff will gain much of the knowledge they need as the planning progresses. User acceptance and enthusiasm for your new automated system is certainly an important ingredient in a successful planning effort. If you are implementing a public access catalogue, it is probably the most important measure of success.

Public relations can allow you to accomplish three things:

- Make users aware of your new system and services;
- Motivate them to use the system; and
- Train them in using the new system and services effectively.

RETROSPECTIVE CONVERSION

In the rush to acquire hardware and software, librarians often forget that their most valuable product is the library's database. The creation of a high-quality machine-readable database provides the cornerstone upon which all present and future automation efforts rest. Vendors will come and go, hardware will become obsolete, software will be replaced, but a well-constructed, well-maintained database, with its accompanying local holdings, will be the library's transportable and viable link from system to system. Moreover, as library users begin to access not only their local system but systems in other libraries as well, the quality of respective databases will influence both the outcome of search strategies and the availability of materials.

Database readiness has several important facets:

- Catalogue records must be carefully converted from manual to machine-readable formats.

- Collections must be prepared for conversion through effective and ongoing weeding and inventory programmes.
- Once converted, collections must be properly maintained as titles are added, withdrawn, transferred and recataloged.
- Standards—for bibliographic, item and patron records as well—must be adhered to. In particular, adherence to well-established and accepted standards of description for bibliographic information in a machine-readable database is critical because: without standards, files cannot easily be transferred from one automated system to another.
- It is essential for libraries wishing to participate in resource sharing arrangements with other libraries, who will require such adherence as a condition of participation.

LIBRARY AUTOMATION IN DEVELOPING COUNTRIES *THE LAST 25 YEARS*

When Information Development was launched in 1984, library automation was, looked at from today's perspective, very much in its infancy. The largest libraries in the world such as the Library of Congress and the British Library had sizeable databases of catalogue records. University library catalogues were available on-line within their institutional four walls and library circulation was also automated, but data was generally confined to the institution that held it since, there was no network resembling the internet. In 1983 the JANET network had begun to connect the universities in the United Kingdom, and some catalogues were beginning to be available online from other institutions.

The most common way of accessing remote data if there was a possibility at all was by dial-up modem using ordinary phone lines and a modem or an acoustic coupler in which the phone handset was pushed into a rubber holder to ensure no extraneous noise seeped into the phone line when it was transferring electronic signals between computers. Businesses including libraries were also connected by dedicated phone lines to locations where their computers were located when they were remote. But most automation was firmly confined to the institution where it was based. Twenty five years ago was also the beginning of the period when computers were being introduced as desk top computers, with IBM PCs and subsequently IBM PC lookalikes. Personal computers were about to make a huge impact on automation in libraries as no longer was it necessary to have a dedicated air-conditioned room to house computers.

In the early days cataloguers had to have terminals on their desks to enable access to the catalogue but eventually all staff had PCs for general administration so no longer was it was the responsibility of the library budget to purchase desk-top computers. Modems were in fact used to access remotely catalogues for bibliographical purposes, to search databases like Medline. It was already possible to dial up databases such as the British Library's BLAISE database or the US National Library of Medicine's Medline. But these facilities required good phone lines and were not available outside Western Europe and the United States.

There was no such thing as 'full text' then. Computers did not have the capacity to store so much data and data stored was often coded to ensure that it did not take up more space than was necessary. 25 years ago, while most libraries in industrialised countries had not only computerised their catalogues but also computerised their circulation, in developing countries there was very little library automation outside that organised by the United Nations agencies such as FAO's AGRIS and IAEA's INIS and these were very much in their infancy or in their planning stages.

To return to the situation in industrialised countries. In the early 1990's catalogues began to be accessible on the internet but were not web-based and required the catalogue software to be run interactively across the Internet using various different protocols. By the end of the decade, true web-based catalogues using the power of hypertext were available. Libraries began to include in their catalogues digital resources internally held and externally held (predominantly external). MARC formats thenceforward incorporated a field 856 used to link to an external resource by means of a URL (the internet address).

Users of the catalogue could click on a link and go straight to a digital resource that could be anywhere in the world. Subscriptions were possible to electronic journals but they were often not available in developing countries or if they were available the bandwidth of tehinternet in those countries was not enough to enable the materials to be read. Digital library software became available and UNESCO encouraged its implementation in developing countries by making Greenstone available free-of-charge, a digital library software package developed at Waikatu in New Zealand. Links could be made from a library catalogue to material in such a digital library. Material available on the internet which might not be easily accessible in institutions in developing countries with low bandwidth could be downloaded or sent on CD-ROM to the digital libraries and hosted locally.

The Soros Foundation set up eIFL (Electronic Information for Libraries) with the aim of creating national purchasing consortia. They have since, become involved in supporting other activities such as promoting library automation systems, mindful of the fact that without a catalogue of print and digital materials the library user cannot easily find out what is accessible. eIFL supported the European Union funded project to implement NewGenLib, a system under development in India, in Aleppo and Al Baath university libraries in Syria alongside providing them with licences at a reasonable price to access electronic resources.

INASP, the International Network for the Availability of Scientific Publications, was set up by the International Council of Scientific Unions (ICSU) in 1992. Aware of the need to establish good catalogues in order to access scientific litreature, they have also participated in some library automation projects. The Andrew W. Mellon Foundation, well known for philanthropic projects in developing countries, is also supporting the development of a new library automation system at Duke University, the Open Library Environment (OLE). Although there is no participation from developing countries at this stage it is likely that any open source package developed would be supported with necessary tailoring in line with the needs of developing countries wherever they might be different.

The main feature in the last 25 years then has been in the expansion of computers into every aspect of libraries. Possibly the biggest change has been the development of digital libraries, acquiring, transforming or accessing data in digital format. In developing countries this methods of digitisation has taken place to a certain extent.

TRENDS IN THE INDUSTRIALISED WORLD

Library systems in developing countries have obviously developed alongside systems in the industrialised world. First we should look at systems for large institutions. The majority of library systems have been developed in the United States. Many commercially available integrated library systems were developed by universities for their own use and later made available to a wider audience. Dynix was one such, developed for a university library and later sold around the world to universities, public libraries and special libraries. Other systems were based from the outset on cooperatives, such as TALIS which originated as BLS, the system of BLCMP (Birmingham Libraries Cooperative Management Project) which was a cooperative set up with government funding in the 1960s.

This project was one of two established from the beginning by OSTI, the UK Office of Scientific and Technological Information, to support cooperative cataloguing. They had less incentive to expand outside their country of origin as it was their aim to serve a cooperative all of whose members were equal. In 1967, the Ohio Colleges Library Centre was established to bring library automation to Ohio academic institutions by sharing costs. OCLC as it is now has developed from being a cooperative between libraries in Ohio to being an international cooperative, and at one time promoted a library management system.

Then they ceased to support it returning eventually to the market by acquiring OLIB, an Oracle based library system. Its vision is to connect libraries of the world. Originally, as with BLCMP, it was a shared cataloguing system receiving records from participating libraries and adding them to a database which in turn could be used by member libraries to populate their own catalogues. Records were transferred between computers initially by sending large magnetic tapes, a thing of the past, from the Centre to the remote libraries. Later they were transferred by telephone lines and subsequently the transfer was done by a client computer, a PC in a remote institution, accessing the Centre's servers by the Internet. Jumping to the present, OCLC have established Worldcat which could act as a large union catalogue for the world if every library in the world added its holdings.

This concept is called Cloud Computing, on the basis that the computer is somewhere remote and no one knows or cares where exactly it is! To return to library systems established in individual institutions, VTLS (Virginia Tech Library System), another large library automation system, always had an interest in working with developing countries and have a large number of installations in the Third World after having expanded into Eastern Europe as well. Another popular system, Aleph, is based in Jerusalem surrounded by a number of developing countries some of which have considered installation though by far the largest share of the market is in Europe.

As for cooperatives like OCLC, there has existed for many years in former Yugoslavia a miniature version of OCLC, COBISS (Co-operative Online Bibliographic System and Service), which since, the break-up of Yugoslavia has expanded to include Albania and Bulgaria on the same basis as other ex-Yugoslav states. They act as a cooperative cataloguing agency but they also keep data on research projects. This institution would be a good model for other regions to adopt. Now and again a commercial library system has been licenced to a developing country institution which has subsequently found it difficult to pay the maintenance fees. Maintenance in any case is often more expensive in a developing country because of economies of scale and distance from the supplier. Additionally there may be problems caused by shortages of foreign exchange.

Now the internet reaches much of the world, distance is not so important. But there have been many instances of institutions retaining a package but not paying maintenance fees and therefore not updating it. Marshall Breeding keeps records of as many library automation packages and the sites where they are used as he can find the information. He publishes the results each year in Library Journal. The latest was published on the web in January 2009. He reviews the market as well as providing statistics about library automation suppliers.

This is a useful guide to make comparisons with developing countries. Unfortunately in his tables he makes only the distinction between the US and the rest of the world. However he also includes a general review and this year he reported that the use of Open Source packages is increasing mainly bring provided by third parties. For example, a company called Equinox provides support for the Open Source package Evergreen.

PACKAGES WHICH HAVE HAD AN IMPACT IN DEVELOPING COUNTRIES

Large libraries in developing countries had always had a certain amount of access to library automation systems. For example, the National Library of Venezuela had a system found in many US academic libraries called NOTIS. However this library's catalogue is still not available on the web. A number of countries in the former Soviet Union use IRBIS, the

CDS/ISIS clone developed by the Russian National Library for Science and Technology. But ordinary libraries, public and academic, in developing countries have always lacked a wealth of possibilities for library automation. Hardware used to be expensive, and relatively speaking is still expensive for developing countries. Other problems raised by writers on the subject range from the power supply to the problems of training staff. Another issue not often raised is the need for collaboration both within and between institutions to get library automation project off the ground and then maintain it.

This is a much more complex activity than a pre-automation situation where there is a library card catalogue maintained by cataloguers and used manually by staff and library patrons. Smaller systems than the ones developed for universities or networks have been developed which could be regarded as being similar sized to CDS/ISIS, for instance Inmagic and Tinlib. Some of these were not very easy to use and were not well maintained. Others were adopted by consortia or organisations in the industrialised world with branches in developing countries such as the British Council.

The main problem in developing countries has been support because of their remoteness and so those packages offering less support would be more attractive as they would be less expensive overall. This may well change in the future with the increase in the power of the internet and the next 25 years will surely see a difference in the availability of and the charges for support.

CDS/ISIS

CDS/ISIS has undoubtedly had a huge influence on library automation in developing countries. This author reviewed the package onits twentieth anniversary. Time and again, libraries have begun automation. There is even a reference to a library which began with Tinlib and has migrated to CDS/ISIS. Since, CDS/ISIS is well mentioned in the litreature, concerning library automation in developing countries, it will not be covered here.

However the most interesting feature which has become available over the last five years in CDS/ISIS is a Z39.50 import facility which is available as part of IsisMARC, and which enables MARC records from external sources to be downloaded into a CDS/ISIS database compatible with the version of MARC of the records. CDS/ISIS is not essentially a library management system, rather a database management system aimed at bibliographic records which by their very nature are variable length (with for example book titles being of indeterminate length) rather than fixed length which is the case for most data processing systems. Because it is attractive to small institutions with little funding and because of its parentage (UNESCO), it has attracted a certain kind of institution, for example those in the development community. UNESCO developed a DOS version in 1985 and a Windows version which was available for many years as a beta test version but was eventually released around 1998.

However libraries were already requiring to place their catalogues on the web and a number of organisations began to develop compatible web-based systems which could be used by institutions which were developing databases for in-house use on Windows or DOS versions of CDS/ISIS. The main developer of the official version was BIREME with WWWISIS but already others were available such as Webisis. CDS/ISIS is no longer being developed by UNESCO but BIREME in cooperation with UNESCO is leading the development of ABCD on an Open Source basis.

Tinlib

Tinlib was a package which was used extensively in British Council libraries. In Ilorin Nigeria it was used from 1996 as reported by Adewoye. The library had by 2001 almost replaced its card catalogue by the OPAC. The chapter was optimistic about the future and reporting on the use of other electronic resources. However e-mail and the internet were not then available. However, TINLIB had its problems. It was not an easy system to use and contracts for it dwindled outside developing countries and it ceased to be supported. Adeyoyin describes in 2004 how the Development Policy Centre Library in Ibadan migrated their catalogue from Tinlib to CDS/ISIS.

DEVELOPING COUNTRY SCENARIOS

It is of course a fallacy to make assumptions that all developing countries will have approached and will approach library automation in the same way. The wealth of the country the distribution of that wealth and the culture of the residents will make a difference.

Nigeria and other African Countries

Nigeria has oil money and had automation early, being one of the first users of CDS/ISIS for mainframe computers. Already in1989 Eyitayo could write a paper on the attitude of automated library system vendors to investing in Nigeria. Many respondents hoped to open an office and increase their marketing. Enakrire describes a few instances in Africa where automation has been implemented, indicating that, except for branches of international organisations, it depends on the generosity of donors. In Makerere University in Uganda, the library has benefited from donor funding through the African Virtual University Library Initiative of the World Bank to equip the library with computers and installed Internet connectivity. Other university libraries are developing their information service as they are also benefiting from the Programme for the Enhancement of Research of (PERI) under the sponsorship of the International Network for the Availability of Scientific Publications (INASP).

Through PERI, donors have paid subscriptions on behalf of libraries in Africa to access web-based journals. The University of Ibadan had a long history of automation, having begun in 1979. Georgina D. Ekpenyong wrote in 1997 about the history so far. The University of Ibadan Library was already seen as a leader in Nigeria. At that time they used CD-Rom extensively to provide bibliographic data. They took training seriously but did not yet have an OPAC. In 2008, the

John D. and Catherine T. MacArthur Foundation in Chicago awarded grants totalling US $7.1 million to expand academic and research programme and strengthen staff development at two Nigerian universities as part of the Foundation's efforts to improve higher education in Africa. The result is that they signed up to VTLS, Virginia Tech Library System, a commercially available package developed originally as Virginia Tech's own system.

Thailand

In Thailand there were efforts in the 1990s to computerise the libraries with foreign-based systems being purchased. Thammasat University library had Dynix, supported from Ameritech's Australia office, and planned to move to Ameritech's new system Horizon. In 1997 the university library sent three cataloguers to Middlesex University to learn to use Horizon. Since, then they have implemented Horizon and exchange of experience took place between Middlesex University and Thammasat University until the Systems librarian at Thammasat moved to a different post around 2006. Many universities in Thailand are able to purchase these systems often through local distributors of international or American packages. Early on though, CDS/ISIS was used and at Thammasat University they used it for databases of journal articles.

OPTIONS FOR DEVELOPING COUNTRIES

Developing countries depend on developments in the industrialised world but they do not necessarily benefit from the same options as the industrialised world can use. Moreover, some of the options may be much more attractive in developing countries or at least may seem to be so.

Developing a Library System

One solution for organisations in developing countries which might have problems with paying organisations in foreign currency but which have good local technical staff is to develop their own software system. One interesting example of this is the University of Colombo in Sri Lanka. They had begun to automate in 1991 by using CDS/ISIS and then later adopted CDS/ISIS for Windows when it became available. In 2002, Seneviratne and Amaraweera reported in Information Development that in Sri Lanka there was discussion on developing a library automation system to bridge the gap between CDS/ISIS and what commercial software was able to provide, such as Alice for Windows (UK commercial) and LibSys (Indian).

In 1997 the National Agency for Research Energy, Science and Agriculture (NARESA) now the National Science Foundation, used the CDS/ISIS DOS version to handler acquisitions, cataloguing, serials management, Current Awareness Services as well as cataloguing and indexing; this package called PURNA was then used in 34 special and academic libraries. AGRIS using CDS/ISIS was widely influencing libraries in the agricultural sector and the Windows version was then used in the National Library of Sri Lanka for its union catalogue.

Now they are using Genisis, a package to make it easy to implement BIREME's WWWISIS on the web, development of which was undertaken in France by Pierre Chabet but for which a manual was written in Sri Lanka (partially a translation from the documentation in French) by Ms. Deepali Talagala Director/Information of the Sri Lanka Scientific and Technical Information Centre based at the National Science Foundation in Colombo Seneviratne and Amaraweera discussed in their paper the features a system would need and the platforms, hardware and operating system, most used and as a result decided to make a prototype using MS Access on Windows. Development took two phases.

Firstly a web-based interface to physically dispersed databases with a user-friendly front-end reported by Kumara et al in 1998, and a library automation system described in a BSc dissertation by DMS Dilrukshi, 1999 NetLib—a library management system through the Internet. In 2002 a prototype had been developed and the system was due to be maintained by the Computing Service Centre of the University of Colombo. Unfortunately there is a high overhead in developing and maintaining systems especially for a small client base.

In the UK all university libraries have commercial systems. Newcastle, used to have their own system in the 1980s but only Lancaster remained, eventually contracting with Ex Libris to take Aleph in 2001. By 2008 both the University of Colombo and the National Library of Sri Lanka had signed up to Softlink Europe's Alice system, a system used by the British Council worldwide (for example in Oman, Jordan and Sudan: the catalogue of the British Council in Sudan is available on the internet) and so has proven maintenance in developing countries. So developing one's own system is not to be recommended: Eyitayo noted that despite the availability of numerous off-the-shelf systems, most libraries in Nigeria that have attempted automation have chosen to commission expensive and time-consuming in-house projects, most of which have suffered severe set-backs and in most cases are not adequate for library work and often lack the capability for sharing information and interconnection with other systems.

Open Source

In the context of moving towards commercially supported systems, it is interesting to see that CDS/ISIS was attractive to libraries in developing countries. It was available without charge and so there was no danger of not being able to pay for it. Of course it was supported by an organisation with as much prestige though not so much turnover as many industrial companies. It also operated on a legal footing. Institutions had to sign a licence agreement to use the software. No doubt many institutions obtained the software illegally but the software was protected in law by the licence agreement. UNESCO were more concerned with illegal copies being made and sold for illegal profit than with institutions using the software without being officially licenced since, the spirit of the software following the ethos of the developer Giampaolo Delbigio was that it should enable institutions to participate in worldwide record sharing at many different levels.

Nevertheless there was established a network of distributors which is still in place. Some acted merely as local distributors sending out the software on diskettes by post and thereby easing the burden of the hard-pressed office in UNESCO dealing with this. Other distributors were able to provide support usually of a limited nature though sometimes of a more extensive nature akin to the commercial support that is found in the large-scale library automation systems. The shareware movement was in place when CDS/ISIS was released in 1985.

In 1984, Andrew Fluegleman programmed a communications software package, PC-Talk and Jim Knopf a file management application called PC-File a year before the IBM PC was released and called it Freeware. The developers wanted to avoid commercial distribution networks and distribute the software over the now seemingly primitive and slow dial up systems whereby PC users could transfer programmes by dialling up a central computer using a modem and phone lines. The idea was that users would download the software, test it and if they liked it make a small contribution to the developer to support further development. Knopf established the term freeware as his own and no one else could use it.

There were other microcomputers around at the time, most notably the Apple Macintosh and others which are only part of history such as the BBC Microcomputer, though none ever reached the level of popularity that the IBM PC with the Microsoft Windows operating system has now reached. Incidentally Fluegleman distributed his software with the source code which led to many other developers producing their own versions and PC-Talk was improved and sold on by other developers such that Fluegleman lost control of it. Knopf however established a multi-million dollar company on the basis of PC-File.

In 1983 Bob Wallace created PC-Write which became a well used word processor and was used extensively in developing countries. Because the word freeware was reserved he called it shareware. The concept was pretty much the same. Over the years, freeware and shareware became less used as concepts probably because the most used programmes for business purposes were monopolised by Microsoft with the operating system and Microsoft Office applications. Shareware was in a sense reborn with the open source movement. It is difficult to see any difference between Open Source and shareware but the Open Source Movement has been supported from the outset by large foundations such as the Soros Foundation which founded the Open Society Initiative.

In English 'Open Source' means freely available source software which developers can use to advance the software in question. In all these cases, software developed is free though usually developers ask for a voluntary contribution. They cannot be sold on. Open Source does not necessarily mean free-of-charge but there is an implication that the availability of the source code will enable organisations to acquire and develop it for free. CDS/ISIS was no shareware or open source but many of the features of open source and shareware were responsible for the popularity of CDS/ISIS.

For example, Open Source has the possibility for users with access to programming skills to make their own developments. CDS/ISIS has a feature of being able to write programme exits which enable further development. Unlike open source the source code was not made widely available but UNESCO did make it available to BIREME in Brazil where further developments have taken place. Moreover, in the Soviet Union the Russian National Library for Science and Technology developed with permission from UNESCO IRBIS, a functionally equivalent package copied from the DOS version of ISIS.

The Open Source movement gained much greater political credibility than the earlier movements did and UNESCO came under pressure to support the movement. They now have on their web site a Free and Open Source software portal. Because of UNESCO's lead in this concept, CDS/ISIS came under pressure to be declared open source in the early 2000s. But the source code is still not available.

This author believes it would lead to many different versions of the software that could generate records in databases that were no longer compatible with each other. Moreover, Open Source is seen by some as the solution to some of the problems facing the library software industry. Is Open Source all it promises to be? Over the last few years there has been a spate of mergers in the library systems industry led by the equity market resulting in a trend to discontinue the development if not the support of library systems when a company has acquired more than one such package. This severely inconveniences the using institutions which have to migrate from one system to another. Would open source be a protection against this? Open Source has become so much a fashionable option for library software that the International Federation of Library Associations and Institutions held a meeting in Senegal prior to the annual conference's meeting in Durban South Africa.

The proceedings are illustrative of the views on Open Source. The argument in Savard's introduction goes that Open Source may help to smooth out the inequalities between industrialised and developing countries. The connection with commerce is weaker than with commercial software but it is not non-existent. In industrialised countries libraries often use third-party services to support Open Source. This means the connection with the commercial world strengthens. There is no way put from paying for support. The question is who pays and there is not much difference between paying a developer or a third party.

In the conclusion of these proceedings, Diop feels there are clearly economic advantages to adopting an open source software solution but agrees that mastering open source software can take a lot of time and effort because library and information professionals are often isolated. User communities need to be built up to provide mutual help. However it remains to be seen what will be the impact of open source on library automation, particularly integrated library systems in the industrialised world. A pessimistic outcome might be that the institutions using such software feel no differently being supported by the commercial open source support companies than by the current range of commercial companies who promote systems they themselves own.

THE CURRENT SITUATION AND FUTURE PROSPECTS

Making predictions is a very hazardous occupation in anything to do with computers since, the future only tends to bring surprises. Developments in many developing countries are not as advanced as might be expected and in some places there is still a problem with electric supply: Adebibo reporting on usage of catalogues by students at the University of Ilorin in Nigeria stated: "Most respondents claimed to know how to use the card catalogues and OPAC but only a few use them. The possible reason for this low level use of the OPAC is power outages, which have become the rule in Nigeria rather than an exception. Overall, as the power of the internet increases, particularly its bandwidth and its reliability, library automation in developing countries will have the same capabilities as the industrialised world, but not the finance to support it.

In developed countries it is felt by some that the future of library automation lies in open source (outside the control of commercial suppliers) or 'Cloud Computing' (very much controlled by commercial suppliers who provide software on their own hardware and the clients access the data via the Internet). However if solutions to library automation are hosted services in the industrialised world, the suppliers of the service would be able to charge developing countries as little as they wish on the basis that every amount, however little, is profit. This has happened with hosted electronic journals where deals have been made by publishers to cover entire countries which are less than the licence fee required for a university in the west. As suggested, see if this happens. As with e-journals, it needs a champion like eIFL to promote to the suppliers the benefits of their working with developing institutions in what may be perceived as an altruistic way.

LIBRARY AUTOMATION IN ACADEMIC LIBRARIES IN INDIA
PROBLEMS AND PROSPECTS

The history of library automation is sufficiently old now. It started in early fifties in the Untied States of America. The landmark was the initiation of MARC project by the Library of Congress. During 1960s some experiments were carried out in India in this field but very sparingly. During late seventies there were some achievements like production of National Union Catalogue of Scientific Serials by INSDOC, production of Union Catalogue of DRDO libraries of Western Region by the Institute of Armament Technology at Pune. Then came eighties and the whole focus of the librarians shifted towards library automation.

A number of seminars were organised on the library automation and still being done so. We graduated from simple library operations to specialised functions including networking. Now we talk about digital libraries and e-journals. We have come a long way. But we are a country where bullock cart and cars are seen on the same road so blocking the fast moving traffic and those bullock carts restrict the speed of the cars to its own speed. To overcome this problem there are only two ways. First, replace the bullock cart with a car, and second, bypass the bullock cart and leave it behind. The state of library automation in our university libraries is more or less the same. We have the libraries like IIT libraries which are highly automated and also totally manual libraries which are really restricting the speed of academic and research in the country.

FACTORS RESPONSIBLE FOR AUTOMATION IN ACADEMIC LIBRARIES

There are several reasons which can be cited for this difference.

Some of them are:

- Attitude and awareness of the management
- Attitude and awareness of the Users specially faculty
- Resources available

- Non-availability of suitable software
- Level and skill of staff
- Geographical locations.

Attitude and Initiative of the Management

Attitude and initiative on the part of the management has played major role in library automation in Indian University Libraries. The management here includes both the university management and the librarian as a secretary of the management whose task is to carry out the decisions taken by the executive bodies of the university, such as Syndicate, Executive Council, etc. If the Librarian had the initiative then he was able to convince the authorities about this emergent need. In some of the cases, the initiative also came from top and the Librarian was forced (or bypassed) to do it. But the best blend was when the initiative of both the Librarian and University Authorities was synergised. If there was no initiative on both the ends than there was no progress.

Attitude and Initiative of the Uses

A library may be as smart as its readers. If the readers are smart and well aware they may force the authorities to work towards library automation. If the readers are knowledgeable about the development being taking place in the information technology, they have influenced the use of computers in library to a great extent. This is more true about faculty as they are the people who participate in decision making process. The good examples are the libraries of IITs and other higher engineering educational institutions.

Resources Available

The third important factor is the resources available with the university libraries. The resources include both financial as well as human resources. In most of the universities, the librarians are given funds only for books and journals. Some libraries do not want to or are not allowed the funds received for books and journals to be used for any other purpose, even though the University Grants Commission (UGC) guidelines permit the use of a certain percentage towards such activities (In VIII Plan it was 15 per cent and in IX plan 10 per cent).

Most of the libraries depend on the funds provided by the UGC under Inflibnet project. The distribution of the money under this project was not done logically. Big and small libraries were equated at par and as a result while some libraries remained fund starved some were not able to use the funds. Before distributing funds to libraries there should have been a survey of the requirement and certain guidelines laid down. Besides this there are no other financial resources available with the university libraries.

In order to save the university libraries from going further down UGC must do something in this direction. Another very serious problem, may be more serious than the financial one, is the lack of trained manpower.

Many of our library science schools have not based their curricula on the automation requirement of the university libraries. Some of them are even teaching today what was designed thirty or forty years back although that has become totally outdated. Not many library schools produce a candidate who can straight away go the Automation Department of a University Library and can independently work without any further training. The bifurcation of the library science schools from libraries are perhaps the one of the main important reasons for that.

As a result our profession became the only profession where practice went far ahead of the teaching. In the country people are talking about digital libraries and web-OPACs and we are teaching fundamental of computers in our library schools. This is the only profession where getting a professional degree does not require any professional training. Can you imagine a doctor without hospital training or an engineer without a training in Industry.

Non-availability of Suitable Software

Non-availability of suitable software has also played an important role. Though there are a number of software available for library management but most of them are non-standard. The main reason behind is that most of the software have been developed without the help of a qualified librarian. As a result there were a stream of non-standard software. Some of these softwares have been developed by big corporations like CMC but have not been proved very successful. The software developed by institutions (for example DESIDOC, INSDOC, etc.,) could not be successful as they were lacking in marketing and after sales service. The librarian is confused as he is not in a position to decide what to select.

Level of Skill of Library Staff

The level of skill of library staff also played a very important role. In our country there are no standard for level of subordinate staff to be recruited in academic libraries. There educational and professional qualification vary from state to state. In some of the cases the library assistants are recruited with 12th pass and a six months certificate in library science while in Central institutions like IITs and Central Universities it is minimum graduation and degree in library science. The institutions having better stuff went far ahead (though there are exceptions to that). The better qualified staff was better oriented towards progressive thinking which could move the things fast. This point emphasises the requirement of a uniform qualification policy for the recruitment of staff in academic institutions.

Geographical Location

Geographical location of an institution also played a very important role. The institutions near to a metro city were benefited by the availability of the resources. They were having better approach to hardware and software market and also the manpower for data entry. They were having approach to better training facilities. Hyderabad is a good example which can be cited.

PRESENT STATUS OF LIBRARY AUTOMATION IN UNIVERSITY LIBRARIES

The real boost in library automation came from the establishment of the INFLIBNET Centre. Before Inflibnet scattered efforts were being made in academic libraries specially in the institutions of special characters like IITs, IIMs, etc. INFLIBNET proved a real catalyst. Inflibnet started with scratch. At that time there were no financial assistance available to the University Libraries for automation. For the first time it was established that automation was the need of hour. The finances were allocated for the first time. The standards were established about the data capturing. The format was finalised and the Karvan started. As one estimate at present about 120 university libraries have been using computers in their activities. Some of the University libraries are even establishing digital libraries not only of already available digital resources but are digitising their own litreature. About 50 university libraries have their web pages.

AREAS WHERE COMPUTERS ARE BEING USED

The following are the areas where computer are being used at present:

- Online public access catalogue
- Circulation
- Acquisition
- Serial control
- Intranet
- Internet
- CD-ROM services

Online Public Access Catalogue (OPACs)

The problem being faced by the users in locating the document was the first to be targeted in the library automation. As a result the work first started in this direction. There was one more reason for this and that was the availability of CDS/ ISIS software which had the facility of catalogue only. It was in contrast of the special libraries where the work first started on providing information services like CD-ROM search. Even today this area of automation has more activity than any other area. It has now graduated to Web-OPAC (web based online public access catalogues) where university libraries have made their databases available on their web sites. This has eliminated the need of installation of search software on the user's terminal. One potential which remains unutilised is the use of search data for research purpose as the search history can provide very useful tools for the librarians to formulate their collection development plans.

Circulation

Circulation is one of the main activities of a university library or any library per say. In university libraries, however, the number of books issued and retuned are more than in special libraries. Therefore, the next area which was taken up was the circulation. In some of the libraries the number of books issued/returned may be more than one thousand per day. We at IIT Roorkee (formerly University of Roorkee) has experience of issuing 1500 books in six working hours. Sometimes there used to be a queue of more than 100 students, since, the free hours for all students used to be the same, before automated circulation started.

Use of barcodes had made the life very simple due to added accuracy and speed. Besides speeding up the issue/return, printing reports, sending reminders also become very easy. Circulation data also provides a very important insight into the book use pattern. Librarians should try to use this data for research and development purpose.

Acquisition

Use of computers in acquisition remains a low priority area. Not many libraries are using computers in acquisition. On reason may be the continuously reducing budget for purchase of books. But this area needs to be strengthened. Computerisation at the stage can help not only in order processing but also can be a very effective tool in budget control. You can allocate funds to different departments based on a set formula, can send department heads about non-availability of funds, can control over ordering and also utilise the data entered at this stage for technical processing and OPAC.

Serial Control

Idiosyncracies involved in serial control affects the use of computers in serial control and hence, the area is not very well represented at automation scenario. One more reason is the unsuitability of serial control modules available in most of the library Management Softwares. The procedures developed by these softwares are so cumbersome that sometimes it looks easier to use normal method rather than automation. However, this area provides very good stage for use of computers as it can help tracking the missing issues very efficiently and provide the current awareness services and even the SDI services besides budget control.

Intranet

Making the information available on intranet is also growing popularity as it eliminates the need of installing the software on the users' terminals. Users can access the catalogue through intranet or they can find the status of the books issued to them through web access. CD-ROM resources and other digital resources can be accessed on intranet. The beauty is that one need not be conversant with the software as the web links are available through the web page. Growing installation of campus wide networks is also playing a positive role in this direction.

Internet

Use of Internet for academic purposes is also increasing day by day. More and more libraries are putting their resources on Internet. Internet is the medium both to access and disseminate information. Internet has emerged as a very big virtual library which has information on practically every subject and in every media may it be text, audio or video. Libraries should use this facility to the best of their capability. They should provide links to similar type of libraries through web pages. One very good use can be designing of e-gates where user can have access to the electronic resources through a common user interface.

Digital Libraries

Digital library has recently become the buzzword for librarians. In the last year most of the seminars and the conferences had 'digital libraries' as their theme. Digital libraries can be of two types, *i.e.*, digital libraries of the digital text available in the market such as e-journals, CD-ROM databases, e-books, software, etc., or it can be developed from the printed text available in the library. If a library takes a decision to develop a digital library of its collection specially theses, dissertations and old journals, it can solve the problem of space and preservation both. But the decision about creating such decision is taken to be very carefully as it will prove a very costly venture both in terms of money and manpower.

PROSPECTS

Having talked about the problems and areas of applications let us talk about future prospects. I can definitely say that the things are changing for the good. Now University authorities are realising that there is no way to escape library automation. They are finding various ways to finance their library automation projects. Librarians are also realising that they can not remain indifferent to the change, otherwise they will be labelled outdated. One area of concern is the library science graduates being produced by our library schools It is surprising that UGC is giving responsibility of refresher courses of library science to the library science school and not to the libraries who are established themselves as advanced libraries and uses the technology far ahead than the library science schools. Existing staff is getting rid of the fear of computerisation. They are coming forward to learn and make themselves suitable to face the challenges of the new millennium. Standardisation is increasing and the better softwares are available.

2

Library Automation and Organisational Change

IDENTIFICATION OF THE ISSUE

The example is only one instance of the large-scale changes that affect people's work lives. These types of changes raise many important issues for managers, from the level of director to unit supervisor. Some issues are primarily technological. What equipment will be needed? Is the technological infrastructure in place? Will the system crash when the date changes to January 1, 2000? Other issues are more social. How will the employees react? Will they accept the change or resist it? Can the change process be made easier? Unfortunately, this second group of issues can be easily overlooked. Managers often do not address human issues adequately, even though they are aware of them, and even though they consider their employees, clients, and other people to be important.

CHANGE ISSUES IN THE PUBLIC AND PRIVATE SECTORS

While the specific issue of library automation is located principally in the public sector, the processes and challenges of change are common to both areas.

HUMAN FACTORS IN LIBRARY AUTOMATION

Librarians, staff and patrons must make a number of adjustments as a result of any library automation project, whether it is an original implementation or a migration. One key area is the relationship between people and technology. People have to change the way they behave and think to work effectively in an automated environment. They skim through cards to find a catalogue record in a manual system. To find a catalogue record in an automated system they use computer commands.

In a migration scenario, this might be a change from typing keyboard commands to choosing buttons or menu items on a graphical interface. For long-term employees, this requires yet a third 'mental map.' These demands for change easily lead to stress reactions of fear or anger, especially when they are large-scale or frequent. Smith mentions several sources for these emotions, such as loss of control, worries about identity and security in the workplace, and breakdowns in interpersonal relationships. It is no wonder that people often resist change. However, Smith cautions against regarding human responses solely as a barrier to change. For leaders who pay attention to social issues, these responses provide valuable feedback and help to implement a more successful system.

HISTORICAL PERSPECTIVE

The early history of library automation can be divided into three phases, the Developmental Phase, the Operational Phase, and the Integrative Phase. The development phase was the period of early experimentation up to the early seventies. During this period a small number of institutions engaged in automation projects. While management hoped that systems could be transferred from one institution to another, this was not the case with these early efforts. Libraries did not have similar computer operating systems, they did not have standardised procedures, and they could not agree on outputs.

However, the development of the MARC record was a significant development that allowed libraries to communicate bibliographic records in a standard format. The operational phase, in the mid-to-late seventies, saw the expansion of automation in a wider variety of libraries. Vendor-supplied systems, shared computer resources, and networking made this possible. Since, libraries were no longer forced to develop their own systems from scratch, it was an easier and less expensive task. During this phase most library automation projects still focussed on discrete tasks, such as check-in or circulation. Operational areas were not integrated, and the overall workflow stayed basically the same, "it has been utterly possible to use the automated system as inefficiently and ineffectively and with as little knowledge of what is going on as with the manual system". Montague proposed that the next phase would be an integrative phase, in which the automation systems would cut across operational lines, actually change the way libraries do business, and improve service.

There were a number of obstacles during these stages of library automation:

- Lack of direction and oversight from library managers to systems staff;
- Lack of technical training for library managers;
- Failure to develop long-range plans;
- Lack of up and down communication between managers and staff;
- Lack of staff input;
- Lack of staff training;
- Lack of feedback mechanisms.

Overall, it appears that the several problems, training, oversight, input, feedback, all involved a general lack of communication.

MIGRATION—SECOND GENERATION SYSTEMS

Since, many libraries, including Notre Dame, have or plan to migrate to second generation library systems, it is important to consider whether the obstacles are the same. One view is that they are not the same. Migrations are said to be easier than initial implementations. Although there may be some staff apprehensions, staff morale is reported to improve. A significant advantage is that second-time buyers have a better understanding of what they want in a system, and focus more on quality and customer support, instead of low bids. There is one potential source of resistance, which is never present in an initial automation project, that is a hostile 'soon-to-be former vendor.' Another important distinction is whether the library is migrating after successful implementation of a system which simply no longer meets their needs, or whether the library is desperately seeking a new system after a failed effort.

The reaction of librarians to this viewpoint is to be mixed. Some libraries have reported a very similar degree of 'techno stress' during migration projects, with similar emotional responses. Staff are required to change procedures, and in many cases the new procedures are not clear-cut—of course, the procedures in the 'old' system were not clear-cut in the beginning either. On the other hand, the majority of directors in a survey of 33 libraries that had undergone system migrations felt that 'promoting' the system change to the staff was unnecessary. This seems to be primarily due to staff frustration with the old systems, providing a clear motivation for change.

The worse the original system, the less staff resistance there was to migration. However, there were still some symptoms of technostress. Many found the vendors training programmes to be inadequate, consisting of 'canned' presentations were did not apply to local needs. Due to 'rush jobs,' the staff at many libraries did not have adequate time to become familiar with the new system before it was made available to the public. In one particularly egregious case, the staff and patrons were given access to the system at the same time. The staff 'hated this.' A two-month lead-time between staff and public access gave optimum results.

PRIVATE SECTOR EXPERIENCES

While library automation, *per se,* is not a major issue in the for-profit world, automation in general definitely is. As such, experiences in the private sector provide helpful comparisons. One very familiar theme from corporate settings in the need to consult with users prior to any sort of migration or automation project. This is true even with systems that are not central to the users' jobs. Gaudin relates several stories of companies that tried to implement new systems without consulting users. One case involved replacing a mainframe e-mail system with a desktop system. After the company spent $3 million, the employees rejected it because it was not fast or stable enough.

In another case, FedEx introduced a scheduling system without consulting their own employees. This became one of the issues in a potential strike against the company. One manager pointed out the importance of remembering that 'users might like their old systems'. This is an important lesson for library managers to remember in a migration, especially when the original system was basically successful. Even a failed system may have features the employees liked. Another illustration is provided by Norman's study of a failed automation effort. An attempt to introduce the CASE system in a management information firm provides valuable lessons for both sectors.

The goal of the CASE project was to establish a 2-1 ratio of CASE workstation usage among the MIS staff and achieve a 10 to 15 per cent increase in productivity. The project is considered to be a failure, because people are not using it. The company has lost business to competitors who do use the system. Norman identifies a number of factors in the CASE implementation, which contributed to its failure. From the beginning, the decision to implement CASE was made by a small high-level committee, without involving staff. There was a successful pilot project, following which the company attempted to expand the system.

Their main methodology was a staff-training programme. Management assumed that if they provided training, the programmers would use the system. While the training was described as 'adequate,' it was informational only, and there was no effort made to change attitudes. The most critical barrier identified in the study was the high learning curve for using CASE. Management did not make any effort to reduce this learning curve. Instead, each work group that attempted to use the system had to learn it on their own. There was no sharing of tricks or shortcuts, or any help given by those who had already started using the product to new users. Interdepartmental friction and a rigid chain-of-command that stifled communication between units prevented this type of cooperation.

A related factor was the lack of any visible benefits or rewards for using CASE. Instead rewards were based on completing projects under-time and under-budget. Since, CASE is intended to increase productivity, it might seem that this would reward its use. But "this means that the rewards are indirect and totally dependent upon the successful use of the tool". In conjunction with the high learning curve, this becomes a negative incentive – the system is likely to slow production in the short-term, until the learning curve is past. If the programmer fails to learn it quickly, rewards are lost rather than gained.

THEORIES AND STRATEGIES FOR CHANGE

In discussing theories of organisational change, many theorists divide changes into different types. Before delving too deeply into specific strategies for change, I would like to examine the relationship between library automation projects and descriptive theories.

CONTINUITY

In the Age of Unreason, Handy tells us that "Change is not what it used to be". He distinguishes continuous and discontinuous change. Continuous change is gradual and predictable, with one situation leading into the next. This is relatively comfortable for most people. But he asserts that the changes in the workplace now are discontinuous. That is, changes are abrupt and unpredictable, and hence, far less comfortable. Handy frequently links discontinuous change to technology. As such, it is easy to reach the conclusion that a library automation project is a discontinuous change. People who worked with paper switch to online systems, and their jobs are altered or even eliminated. But we should not be too quick to classify it this way. Particularly in the early automation projects, automated tasks were substituted for manual tasks on a one-to-one basis. Because of this, there was no drastic change in the overall workflow; even when specific tasks were drastically altered. It could be argued that automation has had a more significant impact since, that time, as library systems have become integrated.

CALM AND TURBULENT WATERS

Robbins focuses on the frequency of change. He uses two metaphors, 'calm waters' and 'whitewater rapids.' In the calm-waters scenario, change is the exception. Most of the time is spent in a state of equilibrium, until some crisis forces a change. After the change is past, the organisation regains a new state of equilibrium. In the white-water scenario, change is continuous, though in a different sense than Handy uses the word.

There is no state of equilibrium; instead one period of change is followed directly by another. It is very tempting to identify library automation projects with the 'calm water' metaphor. In fact, Saunders uses a very similar model in her article on library system migration. First various forces bring about a need for change, which requires unfreesing process. This is followed by a period of instability. When this is over, the library establishes a new state of equilibrium, as new patterns and procedures are frozen into place. Because automation efforts are not made frequently, this model appears to be a good match.

In an original automation project, the library has been using a manual system as long as it has been in existence. Once the project has been completed, the library will continue to use the new system indefinitely. Even in a migration project, the library may have been using its old system for many years, and certainly would hope the new system would be long-lived. One potential problem with this model is that it ignores the wider picture of overall changes. At the same time as a library is contemplating an integrated library system, the staff may be dealing with new online indexes, electronic journals, e-mail systems, computer operating systems, and even a building renovation. Taken in this larger context, the white water metaphor seems more appropriate to the library environment. It is often not just the project at hand that causes problems for staff and users, but the 'unrelenting demand' of changes in many areas. Another issue is the continuing change following the implementation of an automated system due to new releases and upgrades to the system.

Even after a new system is fully implemented, it may not be as 'calm' as the old manual system. One significant problem with the white-water model as a model for change is that it suggests a reactive style of management with unplanned changes. But most library automation and migration projects are planned, as are many of the other changes affecting the library staff. This model seems most apt for dealing with the external changes impacting an organisation.

THE FOUR MOTORS OF CHANGE

Van de Ven and Poole give a more fully fleshed taxonomy of change. They identify two crosscutting distinctions, the level and the mode of change. The level of change is whether the change involves single or multiple entities. The mode of change is either prescribed or emergent. A priori changes are planned, predictable or follow set rules or patterns. Emergent change is discontinuous and unpredictable.

This combination yields four 'motors of change:'

- Life-cycle (single entity, prescribed);
- Teleological (single entity, emergent);
- Dialectical (multiple entities, emergent); and
- Evolutionary (multiple entities, prescribed).

While these motors can be separated in theory, most real-life changes involve interaction between them. The four motors model provides a more complete description of organisational change, and avoids over simplification problems. If we examine library automation projects in this e-context of the four motors of change that Van de Ven describes, as suggested, find rather complex interactions. The teleological theory, which is characterised by planning and goal setting, provides the closest description of the first stage in an automation project. Libraries may have a variety of motivations for undertaking an automation or migration project.

In the case of migration, this might include negative factors, like dissatisfaction with the current vendor, as well as positive ones, like a desire to expand capabilities. These motivations provide the Aristotelian final cause for the project. Most libraries engage in goal setting activities, such as compiling lists of desired features. This stage may be described as teleological in Van de Ven's scheme because it primarily involves one entity and the process is emergent. At the beginning of this stage, it is not clear where it will finish. Although the process is planned the goals are identified during the process, and may provide a dramatic break with the existing manual or automated system.

The dialectical motor may be present to a lessor extant, as different stakeholders interact with each other, and occasionally present conflicting goals. This teleological description fits most, but not all migration projects. For 79 per cent of cases in a migration survey, the projects were planned. But in some cases, the libraries did not have time to develop plans due to legal or financial problems. In those cases, the teleological motor would only apply in a trivial sense, if at all.

Those cases are obviously not ideal scenarios. Towards the end of the selection process, the library must compare its goals and desires to the actual systems available. At this point, the process could be described as dialectical, involving the library and the vendors who would like to supply the system. Vendors and librarians both regard this process as different for migration projects compared to first-time automation efforts.

In a first-time automation, libraries tend to rely on numerical evaluation of vendors' proposals and claims. In migration projects, libraries find site visits to be the most effective way to evaluate quality and hands-on work issues. At some point either during the final selection process or shortly after a vendor is chosen, the process shifts to a life-cycle model. The life-cycle motor is also primarily concerned with the library as a single entity. At this point, the plan, which was developed in earlier stages, becomes the guide for the process.

The library engages is a series of steps that were laid out in the plan, possibly on a strict timeschedule. This includes all of the steps technically necessary to implement the system as well as steps to prepare the users. This process is imminent in, or prescribed by the plan, and is much more predictable than the earlier stages. The library may have even planned for contingencies. Once the actual conversion in done, and the new system is live, the process become somewhat less predictable. Procedures that worked on paper or in test may fail under the pressure of real-life use.

While none of the motors seem to be completely dominant at this point, the evolutionary theory is closest. Procedures that work 'survive' while others are discarded. The changes may still be described as imminent, however, because they are constrained by the system. The others motors continue to play some role, as plans are made and carried out, and different stakeholders disagree on various issues. The dialectical motor may become dominant from time-to-time as the vendor announces new releases, or the library recommends enhancements for the system. At these times the possibilities for change are less constrained, and the results become more emergent.

STRATEGIES

The authors who describe actual automation projects also list key lessons and make recommendations. There are a number of general, and some very specific, suggestions along with a couple of common threads. One of the common threads is communication. Whether it is between management and employees, between systems and users, or between the employees at large, it seems that more communication is always better. A related thread is the need to involve the users in the process as early as possible. Several of the authors suggested that users should be involved at the very beginning, during the selection process. Montage, Norman, Gaudin, Hallmark and Smith all cite lack of user involvement in the selection or planning stage as an obstacle to successful implementation. Since, these two threads stand out, we may conclude that if any overall strategy is too be effective, it must include a high level of communication and user participation.

STRATEGIES FROM THE CASE IMPLEMENTATION

Norman described three change strategies in his evaluation of the CASE implementation. These strategies could be used independently or in conjunction with each other.

Rational-empirical

This strategy focuses on training and information. It is presumed that teaching people to use the system and providing a rational explanation of why it is better will lead them to use it. This strategy could easily be applied to a library automation or migration project, as many of the authors indicated the importance of training programmes.

Normative-educational

This strategy focuses on group strategies for promoting acceptance of the new systems and providing motivation to use it. First, identify the attitudes that create resistance, and then develop programmes to change them. This is similar to developing training sessions in the rational-empirical strategy. The difference is that the sessions are intended to develop positive attitudes instead imparting information.

Power-coercive

In this strategy individuals are induced to use the new system by the threat of loosing their job or other benefits. This can be a fairly direct approach to implement change, but it also runs a high risk creating bad feelings, job dissatisfaction, and tension between management and employees. Threats, whether explicit or implicit, will also add to the fear and anxiety already identified as an obstacle to change. A variation of this strategy can be applied in a positive way by offering employees incentives for change. While this is can be regarded as a power-exercise it is less confrontational. In the CASE implementation, the main strategy that was applied was the rational-empirical strategy.

The normative-educational strategy was largely ignored, and the power-coercive strategy was inconsistently applied. Management made statements that employees were required to use the system, but did not follow-up when it was not used. Management also did not provide any direct positive incentives. This strategy may also be applied to library systems in the sense that when the old system is shut-off, employees will not be able to perform their duties without using the new system.

PHASED IMPLEMENTATION

Saunders recommends a strategy of phased implementation. The idea of this strategy is to minimize the impact of the new system has on staff by introducing modules in a gradual fashion. For example, a library might implement cataloguing or acquisitions functions first, and circulation latter. This strategy has some advantages. Successful implementation of one module should increase staff willingness to use another. Also, management can deal with the staff in smaller groups, concentrating on the area currently being automated, instead of dealing with all areas at once. The chief drawback of this strategy is found when the current system is already well integrated.

In this case, phased implementation may mean that user's are initially presented with a system that has fewer features than their previous system. There may also be technical difficulties that preclude phased implementation, as the two systems are not likely to communicate with each other well, if at all. Where it is usable, this strategy should also be combined with other strategies. Saunders specifically emphasises the importance of training and communication issues.

PARTICIPANT-ORIENTED CHANGE

Zeffane advocates the strategy of participant-oriented change, which is based on the premise that change works best when comes from the bottom up rather than from the top down. One reason for this premise is that if the employees introduce change, then they will not have an authority figure to rebel against. It is also based on the idea that collegial affiliation is a positive motivation for change. That is, employees will be more motivated to help with a changes initiated by someone at, or close to, their level. To use participant oriented change, management needs to shift the responsibility for change away from themselves and towards the employees.

This strategy goes beyond considering the users' needs, or soliciting input, to actually delegating authority to the participants. This strategy takes advantage of the fact that the employees who are closest to the hands-on work have the most detailed knowledge about it. This also frees the upper management from concentrating on this level of detail, and to concentrate on overall strategic planning. This strategy may not be effective in all types of organisations.

There are some essential elements for participative strategies to work. First, the employees given responsibilities for change must be well informed. Second, the employees must understand and agree with the mission of the organisation. Unless these requirements are met, management cannot expect that the decisions will be beneficial to the organisation. The third requirement is that this style of change must be supported by the organisation culture. The management must be comfortable with this type of delegation.

MANAGEMENT FUNCTIONS

The traditional roles of management are planning, organisation, coordination and control. These can be applied to these change strategies.

RATIONAL-EMPIRICAL

The rational-empirical strategy is primarily concerned with dispensing information, presuming that the plans for change have already been made. It involves the organising function of management, in the sense that the managers determine what information needs to be given to which employees in order to implement the changes. It also involves the control function, in that the management is seeking to influence behaviour through the information it dispenses.

NORMATIVE-EDUCATIONAL

The normative-education strategy is concerned with influencing attitudes and behaviour. As such, it involves the control function of management, but in an indirect manner. That is, rather than controlling behaviour directly, the management attempts to instill attitudes which are likely to result in the desired behaviour. Like the rational-empirical strategy, it also involves the coordinating function, as managers decide who should be involved in which programmes.

POWER-COERCIVE

The power-coercive strategy concerns the management role of control in a straight- forward fashion. It is mainly concerned with seeing to it that the change decisions are carried out as directed. To ensure this, it dispenses rewards or penalties to individuals or groups depending or whether they have implemented the changes. In the extreme, employees who fail to change are fired.

PHASED IMPLEMENTATION

Phased implementation involves both the planning and coordinating functions to a large degree. Planning includes determining the order in which to implement the modules and setting timetables for each phase. Coordination includes meshing together the efforts of different groups associated with each phase, and ensuring that each module is integrated with the previous ones when it is brought into production. As more modules are brought into the 'live' mode, coordination becomes essential in order to see that the different areas function smoothly.

PARTICIPANT-ORIENTED CHANGE

Participant oriented change involves the coordinating function of management. Since, much of the planning and decision making is delegated downward to the staff, management must integrate these plans and decisions. This is particularly important when implementing an integrated library system, as the activities of staff in one area will have more impact on other areas than they are accustomed to. The actual delegation of these responsibilities to employees involves the organising function. Determining how and to whom these responsibilities are delegated is in important part of the change process.

This may involve organising employees into self-managed teams, work groups, or interdepartmental task forces. How these groups are organised, the amount of authority they have, and how they will interact with each other are crucial decisions.

CONCLUSION

The participant oriented change strategy provides the best overall approach to managing library automation and migration projects. Of the strategies which have been outlined, it offers the highest degree of employee communication and participation. These are the same areas that caused the most problems if they were inadequate. One of the chief advantages of this strategy is that it involves the users of the system at the earliest possible stage of the project. That is during the teleological process of identifying reasons for the project and setting goals or criteria for a new system. Involving the employees at this stage reduces the need for normative attitude-adjusting sessions latter in the process.

This is not to say that managers who adopt this strategy can just ignore employee attitudes later on. Change will still be stressful, and people may still resist it at various points. But, management will not have to invest as much effort in convincing staff that the new system is better if the staff were involved in selecting it. The rational-empirical strategies of employee training programmes will still have a role to play, as the process moves on. As was demonstrated in the failed attempt at implementing the CASE system, this strategy is not sufficient by itself. But users must learn how a new system works if they are to use it at all. Within the overall context of participant oriented strategy, other employees provide much of that training. With their hands-on experience, employee led training can be more effective than vendor supplied 'canned presentations'.

This also promotes an atmosphere in which employees will be comfortable sharing their learning experiences, tricks and shortcuts following implementation. The other two strategies, phased implementation and power-coercive can not be recommended across the board. The power-coercive strategy is divisive, and is likely make the change harder instead of easier. This strategy aggravates fears about job security, which is one of the sources of change anxiety. While a degree of control needs to be maintained, a threatening approach is not desirable as a general strategy.

The strategy of phased implementation will be helpful for some situations, but not for all. For libraries currently using manual systems or automated systems that are not integrated, this method may help to ease the transition. For libraries that already have a well-integrated system, it could create even more chaos. Within the context of participant-oriented change, the choice of whether to include it rests with the employees who actually work with the system.

3

Problems of Library Automation

In old civilizations like India and other Asian countries, libraries have been in existence since, early times. Recent political and economic developments which have brought about various types of changes in these countries are also reflected in the evolution of information systems. India's educational system had a definite elitist slant in mediaeval times and the legacy of feudalism during the British period nurtured this trend. Libraries with very rich collections of manuscripts and other rare reading material were mainly the property of the elite. The infrastructure of the country was, moreover, not congenial for the kind of wide-ranged library system which one can envisage today. Library development has shown a marked change since, 1947. It is estimated that India now has approximately 90,000 libraries of different types. The Indian library system can be divided into four broad categories: public, academic, special and national libraries.

PUBLIC LIBRARIES

India is divided into states, union territories, districts, sub districts and villages. The state central libraries serve as public libraries. There are also district central libraries, but village libraries are few and far between. Libraries and library development are included in the broad category of education which, under India's constitution, is considered the responsibility of each state. Some states, namely Tamil Nadu,

Karnataka, Andhra and Maharashtra, have very progressive library legislator! which provides the necessary framework and finances for developing good state public library systems. Despite this, only a very small percentage of the total population of India has access to public libraries.

ACADEMIC LIBRARIES

There has been some improvement in the standards and status of university and college libraries in recent years. At present there are more than 100 universities and 8000 colleges throughout the country. Most of these have library facilities which are in different stages of evolution. School libraries, however, have not been given sufficient attention. Primary and middle-level schools rarely have library facilities, and barely 20 per cent of the secondary schools have adequate library facilities.

SPECIAL LIBRARIES

These are mainly the boon of the post-independence period. Government departments, research institutions, business and industrial houses have established libraries for their own research and development programmes. Currently there are approximately 1500 of these special libraries in India; they are also at different stages of development.

NATIONAL LIBRARIES

Under the national library system, the National Library of India is situated in Calcutta. There are regional libraries of national stature at Bombay and Madras. Some libraries on special subjects are now being given the status of national libraries, *e.g.*, the National Medical Library and the Indian Agricultural Research Institute Library. The major activites of the different categories of Indian libraries are mainly routine work, such as acquisition, circulation, management, processing, reference and bibliographic service, periodical holdings, information retrieval, inventory, and so on.

The services and techniques utilised in the different libraries, however, tend to make these activities very cumbersome and slow. The acquisitions of most libraries are done independently, and involve unnecessary duplication of work and lengthy procedures. Cataloguing and classification methods differ from one library to another and are generally time-consuming and labour-oriented. This is very confusing for the users as they must thus switch from one classification and cataloguing system to another when using more than one library.

There is also a lack of bibliographic control at the national level. The Indian National Bibliography suffers from a large time lag. Almost all library activities involve long hours of manual work, tending to make library service very unpopular. Therefore, users still cannot envisage a librarian as a giver of information but consider him or her a custodian of books. In order to improve the services of libraries, application of newer methods, such as information, computer and communication technologies, will be needed. I am only concerned here with computer applications in libraries and believe that for efficient functioning of our library systems, as suggested, need automated services at some point. But serious thought must first be given to which areas will be automated, while keeping in mind the national need.

NATIONAL SCENE ON LIBRARY AUTOMATION

Elaborate automated library systems are still far off in the context of any developing country. The priorities of each country may vary, but the emphasis is mainly on providing the basic necessities of life to its people. The use of computers started in India with the establishment of computer centres at the Indian Institute of Technology and the Tata Institute of Fundamental Research during 1963-64. At present, there are about 400 computers installed at different places. The size and variety range from a Honeywell 400 to the large IBM 370/155 and DEC-1077.

These computers are used mainly for scientific calculations, business applications and data processing for decision-making. Computerised library activities are found in very few organisations, and consist primarily of the use of spare capacity of available computer facilities suitable for off-line use. Although the number of institutions which have computerised library applications is still very small, the awareness of quickly and easily available information is gradually increasing.

I conducted a short survey in this connection through a questionnaire and personal letters sent to different institutions and business houses outside Delhi which have automated library facilities. Like most questionnaire surveys, this one did not prove very successful, although the personal letters I received from some heads of institutions were encouraging. I then visited some of these major institutions in and around Delhi, and interviewed many of those who work with computerised systems or have plans to do so in the future. The institutions visited were: Indian National Scientific Documentation Centre (INSDOC) and National Informatics Centre, New Delhi; Bhabha Atomic Research Centre (BARC) and Tata Institute of Fundamental Research (TIFR), both in Bombay; Documentation Research Training Centre (DRTC), Hindustan Machine Tools, Ltd. (HMT) and Central Machine Tools of India (CMTI), all in Bangalore; and Small Industries Extension Training (SIET) Institute and the Administrative Staff College of India in Hyderabad.

Altogether, twenty-five organisations were contacted. While this survey may not have been comprehensive in its coverage, the extensive discussions gave a good picture of the problems facing Indian organisations using library automation.

INSDOC, NEW DELHI

Automation is used for indexes, a union catalogue of serial publications, data processing of Indian periodicals on science and technology, directory compilation, and the centralised acquisition of periodicals for thirty laboratories. The IBM 360 model 44 and IBM 1620 are used on a rental basis.

TIFR, BOMBAY

Automated operations include recent additions list, cumulative classified catalogue of books, weekly list of preprints/reports of TIFR, catalogues of progress serials and periodical holdings, and evaluations of journals from the user's point of view. The CDC 3600/160-A and DEC- 1077 computers are available in-house.

NATIONAL INFORMATICS CENTRE, NEW DELHI

Bibliographic citations are available so far only for books in its library; periodical articles are to be added. The centre is a member of INSPEC tape service and a subscriber to a patent bibliographic information system since, 1978. The HP 2 I/MX is used.

INDIAN INSTITUTE OF TECHNOLOGY (IIT), MADRAS

In collaboration with INSDOC, IIT handled the CHEM/SDI project, a computer-based SDI system using the IBM 370 model 155 system and the CA Condensates data base. The CHEM/SDI uses a subset of CAN/SDI software made available by CISTI through UNESCO for its regional pilot project. The project was also handled by NISSAT during 1976-77. The project has been upgraded into a national SDI service using CAC, INSPEC and Compendex data bases; there are more than 500 users.

DRTC, BANGALORE

This group provides education and training, and researches methods for designing and developing computer-based information systems and services. A set of fourteen programmes have been developed in COBOL for creation and updating of the data base, retrieval of bibliographical references in response to specific queries, provision of current awareness and SDI services, retrieval of factual data, provision of a referral service, the semi-automatic generation of a microthesaurus, indexing, and so on.

BARC, BOMBAY

The computer unit of the Library and Information Services of BARC uses the in-house computer Honeywell 400 and BESM 6 for information processing. Computerisation activities include: preparation of a monthly current awareness bulletin, Bibliography of Current Reports; an SDI service offered regularly to some seventy-five users since, May 1972; retrospective litreature searches based on stored data on request from BARC scientists; subject bibliographies; documentation lists; compilation of periodical holdings; loan and issue system of the library; and inventory. An SDI service using the DEC-1077 computer of the National Centre for Software Development and Computing Techniques and TIFR and the magnetic tape output of the International Nuclear Information System is being developed and will be in operation shortly.

SIET, HYDERABAD

This group has automated its Index to Product Profile, which is a list of literature available in the library to April 1976. A TDC 12 is used on a rental basis.

CMTI, BANGALORE

Here work is being done on automating an in-depth index of periodical articles to compile a data base. They have a PDF/ 11 in-house. Future plans include classifying the trade catalogue.

HMT, BANGALORE

Currently under consideration is computerisation of the comparative product profile and the issue system. The computer used is ICL 1903.

PHYSICAL RESEARCH LABORATORY, AHMEDABAD

This laboratory has a mechanised catalogue of its publications holdings and information retrieval facilities. They have discontinued CAS and plan to start SDL In use is the IBM 360 model.

OTHERS

Some industrial units, such as Asian Paints India, Ltd., Hindustan Zinc, Ltd., and Institute of Armament Technology have automated catalogues of holdings. Along with all these ventures in automated library services, a weeklong on-line demonstration of the ESRIN/RECON data base system used at Frascati, Italy was arranged at TIFR during September 1976, with the assistance of UNESCO and the European Space Agency. The Frascati centre had 10 data bases and provided access to about 7.5 million references at the time.

NISSAT

Although these organisations and some other institutions have plans for future automation, the most important plan in India is the National Information System for Science and Technology (NISSAT). In 1971, for the first time, it was seriously felt that a strong national network of documentation and information services was necessary to meet the evergrowing need of scientists and research scholars. The Indian government created the high-powered National Committee on Science and Technology in October 1971. A report submitted by the committee in 1973 recommended the establishment of NISSAT under the Department of Science and Technology. The NISSAT network comprises a sectoral system, a regional system and other specialised services.

SECTORAL SYSTEM

All major areas of science and technology are classified into information sectors based on discipline, mission and product, *e.g.*, leather technology, machine tools, drugs and Pharmaceuticals, etc., Organisations of national stature, such as INSDOC, Defence Scientific Documentation Centre, BARC and Small Enterprises Documentation Centre, will continue to provide services at the national level.

REGIONAL SYSTEM

Because of India's size, more than one sectoral centre for each discipline is necessary. Therefore, regional centres will act as NISSAT contact points. These will be located in major areas of research, development, educational and industrial activities, *e.g.*, one centre is in Delhi and another in Bangalore.

Similar centres will be started in Bombay, Calcutta, Madras and Kanpur.

OTHER SPECIALISED SERVICES

Efforts such as the experimental computer-based SDI services of IIT and the on-line demonstration of ESRIN/ RECON at TIFR fall into this category. The ESRIN/RECON demonstration was a success and attracted considerable interest, and there is now a proposal to provide permanent terminals at Bombay and Delhi. NISSAT also includes plans to create and maintain data bases on themes of national importance, and technical and statistical data banks on such topics as minerals, resources, etc. NISSAT is the most ambitious information network plan in India today. Although the social sciences have also been brought within its fold, its emphasis is mainly on science and technology.

Therefore, social scientists are of the opinion that a parallel system for the social sciences and humanities would make the circle effectively complete. India's library system, as described earlier, can make use of automation in different ways for more effective functioning. Thus far, the specialised libraries and documentation centres have laid emphasis primarily on information retrieval, which has been substantially developed in many areas. The major need for computerised bibliographical control has not yet been satisfied.

Table 3.1 Possible Computerized Activities for Different Types of Libraries

	Type of Library			
Activity	Public	Academic	Special*	National
Acquisition and distribution	x	x	x	x
Management and administration	x			x
Cataloguing and bibliographies	x	x		x
Periodical holding		x	x	x
Information retrieval		x	x	
Circulation	x	x	x	

*Special libraries include documentation centres

PROBLEMS OF LIBRARY AUTOMATION

Presently, the system of computerised library activities is growing, although it is still in its infancy compared with system in developed countries. While at the sophisticated research level there appears to be general acceptance that computerised library activities will lead to increased efficiency, the hindrances to such a goal are many and any efforts to achieve it are the exception rather than the rule. Computerised library service is likely to be beset with technological, economic and attitudinal problems peculiar to most developing countries.

TECHNOLOGICAL PROBLEMS

Technological problems include both the hardware, *i.e.*, the computer as an instrument for information processing, and the software, *i.e.*, the methodology which is applied. The major problems faced today in terms of the hardware are due to the variety of computers being used in different types of research and business institutions. The computers, manufactured by various firms are not compatible. Developing countries sometimes receive sophisticated technology like computers as gifts from more developed countries; these often become obsolete from the manufacturer's point of view.

Such machines are not only unsuitable for most complex work but any technical problems which come up cannot be repaired. Information retrieval work requires machines more sophisticated than those manufactured indigenously, and few imported machines are capable of handling information retrieval applications. The random access facility and disks large enough for storage of bibliographic information are not readily available.

In most institutions, organisational goals receive priority over the library's requirements, meaning that the librarian must use the computer available rather than what is actually required according to specifications. Library activities in all institutions are done through sharing disk space as well as computer time. Therefore, when the storage capacity is not large enough to accommodate various types of data, bibliographic data are given the lowest priority. On-line facilities are rare in India. In fact, only TIFR's library has access to an on-line terminal for bibliographic data, the DEC-1077 computer of the National Centre for Software Development and Computing Techniques.

The communication infrastructure of India is still not suitable for extensive on-line information facilities; the telephone system is not reliable enough to support an effective network facility. Software problems arise because programmes must be developed in terms of the machine on which they are to operate. Therefore, the incompatibility of equipment tends to make the software incompatible as well, especially when programmes are written in machine or assembly language. While using languages which are not machine-bound, such as FORTRAN, COBOL, ALGOL, etc., may seem like a solution, in actual practice such languages cannot be interchanged without suitable modifications.

A software package developed for the IBM 360 model 30 would require many changes not only in the programme but also in the programming language if it were to run on any other computer. Development of a programme suitable for the available machine is therefore preferable to acceptance of a package programme. This makes the development and use of package programmes difficult and leads to a lack of standardisation in programming language as well as in output. Machine-readable data bases are byproducts of international information network systems and are available on magnetic tapes.

These are useful in building information resources and for retrospective search and current awareness services. Again, however, the tape service is expensive and suitably sophisticated computers are scarce. The data bases have a standard format which requires extensive changes to fit existing hardware and other system requirements. Also, relevant bibliographic information has to be selected from the data base and stored. Often this storage space is scarce and expensive.

ECONOMIC PROBLEMS

The major obstacle for any innovations in developing countries is the lack of resources. The initial cost of establishing a computer system is beyond the reach of most organisations and institutions. Library and information processing is done either with spare computer capacity made available by the institution itself, or with computer time hired from another institution. The cost of hiring computer time and storage space is very high and often cannot be justified at the management level by cost-benefit analysis. At IIT, for example, CPU time per hour costs ₹ 1000 for educational purposes and ₹.2000 for business and industrial use.

Moreover, the computer provides only paper printout, and the paper often costs more than the processing. Few developing countries can afford the machine-readable data bases, either. The tapes are very expensive and because foreign exchange is involved in subscribing to them, it is even more difficult for most organisations in India and other developing countries to afford them. The annual subscription rate of one data base is now $8000. Library tasks often overlap and their peculiar nature seldom makes the advantages of computerisation seem very convincing in the light of cost-benefit analysis.

In India, libraries and information centres are attached to government organisations or research institutions, so library services cannot be calculated on a profit/loss basis. Long-term benefits have to be kept in mind while justifying such services. The libraries that have computerised some of their services or operations often have not taken such steps as a result of serious thought. Computerisation has a glamour of its own in the minds of many librarians. Overly enthusiastic librarians often run uneconomical programmes, producing lengthy listings, for instance, in the name of computerised service.

Often the manual method is used concurrently with the computerised system because of a lack of faith on the part of staff and users. The duplication of work and the cost involved in these cases is obviously unjustifiable; the librarian should know which aspects of service should be mechanised. An example of an economically viable computerised library activity is the centralised acquisition of periodicals in operation at INSDOC. This facility serves thirty laboratories, which not only frees the facilities from the tedious task of periodical acquisitions but also eliminates the cost of duplicate purchasing.

ATTITUDINAL PROBLEMS

Computers appear very awesome to developing countries. They are powerful machines which can perform many functions and therefore offer a solution to the many types of manual inefficiency which often plague the developing countries. Among librarians there are two different attitudes towards computerised facilities. One group is taken in by the glamour of modern technology and believes that computers can perform miracles. Members of this group often give insufficient thought to the real value of the computer to the organisation/institution and make uneconomical, haphazard use of the facility.

The other group, still the majority in developing countries, lacks knowledge of the potential and consequences of library automation. There is constant tension between this traditional librarian group and the 'new-wave' librarians. Professionals of the majority group do not realise that computers cannot replace human intelligence. Due to the accuracy essential for data input in library services, the librarian/information scientist is indispensable. The National Library of Calcutta conducted an experiment to computerise the Indian National Bibliography in 1968.

The scheme failed, however, because labour unions opposed it fearing retrenchment of library staff. Among developing countries, the attitudes of India's librarians are typical. They are not confident about automated services. Library staffs should therefore be trained in programming and thus be made aware of the work involved in automation. They will then realise that automation will not take away their jobs. They will also realise that computers are machines which have their limitations as well as their advantages. The communication gap between the librarian and the computer specialist is another major hindrance in establishing any effective automated system in a library.

There is often disagreement among the librarian, the programmer and the systems analyst. Librarians should be trained in computer programming and computer specialists should be versed in the special needs of library automation. Only then can a common language evolve among the three and a project be started. Administrative personnel assume a very important role in decisionmaking. Their enthusiasm, support and conviction can help realise any new plan, just as their apathy and lack of understanding of the need for accurate and speedy information can jeopardise any effort. Although many things have taken a favourable turn in India, the majority of those at the management level unfortunately are not conversant with the development of information science and are unaware of the important role of information in all areas of national development.

This very often results in insufficient planning, which in turn curbs the enthusiasm of imaginative information scientists and librarians. Due to this lack of appreciation, priorities are poorly ordered and funds are not well allocated. Administrators also have a tendency to underestimate or overestimate the capacity of automation. Any information system or service is planned for the best possible benefit to its users. Unless the users are mentally prepared to accept a new system, however, it cannot be effective. Indian users are still unfamiliar and overawed by computers, so computer awareness and interest has to be fostered to enable proper utilizaton of a system.

They should neither overestimate computer capabilities nor be afriad of interacting with the computer systems. Another obstacle is that, because batch processing systems are still in use in India, there are bulky printouts in monotonous type faces and formats which prove to be a headache not only for the librarian, but also for the user. There is no dearth of manpower in systems analysis and computer programming in India. We are already exporting software packages to countries that find them less expensive than developing their own. Library automation is still neglected, however; it is an area which has not attracted young people with appropriate expertise. Training should be given to both the librarian and the computer specialist about each other's functions and possibilities. Both INSDOC and DRTC conduct courses on automated systems in libraries. Under the forthcoming NISSAT plan, steps are being taken to build the requisite technical manpower.

Moreover, the Indian government's Department of Electronics is developing training programmes for the National Informatics Centre. There are two main objectives in training for library automation: to orient the programmers and system analysts to writing programmes suitable for automating library facilities, and to persuade librarians to accept the utility of automation and teach them to prepare accurate inputs to make the system worthwhile.

RECOMMENDED IMPROVEMENTS

- The computers used in India should not vary so widely. Production of computers with special capacity for library automation should be taken into consideration.
- Government policy has taken a positive step in establishing large computer systems, with one sophisticated central computer capable of handling complex information to be connected to indigenous minicomputers. The National Informatics Centre project dealing with agricultural and other governmental data processing is designed along similar lines. Such plans should be pursued.
- Indigenous, inexpensive library package programmes are very necessary. These should be usable on a large variety of machines and be capable of handling different activities in the library. The MARC format would be ideal if it could be adapted for the smaller indigenous computers. DRTC is currently involved in preparing software packages for information retrieval.

- The international data bases are being used by some organisations. However, these are expensive and often not applicable to Indian research needs. Indigenous data bases with our specific requirements should be prepared. Core periodicals in each subject relevant to India, and litreature from important Indian periodicals, should be used as input for such data bases.
- A national standard or common language for bibliographic information exchange is necessary. Efforts are being made to achieve a standard language compatible with any international standard.
- Training of personnel, *i.e.*, proper communication among the librarian, computer programmer and systems analyst is very important. Courses offering training in library automation are being taught, but there is a general need for better understanding among these three architects of library automation.
- User awareness and orientation is very much needed. The users comprise managerial policy-makers as well as the research scholars and regular clientele of a library. The need for, as well as the possibilities of, automated library facilities have to be highlighted by professionals and experts in this area. A few seminars and workshops have been conducted at New Delhi and Bangalore, namely the UNISIST workshop in August 1975 and the Indo-U.S., seminar in 1977; however, little else has been accomplished in this area.

CONCLUSION

Do we need library automation now? In developing countries the problems are many and though they are not insurmountable, they are certainly very difficult to face and live with. The most pertinent question for our profession in this regard, however, is whether we really need computerised library services on a large scale. A colleague from Bangladesh said: "The library and information sciences are a 'least-priority area' in this country. Only 20 percent of the people can write their names. There is an acute shortage of readers.... Most of the nation's resources are utilised for food, shelter, flood control and health problems."

Although the Indian situation differs from that of Bangladesh in many ways, the first priority of any developing country is to provide the basic necessities to its people. Litreacy and education are still at the primary level. Information of a very basic nature, such as the essentials for healthful living, must be presented in simple terms and communicated through media which will reach the people. Library activities of even the most primitive nature will not be within the intellectual grasp of most people unless the library is turned into a proper communication centre. We cannot take as our model the community information centre as developed in the West. The economic and social problems here are so acute and diverse that no one model for all parts of the country can be established.

As discussed earlier, library facilities may have to cater to a sophisticated and highly academic clientele in different organisations even though it is a minority. Libraries have had a long tradition here, but academia has yet to develop a tradition of data-oriented search for knowledge. The concept of libraries as storehouses of books remains very strong. Information is still sought in books rather than in microform. Because profundity in knowledge is the tradition of Eastern culture, the modern trend towards fast, accurate information is still not expected.

That is exactly what a computer is supposed to provide for a scholar. Information is often treated as a commodity in the West. In industrially developed countries it is believed that any information which is economically profitable should be considered worthwhile and made quickly available. Can the same be said of the Indian situation? In highly developed industries, such as Hindustan Machine Tools, Ltd., a survey of the information needs of engineers revealed that the time factor was not important. Even if the information were received a day or two after it had been requested it would still be accepted and used. The competition in the industrial field is not sufficiently keen to require immediate information. Industrial research is done in a relatively leisurely fashion in India.

At the documentation centre of SIET, the need for computerising library and information work has not been perceived. I quote: "As of today, there does not seem to be adequate justification for computerising library and information work here. Our intake is not that sizable, nor are the demands on us yet so enormous that we should think of using computers."

The genuine need of the country is to provide usable resources for spreading litreacy and to develop libraries at the school and college levels in order to give students the opportunity to acquire the taste for information. I do not intend to belittle the efforts to build a sophisticated information system such as NISSAT. India is a country in which the levels Proposals of development are varied in different areas. Its planners must therefore cater to the needs of each area in its own right. On the whole, however, our priorities still differ. Both librarians and clientele must be made information-conscious before anything as expensive, sophisticated and dumb as a computer can become a tool in their hands.

4

Supporting Multilinguality in Library Automation

Today's libraries have automated their everyday transactions such as acquisition, cataloguing, and circulation. An automated library appears to users as an online public access catalogue (OPAC) through which they can quickly search and obtain the desired information. Such systems support bibliographic search according to author name, title, publication year, etc., and provide free text and keyword facilities. Hence, computer systems have replaced the librarian's role as intermediary between user and library, and expert systems that simulate this role providing general information to the user have been developed.

Moreover, the application of AI to information retrieval has recently attracted the attention of information scientists. Advanced applications of natural language processing (NLP), such as machine translation, have already improved the capabilities of several systems in this area. Translation-based methods for translingual information retrieval require the query be translated into the target language.

In this case, full-fledged machine translation is not applicable. Experience shows that of three well-known translation approaches, which is dictionary-based term translation (DICT), example-based term translation (EBT), and example- based term-to-sentence (EBS), DICT presents the best solution for queries consisting of isolated words, or at best, short phrases. Other approaches in information retrieval are concerned with systems with cross-language functionality. A few of them, especially in trade trans-actions and Web-based information services, make use of a controlled language in order to improve the recall and precision rates. The majority of these systems utilise free text retrieval.

The corpus-based approach, MIRTH, supports within-language retrieval in English and Chinese and in specific areas, such as computing, linguistics and litreature. The limitations of this system lie in the lack of a complete linguistic tool to guide translation, as well as in the absence of any maintenance system to deal with tasks such as add, insert, delete, update, replace, and sort links with their keywords. Knowledge- based information retrieval is used in Gilarranz where the features of the EuroWordNet multilingual lexical knowledge base are described.

However, although both approaches tackle the cross-language functionality of the retrieval, they do not consider as yet the localizability of their system by adopting, for instance, an internationalised methodology in their design. In addition, libraries have not paid special attention to multilingual features of OPACs, despite the fact that it is a serious problem. The National Library of Canada was one of the first libraries to offer multilingual access to its users, in the form of controlled bilingual that is English and French, authority files. It is also worthwhile mentioning the ETHICS project that produced an OPAC with multilingual user interface and help screens and a subject index in three languages.

So far, multilinguality in OPACs has been dictated by the needs of a specific multilingual community and restricted to the provision of bilingual or multilingual lists of controlled terms such as controlled authority files, subject headings, and thesauri. Multilinguality as a potential problem for the common user of the library was only explicitly investigated in the NORDINFO survey. According to the results of this survey, multilingual access to online catalogues can improve remarkably the quality of the provided services. Similar user surveys were undertaken by the Central Library of the University of Patras, the Library of the Spanish Agency of International Co-operation, and the Municipal Library of Patras.

The main outcomes of the surveys have been as follows: in a conventional OPAC by using controlled:

- Searching or uncontrolled terms is time consuming, requiring repeated effort from the user who in a lot of cases remains unsatisfied.
- The libraries express their interest in a multilingual access tool, because they understand that multilinguality poses problems to their users as well as to the interconnection with libraries from other countries.
- The translation tool, if any, should be able to retrieve information from the title, subject, and author fields.
- An important indication is that the specific national conditions should be taken very seriously into account, especially with respect to dialects and unofficial languages. A very good example is the relatively high interest of the Spanish library in the Catalan language.

These surveys were aimed at an analysis of the attitude of the users towards the OPAC they used and investigation about their eventual need for a multilingual tool. The results of these surveys are essentially independent of the sex, educational status, familiarity of computer use, and frequency of the use of the OPAC by sample users.

The analysis of the results was very illuminating:

- Approximately 75 per cent of the users were either moderately satisfied or dissatisfied with the results of their searches in the OPAC.
- Over 80 per cent of the dissatisfied users noted that the hits were not in the user's native language or that the search was based only on a single language;
- Approximately 70 per cent of the users were interested in bibliographies written in foreign languages.

- 65 per cent of those who used books in only one language considered being able to search in multiple languages either useful or very useful.

In this chapter, we present Translib, a multilingual interface system to library automation systems. It takes full advantage of tools such as bilingual dictionaries, conversion tables, terminology lexica, intelligent thesauri, and simplified translation tools in order to support multilingual access to library catalogues. This system stemmed from the integration of new and existing multilingual information tools and has been tested in existing medium- sized bibliographic databases in Greece and Spain. The tools are characterised by a high degree of modularity and user-friendliness that allow easy and low-cost maintenance. The following section contains an overview of the Translib system, describes briefly its architecture and gives its basic features.

OVERVIEW OF TRANSLIB

The global Translib perspective is shown in figure.

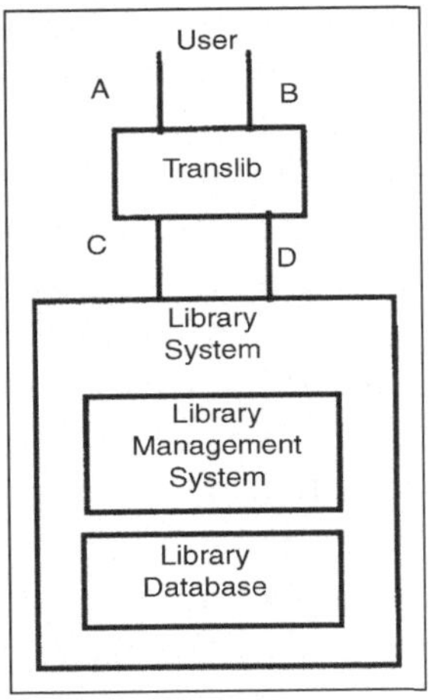

Fig 4.1 Translib Perspective

Notes: *A*: Input, message, search, output language (S).
B: Presented query results, fields, labels, message.
C: Search topic query D: Received records.

The user interacts with the Translib module by choosing the languages to be used as well as the search fields, the search key topics, and the type of searching to be initiated. Translib combines all this information to support multilingual access to the library system, by sending it a query for each key topic and receiving from it the records that match the users' query. Finally, Translib presents the query results to the user in the preferred language as well as the predefined search field labels, information windows, and all messages. If the query results are empty, Translib allows the user to repeat the search using synonyms, super categories, or subcategories of the search keywords. Translib is an OPAC that provides the users with a capability for multilingual access to library catalogues.

Translib is fully implemented, runs under Windows 95, and currently supports three languages, that is English, Greek, and Spanish. These three languages are considered to be sufficient to both demonstrate the feasibility of this type of multilingual access and to highlight potential problems in the future adoption of additional European or non-European languages. An outline of the system is given in figure.

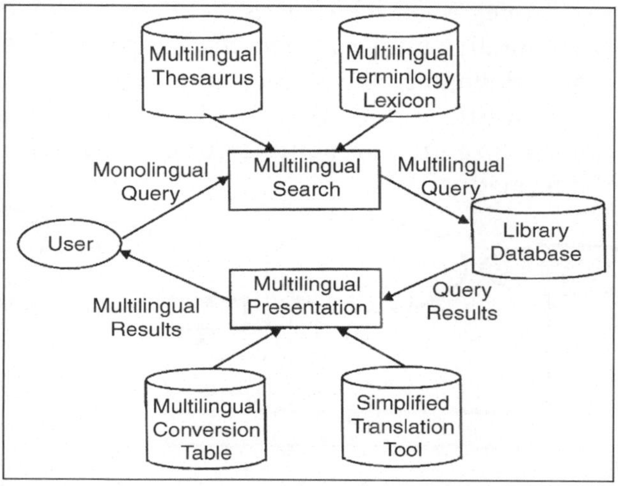

Fig 4.2 An Outline of the Translib System

Translib offers bibliographic information retrieval, whether from a local library database or from remote databases, through servers that support the Z39.50 standard, that is, a standard specifying a client/server- based protocol for information retrieval that was originally proposed for use with bibliographic information. One of the main characteristics of Translib is its ability to be easily integrated into the majority of library automation tools.

In order to achieve this objective, we have had to consider seriously the following problems:

- All library automation systems do not use the same type of database;
- There will be libraries that will not give access to their databases to developers' groups so that they can be connected with the Translib system.

Our solution has been to integrate a Z39.50 client tool into Translib. Thus, the Translib interface can now connect with any library automation system that supports the Z39.50 protocol. All other processes, such as retrieving bibliographic information in any language and translating the titles and keywords into English are also supported by the new Translib with the Z39.50 client module.

Translib comprises two basic tools:

- The multilingual search tool that supports the retrieval of multilingual bibliographic information; and
- The multilingual presentation tool that allows multilingual presentation of the retrieved information.

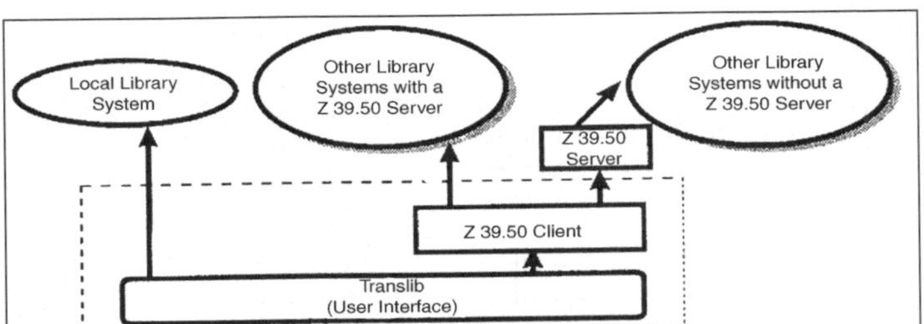

Fig 4.3 The Translib System with the Z39.50 Client Tool

The following subsections illustrate the features of these tools.

By taking advantage of them, Translib offers the following facilities in contrast to up-to-date library systems:

- Localisation of user-interface is supported.
- The user is able to enter a query in his/her native language and search for entries that match this query in all the possible languages for which there is at least one entry in the current database.
- The retrieval of all the entries for a given query as well as for its synonyms in any language is possible. Furthermore, the user is able to indicate the type of search, which can be based on narrower and/or broader terms of the query.
- Finally, translation of the retrieved books/journals titles and keywords in any language is provided in order to give the user an idea of the content of these books/journals.

MULTILINGUAL SEARCH TOOL

This tool enables the user to enter the query in the language (s)he prefers and select the languages in which the matching entries have to be found. Essentially, this tool performs a conversion from monolingual to multilingual queries.

The user can select the input language and the search languages (s)he prefers:

- *Input language*: The language used to introduce the search criteria, that is, the title, author, publication year, etc.
- *Search language(s)*: One or more languages in which the user wishes to find some documents matching his queries.

Furthermore, the user is able to determine the search depth by selecting to search with synonyms, and/or narrower terms, and/or broader terms of the search criteria.

The multilingual search tool utilises:

- A multilingual terminology lexicon, allowing the search of keywords in several languages, and

- A multilingual thesaurus, enabling sophisticated bibliographic information retrieval by means of synonyms, narrower and broader terms.

An example of broader and narrower terms of some keywords is shown in table.

Table 4.1 Example for Broader/Narrower Terms

Keyword	Broader Terms	Narrower Terms
Academic	Journal	—
Book	Publication	Manual, Introduction
Brochure	Publication	—
Industrial	Journal	—
Introduction	Book	—
Journal	Publication	Academic, Industrial
Manual	Book	Tutorial, Reference
Publication	—	Book, Brochure, Journal
Reference	Manual	—
Tutorial	Manual	—

The search criteria can be specified in a search screen. A search can be started for publications that match the search criteria. For instance, if the user types part of a keyword in the field Keyword and selects the button Keyword Search, the application searches the multilingual terminology lexicon for keywords to match.

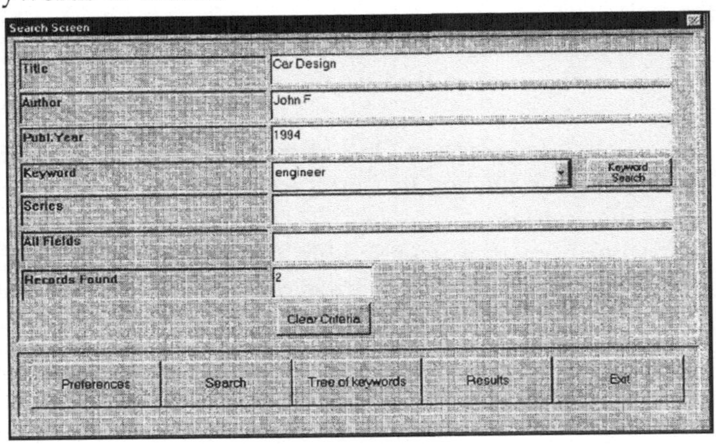

Fig 4.4 Search Screen

The results can be shown in a drop down list. Then a keyword from this list can be selected. The multilingual terminology lexicon contains a list of key topics in three languages, that is, Greek, English, and Spanish.

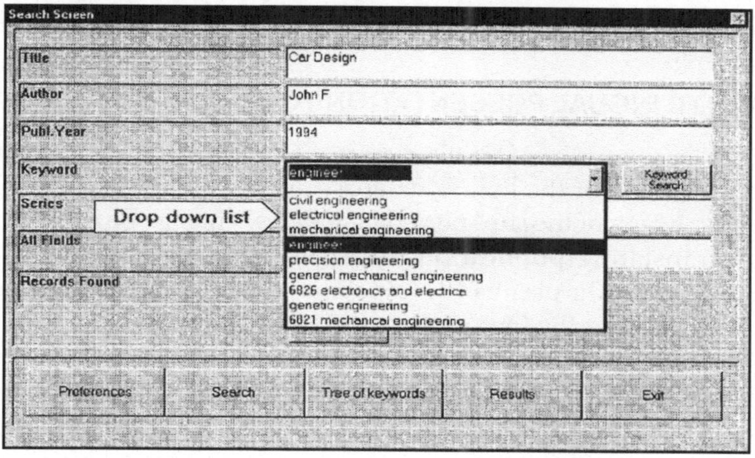

Fig 4.5 A List of Keywords Appear in a Drop Down List

A search for publications that match the search criteria is executed when the button Search is selected from the Search Screen. The number of publications found appears in the field Records Found.

The search fields are as follows:

- *Title*: The title or part of the title of a publications.
- *Author*: The name or part of the name of an author.
- *Publishing year*: The issuing year of a publication.
- *Keyword*: A Keyword or part of a keyword.
- *Series*: The series or part of the series of a publication.
- *All fields*: All the fields associated with a publication.

When a search starts, all the fields associated with a publication are searched for a string that matches the string typed in this field. The application searches for matching publications by using the 'OR' operator between data entered in the search fields. For example, if the search criteria contain the title 'Democracy', the author 'Cat Stevens,' and the keyword 'Ancient Greece,' a search is performed for publications with the title 'Democracy' or publications written by "Cat Stevens" or publications that contain the keyword "Ancient Greece." Finally, fields that are left blank are not included in the search criteria. For example, if the user leaves the fields Publishing Year, Keyword, Series, and All Fields blank, the search criteria include only the fields Title and Author.

MULTILINGUAL PRESENTATION TOOL

This tool allows localisation of the user interface as well as presentation of the library database entries matching the user query in any of the sup- ported languages. This can be achieved by translating publication titles and keywords, if needed. Particularly, the user has the capability of selecting the Message Language and the Output Languages (s)he prefers.

More specifically, these languages stand for:

- *Message language*: The language used for presenting labels and messages to the user as well as help screens.
- *Output language(s)*: One or more languages used for presenting the query results. The multilingual presentation tool utilises.
- A multilingual conversion table, converting labels and messages into the Message Language.
- A simplified translation tool, supporting the translation of book and journal titles and/or keywords into the specified Output Language(s).

A CLARIFYING EXAMPLE

The following clarifying example aims at further illustrating the definitions. Let us assume that the user selects English as the Input Language, English and Greek as the Search Language(s), English, Greek, and Spanish as the Output Language(s), and the search criteria contain the keyword democracy. The multilingual search tool searches the library data- base for entries containing the keywords democracy and the multilingual presentation tool lists the publications that match these keywords and translates their titles and keywords into Spanish as is shown in table.

Table 4.2 A Clarifying Example

Input Language	Search Language(s)	Output Language(s)	
English	English, Greek	English, Greek, Spanish	
Search Criteria (keyword)	**Search for**	**Results** (Title)	(Keywords)
Democracy	*Democracy* *Δημοκρατία*	*Democracy in Ancient Greece* (English translation)	*Democracy, Ancient Greece*
		La Democracia en Grecia Antigua (Spanish translation)	*Democracia, Grecia Antigua*
		Η Δημοκρατία στην Αρχαία Ελλάδα (original language)	*Δημοκρατία, Αρχαία Ελλάδα*

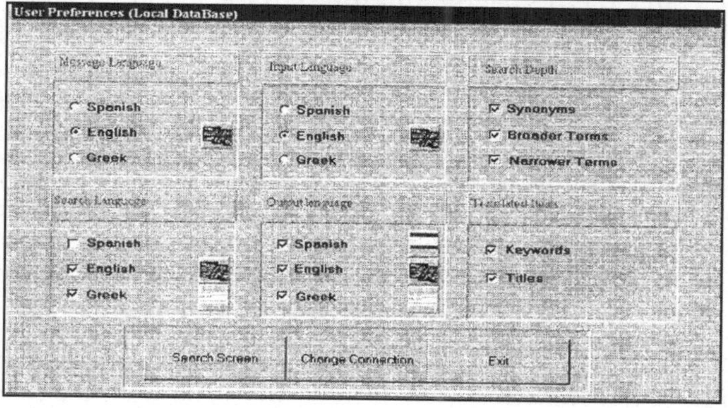

Fig 4.6 The Screen Where the User Enters His/Her Choices for This Search

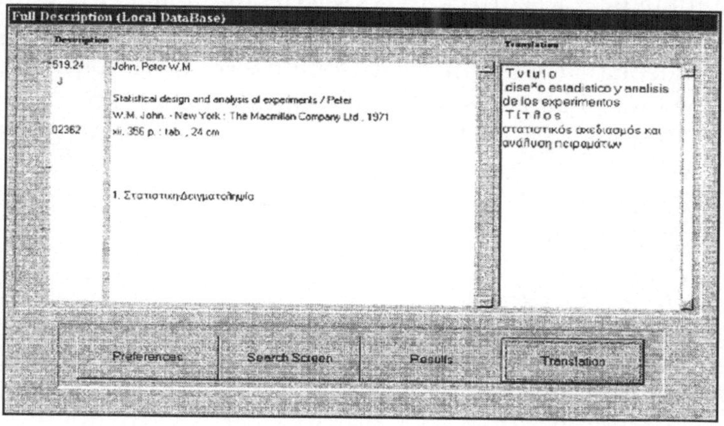

Fig 4.7 Typical Full Description of a Retrieved Book Entry

Figure shows a typical full description of another retrieved book entry that also contains its translation from English into Greek and Spanish.

The system can also present the query results by using a short description of the retrieved book entry. At times a query can retrieve multiple records. In this case, the records are presented to the user ranked in alphabetical order. The original language of these records is also clearly labelled.

MULTILINGUAL RESOURCES

Translib is a system built through the integration of both new and existing information tools. Since, the advantages of the use of reusable resources are well known, we tried to utilise general purpose and state-of-the-art resources where possible, in order to avoid the excessive cost of building a resource from scratch, as well as to ensure the quality and the adequacy of the resources.

MULTILINGUAL THESAURUS

After an extensive market survey and taking into account the advantages and disadvantages of using an existing multilingual thesaurus, we decided that EUROVOC suits the needs of the Translib system. EUROVOC is based on ISO-5964/85, which is an international standard for the development of multilingual thesauri. EUROVOC is a multilingual thesaurus, which was originally built specifically for processing documentation of the European commission. It is implemented in the official languages of the European community.

The edition we used was compiled in 1994 in nine languages:

- Danish
- Dutch
- English
- French
- German
- Greek
- Italian
- Portuguese
- Spanish

Our version of EUROVOC contains only the following languages, which cover the needs of the current Translib system: English, Greek, and Spanish. All these languages have equal status—each descriptor in one language necessarily matches a descriptor in each of the other languages.

At the specific level of descriptors and non-descriptors, the internal structure of EUROVOC depends on semantic relations:

- Scope note (SN)
- Microthesaurus relationship (MT)
- Equivalence relationship (UF, USE)
- Hierarchical relationship (BT, NT)
- Associative relationship (RT)

The EUROVOC thesaurus covers all the subjects that are of importance to the activities of the European community institutions:

- Politics, international relations, European communities, law, economics, trade;
- Finance, social questions, education and communications, science, environment;
- Business and competition, employment and working conditions, transport, energy;
- Agriculture, forestry and fisheries, agri-food stuffs, production;
- Technology and research, industry, geography, international organisations.

We mainly focused on the use of the following subjects: economics, trade, finance, education and communications, science, business and competition, production, technology and research, energy, industry, without excluding the others. Technically speaking, EUROVOC is a single file that contains a significant number of terms relevant to the subjects. EUROVOC's architecture consists of a number of micro-thesauri. Each one of them consists of a set of terms for a given topic.

Each record in a micro thesaurus has several fields indicating the relation between the records and the terms themselves in the nine languages of the European community.

Each term is given in two forms for each language. Two terms can have a hierarchical relation, that is, one can be narrower or broader than the other. Each record in the EUROVOC file fits on a single line. The fields occupy fixed positions on the line and have concrete names. Our goal was to transfer the data from EUROVOC to a commercial database.

A set of routines was thus developed for the compilation of the EUROVOC thesaurus into files with a special format that can be easily read by database procedures. Several files constitute the Translib multilingual thesaurus derived from EUROVOC. There are separate files for the terms of each language. The terms are stored in the same order in each of the three files, so that the files are matching. If a term has no equivalents in one or more languages, there is a blank line in the corresponding position. The line number of each term in the files is used as a unique code during the building of the tree, which is stored in another file and does not include the terms themselves.

Thus, the multilingual thesaurus of TRANSLIB has been designed as a simple ASCII table file which contains all the material that is included in the EUROVOC thesaurus. Software was written in order to be able to extract the terms and relevant terms from this huge data store quickly. B+ trees algorithms have been used to make the extraction process as quick as possible.

In conclusion, the multilingual thesaurus helps the user retrieve bibliography related to the relevant keywords (s)he has entered, as its sophisticated search mechanism automatically builds the tree structure of the keywords in all the preferred search languages and sends a complex query to the data-base. In the case where the user does not use the thesaurus, he may not retrieve all the available bibliographic records, since, the keyword he uses to describe his query may not be the same as that used by the librarian for the record classification.

Even when the user enters a query which has no keywords in the multilingual thesaurus, it is possible to update it by means of an editing tool that caters for a number of data entry fields, such as New Keyword, Related Keyword, Keyword Language, Kind of Relationship, etc.

MULTILINGUAL TERMINOLOGY LEXICON

The result of another extensive market survey encouraged us to adopt EURODICAUTOM as a terminology tool. However, after we had completed the decoding of EURODICAUTOM, a problem emerged. The terms of the multilingual thesaurus were entirely incompatible with those of the multilingual terminology lexicon. This meant that the library database could not be searched using keywords from the multilingual terminology lexicon, nor by using synonyms, broader or narrower terms of it. The solution decided on was to create a multilingual terminology lexicon from the terms of EUROVOC.

This was analysed into two sections:

- The informative part; and
- The data retrieval part.

The former mainly consists of a file containing all the terms that are used as keywords in all the Translib supported languages. This file is a three- column file, which contains the same term in each line for all the supported languages. The latter uses a binary search algorithm to achieve maximum efficiency. In this case, it was necessary to create a sequence of files, which contain an upper case description of terms and a numeric label used to locate the term and its description in all languages.

The multilingual terminology lexicon helps the user choose one term in the preferred Input Language, and search the database for this term as well as for all the equivalent terms in all the preferred Search Languages. Again the user can check the new keywords to be included in the multilingual terminology lexicon by means of an editing tool that caters for a number of data entry fields, such as New Keyword, English Keyword, Spanish Keyword, Greek Keyword, etc.

MULTILINGUAL CONVERSION TABLE

The multilingual conversion table is responsible for the interaction between the user and the system in the user's preferred language. It contains all the label fields, messages, and help screens of the user interface in all the supported languages and provides the user with the ability to both choose the language of the user interface and effectively change it at runtime according to his/her preferences. It is independent of any actual data store that is used as the base of the information storage. Finally, the information kept in the Multilingual Conversion Table is logically grouped into three files, one for each language.

A new file can be used for a new supported language, so that maximum source independence and management can be achieved. The Multilingual Conversion Table is stored at the client's site in relational database tables. One table in the database includes the label fields, messages and on- line help information in the three languages supported by the project. Its internal structure is compatible with a future addition of equivalent terms in other European languages.

The table has the following attributes:

- *Code*: A unique number that acts as the tuple's identifier.
- *Kind*: Reflects the type of the user interface item that is contained in the tuple.
- *EngContent*: Content in English.
- *SpaContent*: Content in Spanish.
- *GreContent*: Content in Greek.

When the user wants to customise any label fields, messages, or help screens, this can be accomplished through an editing tool that caters for a number of data entry fields, such as code label, Greek message, Spanish message, etc.

LIBRARY DATABASE

The Translib system follows the UNIMARC standard so as to be easily portable to all library automation systems following the same standard. Regarding the library database, two medium- sized bibliographic data- bases have been utilised. The Greek one possesses about 10,000 titles concerning mainly engineering and computer science sectors, while the Spanish one possesses about 20,000 titles regarding political and financial topics. More specifically, the Greek library database contains 5,500 Greek titles, 3,500 English titles, and 1,000 titles in other

European languages. On the contrary, the Spanish library database contains 12,000 Spanish titles, 6,300 English titles, and 1,700 titles in other European languages. Both data- bases were considered appropriate and representative to test the performance of the TRANSLIB system.

SIMPLIFIED TRANSLATION TOOL

The translation of the titles carried out by this tool should give the user an idea of the content of a retrieved book/journal. Even when the translation is not completely correct, it should help the user understand the subject of the document. Translating titles is, in general, easier than translating a whole sentence or even entire texts. The simplest title is a single noun while the most complex one may be a whole phrase. Few titles, however, are composed of a long phrase, *i.e.*, the combination of both noun and prepositional phrases. Furthermore, a title is selected carefully by the author to represent the content of a book.

This fact means that a title must not be ambiguous in order to be comprehensible immediately by the reader. In most cases, syntactic or referential ambiguities can easily be solved. Additionally, titles are usually typed carefully by the editors of a book, so that no grammatical or syntactic errors occur. Needless to say, the titles of books and journals are totally different from those found in a newspaper. Looking at the translation of the titles from a computational point-of-view, the translation process can be facilitated further by making a set of assumptions.

These can be described as follows:

- Translation from one language into another is realised via English which is used as an interlingua.
- For each title only one translation is provided. In addition, a set of titles may have the same translation.
- Only the main title of a bibliographic entry is translated. Subtitles, version numbers, etc., are ignored.
- The titles are considered to be linguistically correct. Hence, syntactically incorrect interpretations are ignored.

- No semantic and/or pragmatic information is used. All the titles are referred to the scientific domain of engineering and computer science. Moreover, for every word in the dictionary there is only one translation.
- Finally, the input as well as the output files of the translators are ASCII files containing one title per line. If a title cannot be translated, the output file contains an empty line for it.

The selection of an interlingua was adopted to achieve system robustness and reduce the translation costs. Translation between a pair of languages implies translation to and from interlingua. Additionally, the upgrade of the system with a new supported language would only require the implementation of a ling ware for the new language, able to provide translation to and from interlingua. We selected English as the interlingua, since, it was found that it is the most widespread foreign language among the OPAC users. In fact, our interlingua is not plain English but an artificial language, that is, an abstract form that represents the structure of the title based on the English translations of its consisting words. Thus, the interlingua is composed of a list of structures that correspond to the words of the title.

These structures have the following form in PROLOG language for a given word of the line: where English-Lemma is the English translation of the Greek or Spanish word of the title, and Part-of-Speech, Number, and Case are the corresponding morphological information of this word in the source language. Taking all the points into account and in order to strengthen our claim that an AI-based translation tool is needed in the translation process, we tried two translation scenarios. We first implemented a simple word-by-word translation, in order to simplify the translation process and consequently minimize the computational cost.

The evaluation of this approach* has shown that only a small percentage of the translated titles were comprehensible, particularly in translations from Greek to English, Spanish to English, and *vice versa*. We decided, then, to implement a more sophisticated approach that would improve the quality of the translations by taking advantage of AI- based methods.

For instance, the following tools for the implementation of the Greek and English ling-ware were used:

- An existing two-level morphological analyser for morphological recognition and synthesis of Modern Greek words. This is a PC KIMMO-based analyser that was designed for general purpose morphological analysis of Modern Greek and uses a 30,000-word lexicon. According to the two-level morphological model, the surface form of a word is derived by applying a set of rules to the lexical form of that word and *vice versa*. The main advantage of such a model is that these rules are applied in parallel and in both directions, that is, surface to lexical form and lexical to surface form. In linguistic terms, the two- level rules are not processing rules, but more like the realisation rules of stratification linguistics.
- A public domain two-level morphological analyser for morphological recognition and synthesis of English words. This is a PC KIMMO-based analyser that was designed for general purpose morphological analysis of English and uses a 10,000-word lexicon.
- Two syntactic parsers built from scratch and able to recognise the basic phrase structures of the title. These parsers are based on a context-free grammar model consisting of 28 rewriting rules for each one of them. As an example, the four first rules of the modern Greek grammar are given below:
    - Title ⇐ Phrase.
    - Title ⇐ Phrase, Conjunction, Phrase.
    - Phrase ⇐ NounPhrases, Prepositional Phrases.
    - Phrase ⇐ Prepositional Phrases.
- Two medium-sized bilingual morphological dictionaries containing words from the scientific domains of engineering and computer science found in the Central Library of the University of Patras. In particular, these dictionaries stemmed from the PC

KIMMO-based dictionaries and translation information as well as new words from the previous scientific domains were added.

Similar tools for the implementation of the Spanish ling ware were utilised.

Just to illustrate the translation process from a Greek title into a corresponding English one, we give below the sequence of transitions among the different tools:

- Greek Title→Greek Morphological Analyser→ Morphologically Analyser Greek Title
- Morphologically Analysed Greek Title→Greek Syntactic Parser→ Abstract Syntactical Form
- Abstract Syntactical Form→Greek-English Translator, Greek-English Bilingual Dictionary→Translated Abstract Form
- Translated Abstract Form→English Morphological Analyser→Morphologically Correct English Title
- Morphologically Correct English Title→English Syntactic Parser→Well-Formed English Title

An outline of the simplified translation tool is shown in figure.

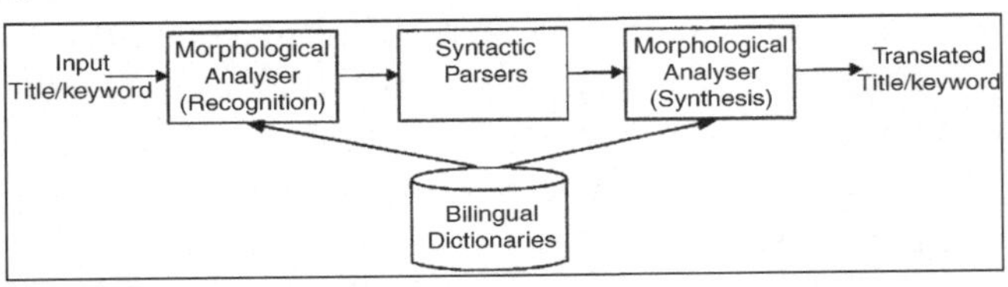

Fig 4.8 Outline of the Translation Tool

In contrast to the word- by- word translation, approximately 86 per cent of the translated titles are comprehensible.* It has to be noted here that the quality and comprehension of the provided translations depend on the scientific domain of the library database.

For instance, the Greek word has two meanings:

- Series; and
- Line.

Hence, if the library database comprises books/journals concerning the scientific domain of mathematics, then the former translation should be included in the bilingual dictionaries. Finally, an editing tool is used for updating entries in the English-Greek and Greek-English dictionaries. The user is able to update the nouns and adjectives that are included in the selected bilingual dictionary.

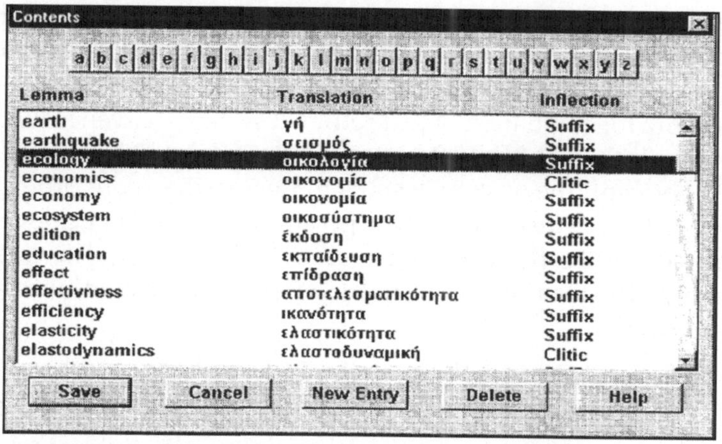

Fig 4.9 Editing Tool for the Bilingual Dictionaries

A new entry may be inserted or an existing one may be changed or deleted. When inserting a new entry, the user must insert the new lemma as well as its translation. Additionally, (s)he should also select an inflectional category in order to determine the various word forms of the new entry.

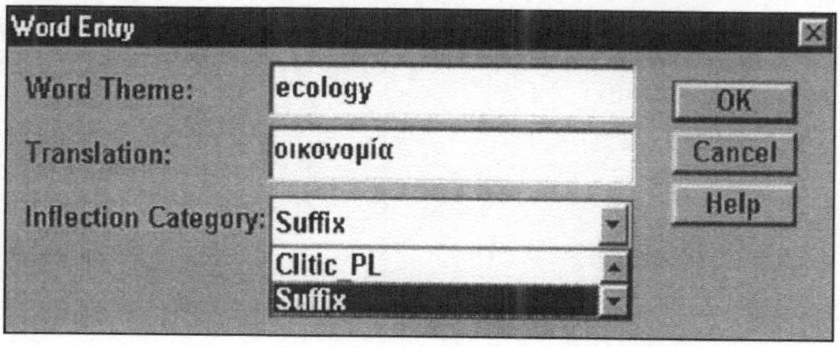

Fig 4.10 Inserting a New Entry

EVALUATION

The Translib system has been tested in the library databases in both Greece and Spain under real life conditions.

Two parameters were evaluated:

- The subject search, *i.e.,* the proportion of citations found by the user referring to a given subject, and
- The user satisfaction, *i.e.,* the impression of the user with respect to the quality of the service provided.

The first parameter was measured by means of the standard 11- point average precision for our DICT method. The 11- point average precision is a conventional performance measure for evaluation of text retrieval systems. Given a query, for recall thresholds of 0 per cent, 10 per cent, 20 per cent..., 100 per cent, the system assigns in decreasing score order as many titles as needed until a given recall level is achieved, and computes the precision value at that point. Then, the precision values of individual queries are averaged over all test queries.

Table 4.3 Recall- Precision Values for the DICT Approach

Monolingual Retrieval		Multilingual Retrieval	
Recall	**Precision**	**Recall**	**Precision**
0.0	0.90	0.0	0.63
0.1	0.86	0.1	0.50
0.2	0.83	0.2	0.45
0.3	0.80	0.3	0.39
0.4	0.77	0.4	0.34
0.5	0.72	0.5	0.30
0.6	0.68	0.6	0.23
0.7	0.59	0.7	0.21
0.8	0.52	0.8	0.18
0.9	0.50	0.9	0.12
1.0	0.35	1.0	0.10

These averaged precision values can be further averaged over the recall thresholds, to obtain a single-numbered global measure. The resulting global average is referred to as the 11-point average precision. We carried out the measurement of the first parameter in the Greek library database, initially with the previous OPAC system and then with the Translib system. We used 1,000 test queries from the scientific domain of engineering and computer science. The input language for these queries was either Greek or English, and the search criteria comprised either a unique search field or a combination of two or more search fields.

The vast majority of these queries consisted of isolated words or short phrases. Only 15 per cent of the above queries formed long phrases. The recall- precision values for these two systems are shown in table.

The DICT approach proves efficient enough for queries consisting of isolated words or at best short phrases. The second parameter was evaluated by means of a short questionnaire which was used to gather the general impression on the system and its features.

This questionnaire comprised 27 questions, which were classified in four distinct parts:

- Personal information regarding the evaluator;
- Results on the use of Translib;
- Personal opinion of Translib.;
- Comments.

In some cases, the questionnaire reply boxes ranged from 1 to 5 by degree of satisfaction. Finally, a total of 42 library users filled the questionnaires.

They were selected on the basis of the following criteria:

- To be familiar with OPACs;
- To possess a good knowledge of English and/or Spanish;
- To have different sex and age;
- To be willing to participate in the evaluation process.

The results of the evaluation are encouraging and pinpoint the strength as well as the potential weaknesses of this system. Some of the most important results are listed below:

Multilingual Search:

- 95 per cent of the users performed multilingual searches in the library database rather than monolingual ones.
- Approximately 45 per cent of the users felt rather satisfied or completely satisfied about the results of their search, while 9 per cent of them were dissatisfied.

- Less than 25 per cent of the dissatisfied users considered multilingual aspects not supported in Translib responsible for their dissatisfaction.
- Approximately 85 per cent of the users considered the search via the multilingual thesaurus more accurate and complete.

Translation of Titles:

- Approximately 80 per cent of the users considered the translation of titles rather useful or very useful.
- Over 55 per cent of the users considered the translations of titles comprehensible. Note that users with high familiarity with OPACs tended to be slightly more satisfied with the quality of the translation.
- Over 90 per cent of the users found the functionality of the translation component very easy.

Multilingual Presentation:

- Over 70 per cent of the users considered the system easy to use by anyone, not just experts.
- Over 60 per cent of the users considered Translib more friendly, useful, and easier to understand than other OPACs they had used in the past. It is noteworthy that users with a high familiarity in OPACs were considerably more satisfied.
- Finally, over 65 per cent of the users found the help and error messages of Translib clear, useful, and adequate.

As noted earlier, the selection of an interlingua affects the quality as well as the comprehension of the translation of titles. Hence, translations to and from English are more comprehensible than from Greek to Spanish and *vice versa*. Nevertheless, approximately 95 per cent of the performed translations are translations to and from English, since, the vast majority of the book/journal titles contained in a library consists of titles in the local language and English.

The satisfaction of the users with the multilingual thesaurus and the overall search results they obtained from the system in contrast to other OPACs was remarkable. The localisation of the user interface was one of the main reasons why the users favoured this system.

In conclusion, the reaction of the users to the Translib system appears to be closely dependent on their previous experience:

- Users find multilingual search very useful.
- Users with a higher familiarity with OPACs find Translib a simple, friendly, and easy to learn system. Users with a lower familiarity with OPACs find it more difficult to use Translib. This is a satisfactory conclusion, as Translib neither intends to replace OPAC nor makes its baseline operation simpler. It is simply intended to overcome the linguistic barriers posed by multilingual library holdings.
- Users appear to search for titles in languages in which they are familiar. For this reason they tend to show limited appreciation of the usefulness of the translation of titles, while they expect a better translation.
- Although the user reaction is positive, there appears to be room for improvement with respect to the terminology used, the help and error messages, and the way that the system keeps the user informed of what is being done at any time.
- The satisfaction of the users depends highly on both the Translib system as well as on the bibliographic database and the library holdings. As a result it is difficult to assess the impact of Translib on the quality of the search results. More extensive experiments would be needed for this purpose, preferably in a distributed, transnational bibliographic database.

CONCLUSION

As we described earlier, despite the fact that there are several OPACs supporting the automation of retrieving bibliographic information, only a few of them support some kind of bilingual or even multilingual access to libraries catalogues. In this chapter, we presented a system that aims at solving this problem. Translib allows multilingual search as well as multilingual presentation of the query results and consists of an integration of state-of-the-art existing information tools and tools built from scratch. The integration of these tools was a difficult task, since, the former were built for different purposes and, some of them, for different operating systems.

The multilingual functionalities of Translib help the user, to a high degree, improve significantly the results of a query and allow him/her to select the presentation of the results in the preferred language. For all these reasons, we feel that libraries, book trade enterprises, appropriate consultancy services and library schools can directly benefit from a system of this type. Translib should have a remarkable impact on the improvement of library services as well as on the easy access to the wealth of knowledge held in libraries. The results of its performance on the Greek library database and its pilot installation in the Central Library of University of Patras strongly encourage us to believe that it will have a successful commercial exploitation in the near future.

Our short-term goal is to endow Translib with the capability to support bibliographic information retrieval from remote databases through INTERNET servers. In addition, we plan to further improve the present system by adding new languages in the existing framework. Our long-term goal is to enrich it with new AI tools. In particular, we intend to provide the translation of entire abstracts rather than just the titles and improve the accuracy of the search results based on intelligent information extraction.

5

Participatory Networks

AN OVERVIEW

Knowledge is created through conversation. Conversations can take place between friends and colleagues in the 'here and now.' But, they can also take place over centuries, with the participants changing but the theme remaining the same, and the conversation being recorded in thousands of artifacts, like books, pictures, and digital files. In many conversations users need sophisticated processes to facilitate the conversation. Facilitation not only enriches conversations with diverse and deep information, it also serves as a memory keeper, documenting agreements and outcomes to facilitate future conversations.

The library serves this vital role for many communities. The implication of this rather abstract concept is that libraries are in the conversation business. This theoretical argument can be seen in traditional brick-and-mortar libraries as library speaker series, book groups, and even the collection development processes. Yet online, the library has fallen far short of this ideal of conversation facilitator. Key library systems, such as the catalogue for example, are at best one-way conversations.

Libraries have a great opportunity to provide invaluable conversational, participatory infrastructure to their communities online. By adopting concepts and technologies from Web 2.0 and tightly integrating them into their services, libraries can advance not just their communities but also their positions within them. The opportunities inherent in participatory networks have not emerged because of current Internet developments such as Web 2.0, but, rather, these technologies make it easier to meet an identified and long-standing role of libraries. Wikis, blogs, and recommender systems replace dial-up bulletin boards and local databases as a means to empower our communities.

What's more, these technologies can bring the ideal of the participatory model to our most fundamental library systems. Libraries should adopt participatory network concepts and software not because they are new or sexy, but because they match our most fundamental mission: knowledge creation and dissemination. This document describes the participatory model of libraries and provides an overview of current Web 2.0 technologies and a brief discussion of how current Library 2.0 efforts point the way to an even greater change in library as a facilitator of conversations. Specific challenges and opportunities of participatory networking are reviewed. Finally, the authors recommend the creation of a shared participatory test bed for libraries.

This network would not only experiment with new collaborative Web technologies, but also work with library organisations and vendors to speed innovation in traditional library systems. Finally, the network test bed would create a shared infrastructure to provide participatory technologies – such as Wikis, blogs, and RSS feeds—to libraries for inclusion in their day-to-day services.

THE GOAL

Knowledge is created through conversation. Libraries are in the knowledge business. Therefore, libraries are in the conversation business. Some of those conversations span millennia, while others only span a few seconds. Some of these conversations happen in real time. In some conversations, there is a broadcast of ideas from one author to multiple audiences. Some conversations are sparked by a book or a video or a Web page. Some of these conversations are as trivial as directing someone to the bathroom. Other conversations centre on the foundations of ourselves and our humanity. It may be odd to start a technology brief with such seemingly abstract comments. Yet, without this firm, if theoretical, footing the advent of Web 2.0, social networking, Library 2.0, and participatory networks seems like a clutter of new terminology, tools, and acronyms.

In fact, as will be discussed, without this conceptual footing, many library functions can seem disconnected, and the field that serves lawyers, doctors, single mothers, and 8 year olds fragmented. The scale of this technology brief is limited; it is to present library decision makers with the opportunities and challenges of participatory networks. It is only a single piece of a much larger puzzle that seeks to present a cohesive framework for libraries. This framework will not only fit tools such as blogs and Wikis into their offerings, but also will show how a more participatory, conversational approach to libraries in general can help libraries better integrate current and future functions.

Think of this document as an overview or introduction to participatory librarianship. Readers will find plenty of examples and definitions of Web 2.0 and social networking later in this chapter. However, to jump right into the technology without a larger framework invites the rightful skepticism of a library organisation that feels constantly buffeted by new technological advances. In any environment with no larger conceptual founding to measure the importance of an advance in technology or practice selection of any one technology or practice is nearly arbitrary. Without a framework the field becomes open to the influence of personalities and trendy technology.

Therefore, it is vital to ground any technological, social, or policy conversation into a larger, rooted concept. As Susser said, "...to practice without theory is to sail an uncharted sea; theory without practice is not to set sail at all." For this chapter, the chart will be conversation theory.

The core of this brief is in four sections that follow:

- A conceptual framework for understanding and evaluating participatory networks;

- A discussion of key concepts and technologies in participatory networks drawn primarily from Web 2.0 and Library 2.0;
- A merging of the conceptual framework with the technological discussion to present a sort of roadmap for library systems development; and
- A set of recommendations to foster greater discussion and action on the topic of participatory networks and, more broadly, participatory librarianship.

LIBRARY AS A FACILITATOR OF CONVERSATION

So let us return to the concept that knowledge is created through conversation. This notion stretches back to Socrates and the Socratic Method. However, the specific foundation for this statement comes from 'Conversation Theory,' a means of explaining cognition and how people learn. It is not the purpose of this chapter to provide a detailed description of Conversation Theory, a task already admirably accomplished by Pask. Rather, let us use the theory as a structure upon which to hang an exploration of participatory networking and, more broadly, participatory librarianship.

The core of conversation theory is simple: people learn through conversation. Different communities have different standards for conversations, from the scientific community's rigourous formalisms to the religious community's embedded meaning in scripture to the sometimes impenetrable dialect of teens. The point remains, however, that different actors establish meaning through determining common definitions and building upon shared concepts. The library has been a place where we facilitate conversations, though often implicitly.

The concept of learning through conversations is evidenced in libraries in large initiatives like information litreacy and teaching critical thinking skills and in the smaller events of book groups, reference interviews, and speaker series. Library activities such as building collections of artifacts inform scholars' research through a formal conversation process where ideas are supported with evidence and methods. Similarly, preservation efforts, perhaps of wax cylinders with spoken word content or of ancient maps that embody an ongoing dialogue about the shape and nature of the physical world, seek to save, or at least document, important conversations. Common use of the word 'conversation' is completely in accordance with the use of the term in Conversation Theory.

The term is, however, more specifically defined as an act of communication and agreement between a set of agents. So, a conversation can be between two people, two organisations, two countries, or even within an individual. How can a conversation take place within an individual? Educators and school librarians may be familiar with the term 'metacognition,' or the act of reflecting on one's learning. Yet, even the most casual reader will be familiar with the concept of debating oneself. The point is that a conversation is with at least two agents trying to come to an understanding. Also note that those two agents can change over time. So, while Socrates and Plato are dead the conversation they started about the nature of knowledge and the world is carried forward by new generations of thinkers...same conversation, different agents. People converse, organisations converse, states converse, societies converse.

The requirements, in the terms of Conversation Theory, are two cognitive systems seeking agreement. The results of these conversations, what Pask would call 'cognitive entanglements,' are books, videos, and artifacts that either document, expand, or result from conversations. So, while one cannot converse with a book that book certainly can be a starting point for many conversations within the reader and within a larger community.

If the theory is that conversation creates knowledge, the library community has added a corollary: the best knowledge comes from an 'optimal information environment,' one in which the most diverse and complete information is available to the conversant. Library ethics show an implicit understanding of this corollary in the advocacy of intellectual freedom and unfettered access. Libraries seek to create rich environments for knowledge and have taken the stance that they are not in the job of arbitrating the conversations that occur or the 'appropriateness' of the information used to inform those conversations. As will be discussed later, this belief in openness of conversations will have some far-reaching implications for the library collection and is an ideal that can never truly be met.

For now, the reader may take away that conversation theory is very much in line with current and past library practice, and it also shows a clear trajectory for the future. The value to this viewpoint is not just theoretical; it has real consequences and uses. For example, much of library evaluation has been based in numeric counts of tangible outputs: books circulated, collection size, reference transactions, and so on. Yet this quantitative approach has been frustrating to many who feel they are counting outcomes but not getting at true impact of library service. Librarians may ask themselves, "Which numbers are important...and why?" If libraries focused on conversations there might be some clarity and cohesion between statistics and other outcomes. Suddenly, the number of reference questions can be linked to items cataloged or to circulation numbers...they are all markers of the scope and scale of conversations within the library context.

This approach might enable the library community to better identify 'important' conversations and demonstrate direct contributions to these conversations across functions. For example, a school district identifies early litreacy as important. There is a discussion about public policy options, new programmes, and school goals to achieve greater litreacy in the K-5 grades. The library should be able to track two streams in this conversation.

The first is the one libraries are used to counting; that is, the library's contribution to K-5 litreacy. But the library can also document and demonstrate how it furthered the conversation about children's litreacy in general. It could show the resources provided to community officials. It could show the litreacy pathfinders that were created. The point of this example is that the library is both participant in the conversation and facilitator of conversation. The theoretical discussion leads us to a discussion about the second topic of this technology brief: pragmatic aspects of the knowledge as conversation approach, or a participatory approach as it will be called.

As new technologies are developed and deployed in the current environment of limited resources, there must be some means of evaluating their utility. The utility of a technology is appropriately measured against a given library's mission, which is in turn developed to respond to the needs of the community that library serves. First, however, let us identify some of the new technologies and describe them briefly.

PARTICIPATORY NETWORKING, SOCIAL NETWORKS, AND WEB 2.0

Let us now move from the theoretical to the operational. The impetus behind this chapter is the relatively recent emergence of a new group of Internet services and capabilities. Suddenly, terms like Wiki, blog, mashup, Web 2.0, and biblioblogosphere have become commonplace. As with any new wave of technological creation, these terms can seem ambiguous and they also come wrapped in varying amounts of hype. They may all, however, be grouped under the phenomenon of participatory networking. While we now have a conceptual framework to evaluate these technologies that support participatory networking, we still need to know the basics of the terminology and technologies. This section outlines key concepts in the pragmatics of participatory networking. The section after this one will join the theoretical and operational to outline key challenges and opportunities for the library world. We begin with Web 2.0

WEB 2.0

Much of what we call participatory networking, at least the technological foundation of it, stems from developments in 'Web 2.0.' As with many buzzwords, the exact definition of

Web 2.0 is not clear. It is more an aggregation of concepts that range from software development to abstractions. What pervades the Web 2.0 approach is the notion that Internet services are increasingly facilitators of conversations.

Web 2.0 Characteristic: Social Networks

A core concept of Web 2.0 is that people are the content of sites; that is, a site is not populated with information for users to consume. Instead, services are provided to individual users for them to build networks of friends and other groups. The content of a site, then, comprises user-provided information that attracts new members of an ever-expanding network.

Examples:

- *Flickr*: Flickr provides users with free Web space to upload images and create photo albums. Users can then share these photos with friends or with the public at large. Flickr facilitates the creation of shared photo galleries around themes and places.
- *The Cheshire Public Library*: The Teen Book Blog at the Cheshire Public Library offers book reviews created only by the students who use the library.
- *Memorial Hall Library*: The Memorial Hall Library in Andover Massachusetts offers podcasts of poetry contests in which the content is created by students.
- *Libraries in MySpace*: MySpace searches show that there are MySpace sites for hundreds of individual libraries and scores of library groups. Alexandrian Public Library. This practice is growing among public libraries and is an attempt to reach out to users in their preferred online environments. In this venue, the more friends a library MySpace site has the more successful it may be considered. The Alexandrian Public Library has 75 friends and 15 comments. The Brooklyn College Library has 2195 friends and 270 comments.

Web 2.0 Characteristic: Wisdom of Crowds

There has been some research into the quality of mass decision-making. That research shows how remarkably accurate groups are in their judgements. Web 2.0 pools large groups of users to comment on decisions. This aggregation of input is facilitated by the ready availability of social networking sites. Certainly, this approach of community organisation and verification of knowledge also has its detractors. Many, for example, question the wisdom seen in some entries of Wikipedia. Yet, recent articles have compared this mass editing process favourably to traditional sources of information such as the Encyclopaedia Britannica.

Examples

eBay

eBay has perhaps the most studied and copied community policing and reputation systems. All buyers and sellers can be rated. The aggregation of many users' experiences create a 'Feedback Score' that is equivalent to a group credibility rating. These kinds of group feedback systems can now be seen in most major Internet retailers.

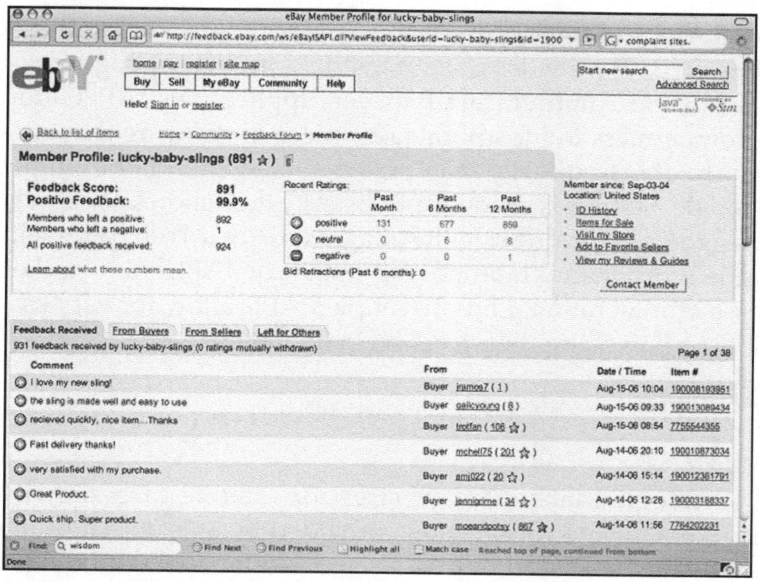

Fig 5.1 A Seller's Profile Shows a Potential Buyer the eBay Community's Current Estimation of a Seller's Credibility.

LibraryThing

LibraryThing.com makes book recommendations based on the collective intelligence of all users of the site. The greater the pool of collective intelligence the more information is available to the user for decision-making.

The Diary Project

The Diary Project Library is a non-profit organisation that encourages teens to write about their day-to-day experiences growing up. The goal of this site is to encourage communication among teens of all cultures and backgrounds, provide peer-to-peer support, stimulate discussion, and generate feedback that can help ease some of the concerns encountered along the way and let them know that they are not alone. To that end, the site comprises thousands of entries in 24 categories. Because of the great number of entries, most youth can find helpful materials.

Web 2.0 Characteristic: Loosely Coupled APIs

API is short hand for 'Application Programming Interface.' It provides a set of instructions that a programmer can use to communicate between applications. APIs allow programmers to incorporate one piece of software they may not be able to directly manipulate into another. For example, Google Maps has made a public API that allows Web page designers to include satellite images into their Web pages with little more than a latitude and longitude. APIs vary in their ease of integration. Loosely coupled APIs allow for very easy integration using high-level scripting languages.

Examples

Google Maps

Google Maps displays street or satellite map showing markers on specific locations provided by an external source with simple sets of longitudes and latitudes. So, it becomes extremely easy to create Geographic Information Systems with little knowledge of GIS principles.

Flickr

Flickr provides easy means to integrate these hosted images into other Web pages or applications.

YouTube

YouTube provides users with the capability to upload and comment upon video on the Internet. It also allows for easy integration of the videos into other Web pages and blogs. With a simple line of HTML code anyone can access streaming video for their content.

Web 2.0 Characteristic: Mashups

Mashups are combinations of APIs and data that result in new information resources and services. This ease of incorporation has led to an assumption of a 'right to remix.' In the world of open source software and the creative commons, the right to remix refers to a growing expectation among Internet users that they are not limited by the interfaces and uses presented to them by a single organisation.

Examples

ChicagoCrime.org

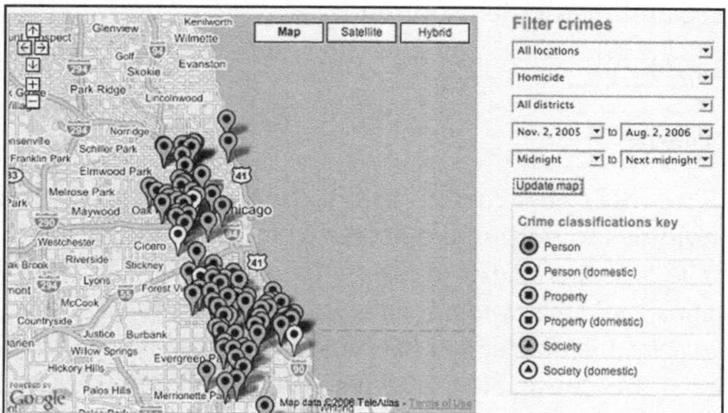

Fig 5.2 Screen Shot of Chicagocrime.org. The Map, Generated by Google Maps, is showing a Marker at the Location of Every Homicide in Chicago from November 2, 2005 to August 2, 2006.

An often-cited example of a mashup is ChicagoCrime.org, which uses Google Maps to plot crime data for the city of Chicago. Users can now see exactly which street corner had the most murders.

Book Burro

Book Burro "is a Web 2.0 extension for Firefox and Flock. When it senses you are looking at a page that contains a book, it will overlay a small panel which when opened lists prices at online bookstores such as Amazon, Buy, Half and whether the book is available at your library."

Web 2.0 Characteristic: Permanent Betas

The concept of a permanent beta is, in part, a realisation that no software is ever truly complete so long as the user community is still commenting upon it. For example, Google does not release services from beta until it has achieved a sufficient user base no matter how fixed the underlying source code is. Permanent beta is also a design strategy. Large applications are broken into smaller constituent parts that can be manipulated separately. This allows large applications to be continually developed by a more diverse and distributed community.

Examples

MIT Libraries

The MIT Libraries are experimenting with new technologies to help make access to information easier.

The tools are offered to the public with an appeal for feedback and additional tools, and the there is a permanent address designed just to collect feedback from the beta-phase tools, which include:

- The New Humanities Virtual Browsery, which highlights new books and incorporates an RSS feed, the ability to comment on books, links to book reviews, availability information, and links to other books by the same author.
- The LibXMIT Edition, which is a Firefox toolbar that allows users to search the Barton catalogue, Vera, Google

Scholar, the SFX FullText Finder, and other search tools; it embeds links to MIT-only resources in Amazon, Barnes and Noble, Google Scholar, and NYT Book Reviews.

- The Dewey Research Advisor Business and Economics: Q&A, which provides starting points for specific research questions in the fields of business, management, and economics.

Google Labs

Google has a site named 'Google Labs' that puts out company-generated tools and services. In fact, part of a Google employee's work time is dedicated to creating the resources and tools through personal projects and exploration. These tools and services remain a part of the 'Lab' until they are finished and have sufficient user bases. Projects range from the simple to the extensive.

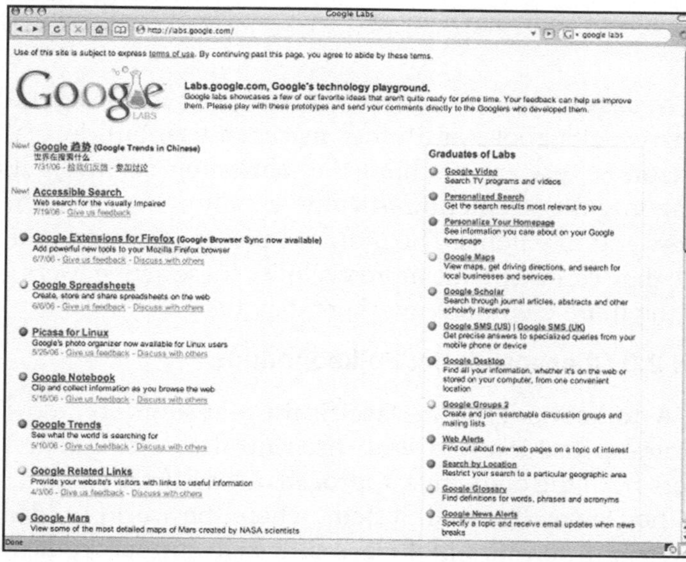

Fig 5.3 Screen Shot of Current Google Lab Projects.

Web 2.0 Characteristic: Software Gets Better the More People Use It

An increasing number of Web 2.0 sites emphasise social networks, where these services gain value only as they gain users. Malcolm Gladwell recounts this principle and the work of Kevin Kelly with an earlier telecommunications network, the network of fax machines connected to the phone system: "The first fax machine ever made...cost about $2,000 at retail. But it was worth nothing because there was no other fax machine for it to communicate with.

The second fax machine made the first fax machine more valuable, and the third fax made the first two more valuable, and so on...When you buy a fax machine, then, what you are really buying is access to the entire fax network—which is infinitely more valuable than the machine itself." With social networking sites, and all sites that seek to capitalise on user input, the true value of each site is defined by the number of people it can bring together.

Examples

Amazon

A classic example of this characteristic is Amazon.com. Amazon sells books and other merchandise, but, in reality, Amazon is very much about the marketing of information. Amazon gains tremendous value by allowing its users to review and rate items. The more people use Amazon and the more they comment, the more visibility these active users gain and the more credibility markers they take on.

Web 2.0 Characteristic: Folksonomies

A folksonomy is a classification system created in a bottom-up fashion and with no central coordination. This differs from the deductive approach of classifications systems like the Dewey Decimal System, where the world of ideas is broken into ten nominal classes. It also differs from other means of developing classifications where some central authority determines if a term should be included. In a folksonomy, the members of a group simply attach terms to items and the aggregate of these terms is seen as the classification. What emerges is a classification scheme that prioritises common usage over semantic clarity.

Examples

PennTags

PennTags is a social bookmarking tool for locating, organising, and sharing one's favourite online resources. Members of the Penn Community can collect and maintain URLs, links to journal articles, and records in Franklin, the online catalogue, and VCat, the online video catalogue. Once resources are compiled, users can organise them by assigning tags and/or by grouping them into projects, according to specific preferences. PennTags can also be used collaboratively, because it acts as a repository of the varied interests and academic pursuits of the Penn community, and a user can find topics and other users related to his or her own favourite online resources.

Hillsdale Teen Library

The Hillsdale Teen Library uses Flickr to post pictures of events at the Hillsdale Teen Library, as in this figure.

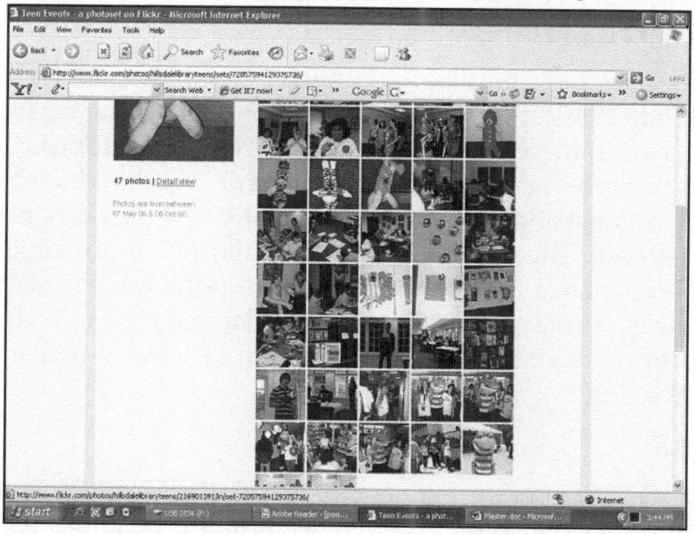

The resulting tag view is represented in the next figure. These tags allow users to easily retrieve the images in which they are interested.

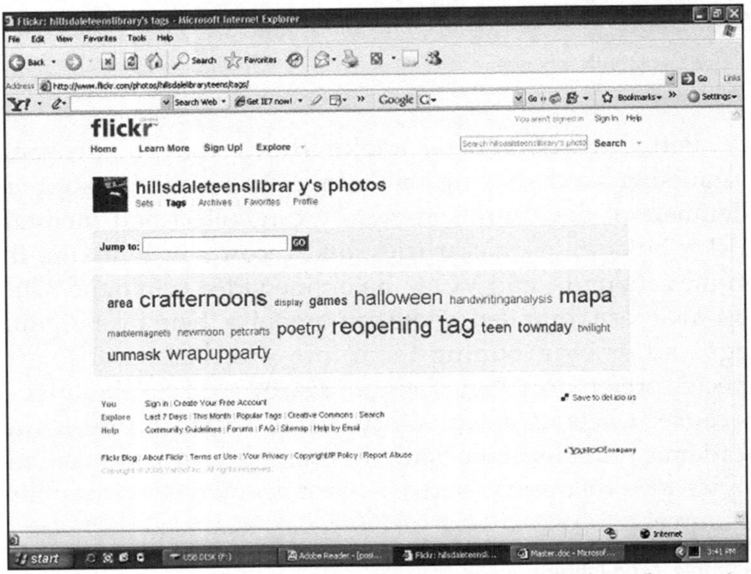

There are more characteristics of Web 2.0, but these give some overall concepts.

CORE NEW TECHNOLOGIES: AJAX AND WEB SERVICES

As we have jut discussed, Web 2.0 is little more than set of related concepts, albeit with a lot of value being currently attached to these concepts. These concepts are supported by two underlying technologies that have facilitated Web 2.0 development and brought a substantially new user experience to the Web. The first is AJAX, which allows a more desktop-like experience for users. The second is the advent of Web services. These technologies are not necessary for Web 2.0 concepts, but they have made Web 2.0 sites much more compelling.

AJAX

AJAX stands for Asynchronous JavaScript and XML. It is a set of existing Web technologies brought together. At the most basic, AJAX allows a browser and a server to send data back and forth without needing to refresh the entire Web page being worked on. Think about the Web sites you work with. You click on a link, the browser freezes and waits for the data, then draws it on the screen. Early versions of sites like MapQuest would show a map. If you wanted to zoom into the map, you would press a zoom icon and wait while the new map, and the rest of the Web page was redrawn. Compare this to Google Maps, where you click in the middle of a map and drag left or right and the map moves dynamically.

This kind of interaction we are used to in desktop applications. Click and drag has become second nature on the desktop and AJAX is making it second nature on the Web, too. Another advantage of AJAX is that it is open and requires only light programming skills. Javascript on the client and almost any server side scripting language are easily accessible languages. This fact allows for both fast development and easier integration with existing systems. As an example, it should now be easier to bring more interactive Web interfaces to existing online catalogues.

Web Services

Web services allow for software-to-software interactions on the Web. Using Web protocols and XML, applications exchange queries and information in order to facilitate the larger functioning of a system. One example would be a system that uses an ISBN number to query multiple online catalogues and commercial vendors for availability of a book. This simple process might be part of a much larger library catalogue that shows users a book and its availability. The point is that unlike federated search systems such as Z39.50, Web services are small. They also tend to be lightweight, and are aggregated for greater functionality.

LIBRARY 2.0

Library 2.0 is a somewhat diffuse concept. Walt Crawford, in his extended essay Library 2.0 and 'Library 2.0' found 62 different views and seven distinct definitions of Library 2.0. It is no wonder that people are confused. However, it is natural for emerging ideas and groups to function in an environment of high ambiguity. For use in this technology brief the authors see Library 2.0 as an attempt to apply Web 2.0 concepts to the purpose of the library. In the words of Ormsby, "The purpose of a library is not to ... showcase new gadgetry ...; rather, it is to make possible that instant of insight when all the facts come together in the shape of new knowledge."

How the applications are used will determine whether they support Ormsby's "instant of insight." Many libraries and librarians are already pursuing this goal. Some, for instance, are using blogs to reach other librarians, their own users, and potential users.

They are using Wikis to deliver reports, teach information litreacy, and serve as repositories. One has developed an API that allows WordPress posts to be directly integrated into a library catalogue. Clearly, the Internet and newer tools that empower users seem to be aligned with the library mission. After all, librarians blogging and allowing the catalogue to be 'mashed up' can be seen as an extension of current information services. But this abundance of new applications poses a challenge.

Given the speed with which new tools are invented, librarians may find it difficult to create strategies that include all the desired services that they make possible. For every new application that becomes available, library administrators must decide whether it can serve the library, how to use it, and how to find additional resources to manage it. This problem stems from focussing excessively on the technology. Librarians should, instead, focus on the phenomena made possible by the technology. Most important of these phenomena, the library invites participation.

As Chad and Miller state:

- Library 2.0 facilitates and encourages a culture of participation, drawing upon the perspectives and contributions of library staff, technology partners and the wider community. Library 2.0 means harnessing this type of participation so that libraries can benefit from increasingly rich collaborative cataloguing efforts, such as including contributions from partner libraries as well as adding rich enhancements, such as book jackets or movie files, to records from publishers and others.

- Library 2.0 is about encouraging and enabling a library's community of users to participate, contributing their own views on resources they have used and new ones to which they might wish access.
- With Library 2.0, a library will continue to develop and deploy the rich descriptive standards of the domain, whilst embracing more participative approaches that encourage interaction with and the formation of communities of interest.

The carte blanche statement that users participating in the library is 'good,' however, is insufficient. Library administers must ask, 'What is the ultimate goal?' In summary, current initiatives in the library world to bring the tools of Web 2.0 to the service of Library 2.0 are exciting and innovative, and more to the point, they are supportive of the library's purpose. They may, however, incur costs, such as monitoring blogs and Wikis and creating content and corresponding with users that stretch already inadequate resources even further. Ultimately, the value of Library 2.0 concepts requires us to answer some important questions: will they be used to further knowledge, or will they simply create more work for librarians? What does the 'next version' of Library 2.0 look like? Is its mission the same and just the tools different? What makes the library different from MySpace... simply a legacy? Should we incorporate new services into the current library offerings? How do we, as facilitators of conversations, point the way to the next generation of library? It is hoped that some of the concepts in participatory librarianship may answer these questions and help further the innovations of the Library 2.0 community.

PARTICIPATORY NETWORKS

The authors use the phrase participatory networking to encompass the concept of using Web 2.0 principles and technologies to implement a conversational model within a community.

Why not simply adopt social networking, Web 2.0, or Library 2.0 for that matter? Let us examine each term's limitations:

- *Social networking*: Social network sites such as MySpace and Facebook have certainly captured public attention. They have also proven very popular. In their short life spans these sites have garnered an immense audience and drawn much attention from the press. Some of that attention, however, has been very negative. MySpace, for example, has been typified as a refuge for pedophiles and online predators. Even the television show Saturday Night Live has parodied the site for the ease with which users can create false personas and engage in risky online behaviours. To say you are starting a social networking site in your library may draw either enthusiastic support, vehement opposition or simply confused looks. Add to the potential negative connotations the ambiguity of the term. Is a blog a social networking site? Is Flickr? To compound this confusion, the academic domain of Social Network Theory predates MySpace by about a decade.
- *Web 2.0*: Ambiguity also dogs the Web 2.0 world. For some, it is technology. For others, it is simply a buzzword for the current crop of Internet sites that survived the burst of the.com bubble. In any case, Web 2.0 certainly implies more than just the inclusion of users in systems.
- *Library 2.0*: As stated before, the term Library 2.0 is a vague term used by some as a goad to the library community. Further, this term limits the discussion of user-inclusive Web services to the library world. While this brief focuses on the library community, it also sees the library community as a potential leader in a much broader field.

So, ultimately, the authors propose 'participatory networking' as a positive term and concept that libraries can use and promote without the confusion and limitations of previous language. The phrase 'participatory network' also has a history of prior use that can be built upon. The phrase 'participatory networks' represents systems of exchange and integration and has long been used in discussions of policy, art, and government. The phrase has also been used to describe online communities that exchange and integrate information.

LIBRARIES AS PARTICIPATORY CONVERSATIONS

So where are we? We started with the abstract statement that knowledge is created through conversation. We then looked at the current landscape of technologies that can facilitate these conversations and showed examples of how libraries, other industries, and individuals are using these technologies. In this section we combine the larger framework with the technologies to see how libraries can incorporate participatory networks to further their knowledge mission.

PARTICIPATORY LIBRARIANSHIP IN ACTION

Let us look specifically at how participatory networks can be used in the library's role as facilitator of knowledge through conversation. An obvious example is libraries hosting blogs and Wikis for their communities creating virtual meeting spaces for individuals and groups, just as libraries do in the physical world. Indeed, these are increasingly useful functions for libraries. They meet a perceived need in the community, and can generate excitement both within the library and in the community.

The idea of creating online sites for individuals and organisations makes sense for a library, although it is not without difficulties. Libraries could also use freely available open source software to create library versions of Wikipedia. Another way for libraries to offer these services would be through a cooperative or other third-party vendor.

Such a service can easily be seen as a knowledge management activity capturing and providing local expertise while linking this expertise to that produced at other libraries. Another reason for libraries to engage in participatory networking is that one library can more easily collaborate with other libraries in richer dialogues. We currently have systems that connect our online catalogues and share resources through interlibrary loan. These conduits exist and can be used for the transferal of richer data, as has been proved through collaborative virtual reference systems.

In our current systems, as in traditional library practice, when users are referred to other libraries, they are sent out and not brought back. In a participatory library setting, libraries would facilitate a conversation between the user, the community of the local library, and then through the developed conduits, other libraries and their communities. The end result would be a seamless web of libraries where the user can ignore the intricacies of the library's organisation structure and boundaries, and in which the libraries are using the best local resources to meet local needs. Bringing libraries seamlessly together to participate in conversations with a single user has another significant advantage: the Library would make it easy for users to join the conversation regardless of where they are, through the presentation of a single façade.

There is, for example, only one Google, one Amazon, and one Wikipedia. Why should users have to search from among thousands of libraries to find the conversations they want? Participatory networking will be most effective when libraries work together, when the whole is greater than its parts. We currently see elements of The Participatory Library in the OCLC Open Worldcat project. For example, users searching Google may come across a listing provided by OCLC.

After selecting the entry for the book, the user can then jump to his or her own local library's information about the book. Users do not have to know which library to visit to find a book near them. Extending this concept to conversations, one goal of these participatory networks is to make it easier for the user to enter a conversation with The Library without having to work to discover their own specific entry points. However, ensuring this effective seamless access to the Library will require more than simply adding elements of participatory networking around the edges of the library. Adding services like blogs and Wikis may be seen merely as adjunct to current library offerings. As with any technological advance, scarce resources must be weighed against a desire to incorporate new services. Do we expand the collection, improve the Web site, or offer blogs to students? A better approach for making these kinds of decisions is to look at the needs of the community served in context with the commonly accepted, core tasks of a library, and see how they can be recast as conversational, or participatory tools.

In point of fact, every service, patron, and access point is a starting point for a conversation. Let's start with the catalogue. If the catalogue is a conversation, it is decidedly formal and, more importantly, one way. Think of today's catalogue as the educational equivalent of a college lecture. A formal system is used to serve up a series of presentations on a given topic. The presentations are rigid in their construction. They follow an abstract model and provide minimal opportunities to the receiver of the information to provide feedback or input.

They provide no constructive means for the user to improve or shape the conversation. Even recent advances in catalogue functions do little more than make the presentation of information more varied. They are still not truly interactive because they do not allow user participation; they do not allow for conversation. To highlight the one-way nature of the catalogue, ask a simple question: what happens when the user doesn't find something?

Do we assume that the information is there, but that the user is simply incapable of finding it? Do we assume that the information does not exist? Do we assume that the catalogue itself is limited? What if we assume that the catalogue is just the current place a user is involving in an ongoing conversation...what would that look like? How can such a traditionally rigid system be made more participatory? What if the user, finding no relevant information in the catalogue, adds either the information or a placeholder for someone else to fill in the missing information? Possibly the user adds information from his or her expertise.

However, assuming that most people go to a catalogue because they don't have the information, perhaps the user instead begins a process for adding the information. The user might ask a question using a virtual reference service; at the end of the transaction, the user then has the option to add the question, along with the answer and associated materials, to the catalogue. Or perhaps, the user simply leaves the query in the catalogue for other patrons to answer, requesting to be notified when an answer is posted. In that case, when a new user does a catalogue search and runs across the question, he or she can provide an answer.

That answer might be a textual entry, or simply a new query that directs the original questioner or new patrons to existing information in the catalogue. The catalogue can also associate conversations with any data point. For example, a user pulls up the record for a book s/he feels might be relevant to an information need s/he is having. This process starts a conversation between that user and the library, its users and authors of associated works. The user can see comments and ratings associated with this book from not only users of this library but users of other libraries. Also associated is a list of related works and the full audio of a lecture by the author. The user might also be directed to an in-person or online book group that is reading that book.

The point is that the catalogue facilitates a conversation as opposed to simply presenting what it 'knows' about a topic and then stepping out of the process. The catalogue, then, does not simply present information, but instead helps users construct knowledge by allowing the user to participate in a conversation. There are other means of improving systems in a conversational library. Take the implicit link between the catalogue and circulation. Of course these systems have always been linked in that items found in the catalogue can be checked out and checked out items have their status reflected in the catalogue. But this kind of 'state' information is a pretty meagre offering.

Imagine using circulation data to improve the actual functionality of the catalogue. Take the example of a user who is searching the catalogue for fictional books on magic. Currently, a relevance score between an item's metadata and the query is computed and then all the items are ranked in a retrieval set. This relevance score can be computed in many ways, but is usually based on the number of times a keyword appears in the record and the placement of that keyword in the metadata record. What is missing is the actual, real-world circulation of an item. Wouldn't it make sense, given such an abstract query, to present the user with Harry Potter first? What if we added circulation data to our relevance rankings: how many times this item has been checked out? It turns out that using a simple statistic is amasingly powerful.

It is akin to Google's page rank algorithm that presents sites most linked to higher in the results. Also, for those worried that users would be flooded with only popular materials, studies show that while these algorithms do change the very top ranked material, the effect quickly fades so that the user can still easily find other materials. Another consideration for adjusting a search is to allow the user to tweak the algorithms used to retrieve works. In the example, a user could turn off the 'popularity' feature. The user could also toggle switches for currency, authority, and other facets of relevancy rankings.

The conversational model requires us to rethink the catalogue as a dynamic system, with data of varying levels of currency and, frankly, quality, coming into and out of the system. In a conversational catalogue there is no reason that some data can't exist in the catalogue for limited durations. Records of well-groomed physical collections may be a core and durable collection in the catalogue, but that is only one of many types of information that could exist in the catalogue space. Furthermore, even this core data can be annotated and linked to more transient media.

So, the user might see a review from a blog as part of a catalogue record on one day, but when s/he pulls the record up again in a few days, that review might be absent, the blog writer having withdrawn the comment. This is akin to weeding the collection; however, it would happen in a more dynamic fashion than occurs with the content on library shelves. The conversational model can also be used in other areas of the library. What do we digitise? What do we select? What programmes do we offer? What do we preserve? The empowered user can participate in answering all of these questions but does not replace the expert librarian; rather, the user contributes additional and diverse information and commentary. In fact, the catalogue scenario just proposed already assumes that the library catalogue does more than store metadata. In order for the scenario to work the 'catalogue' must store questions, answers, video, audio...in essence the catalogue must be expanded and integrated with other library systems so that a final Participatory Library System can present a coherent view of The Library to patrons.

FRAMEWORK FOR INTEGRATION OF PARTICIPATORY LIBRARIANSHIP

As has been noted, participatory networks and libraries as conversations are not brand new concepts sprung from the head of Zeus. Instead they are means to integrate past and current innovations, and create a viable plan forward. The figure below provides a sort of road map of how the library might make the transition from current systems to a truly participatory system. It includes current systems, systems under development, and new concepts. It seeks to capture current momentum and push the field forward to a larger view instead of getting bogged down in the intricacies of any one development activity.

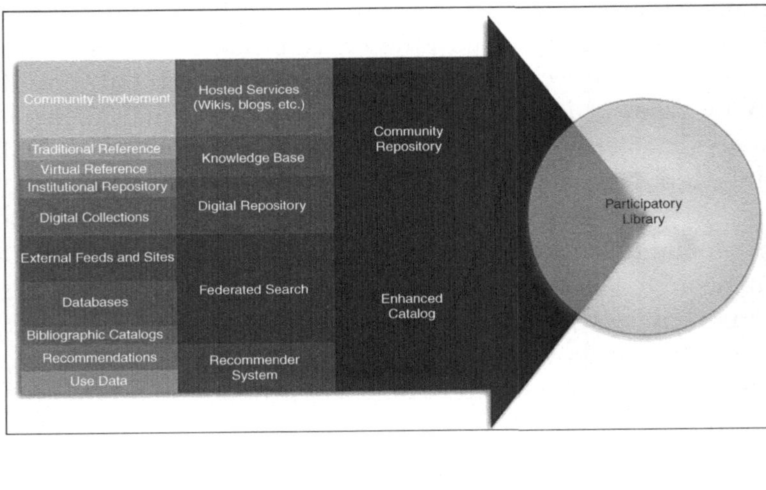

Along the left hand of the graph are current library systems. While the terminology may differ from library to library, nearly every system can be found on today's library web sites. By showing the systems together, the problems of user confusion and library management burden become obvious. Users must often navigate these systems based on their needs, and often with little help. Should they search the catalogues first or the databases? Isn't the catalogue really just another database? Which database do they choose? In our attempts to better serve the users by creating a rich set of resources and services, we have instead complicated their information seeking lives.

As one librarian puts it, "don't give me one more system I, or my patrons, have to deal with." From the array of systems on the left hand, we can see that libraries have not been doing themselves any favours either. We are maintaining many systems, therefore making the calls for yet more systems not only impractical but unwise. The answer is to integrate systems, combining the best of each while discarding the complexity of the whole. The library world is in the midst of doing just that. This section seeks to highlight promising developments in integrating library systems well beyond the library catalogue and to highlight not only an ideal endpoint, but also how this ideal system is truly participatory.

Merging Reference and Community Involvement

The functional area furthest along in the integration of participatory librarianship is reference; since, reference is most readily recognisable as a conversation, this comes as no surprise. Over the last decade, reference services have gone online, and have led to shared reference services. More importantly, reference done online creates artifacts of reference conversations: electronic files than can be cleaned of personal information and placed in a knowledge base, and used as a resource for other users.

A new development in reference is the reference blog, in which multiple librarians and other users can be part of a question answering community with conversations that can live on beyond a single transaction. Another functional area of libraries that is already involved with participatory librarianship is community involvement. For decades, public libraries have supported local community groups through meeting spaces. Some libraries are now hosting Web spaces for local groups.

As libraries incorporate participatory technologies into their offerings, they can create virtual places such as discussion forums, Wikis, and blogs for these community groups to use. If there are standards for these discussion areas, then groups from different communities could also easily participate in shared boards; this makes sense for groups such as Weight Watchers or Alcoholics Anonymous that have local branches and national involvement. In an academic setting, these groups can be student, faculty, or staff organisations or courses. In addition to reference and hosted community conversations, the library has been actively creating digital collections of materials. Parallel to the digital collection building of library materials is an active attempt to create institutional repositories of faculty papers, teacher lesson plans, organisational documentation, and the like.

These services are participatory systems in which collections come from users' contributions, and they may evolve into digital repositories that include both user-created and librarian-created artifacts. These different conversations can be archived into a single repository, and if properly planned, the reference conversations can live alongside, and eventually be intermingled with, the community conversations, and the digital repository into a community repository. Community repositories allow librarians to be more easily involved in the conversations of the community and capture important artifacts of these conversations for later use.

Merging Library Metadata into an Enhanced Catalogue

Participatory librarianship can be supported by another functional area of the library: collections. Traditionally, the collection comprises books, magazines, and other information resources paid for by the library. Electronic resources such as databases that are leased instead of purchased make up a large portion of library expenditures. More recently, Web-based resources have been selected and added to the virtual collection. Several kinds of finding aids are used to locate these information resources.

The catalogue and databases both contain descriptions of resources and searching interfaces. In order to improve access, libraries include records for databases within the catalogue. Conversely, federated searching tools combine the records from different databases and could allow the retrieval of both books and articles by combining records from both the traditional catalogue and databases into one tool. If community-created resources are part of the catalogue, then these resources would also be findable alongside other traditional library resources.

The tools for describing information resources can also be participatory. In traditional librarianship, the librarians provide metadata that patrons then use to make selections. By examining this use data, recommender systems can be created to help users locate new materials. In participatory networking, patrons will be encouraged to add comments about items. If standards are used for these comments, then they can be shared among libraries to create larger pools of recommendations. As these comments are analysed, they can be combined with usage databases to create stronger recommender systems to present patrons with additional choices based upon what is being explored.

The end result is an enhanced catalogue that allows users and libraries to find information regardless of which system the information resides in. However, the enhanced catalogue is still just that, a catalogue. It contains surrogates of digital information and is managed separately from the artifacts themselves. In the case of physical items, this may be all the library systems can manage, but in the case of digital content, there is one more step that needs to be taken. Namely, the artificial barrier between catalogue and content must come down.

Building the Participatory Library

At this point in the evolution of distributed systems into a truly integrated library system, the Participatory Library, we have two large collections: one of resources and one of information about the resources. The first collection of digital content, the community repository, is built by the library and its users collaboratively. The second collection, the enhanced catalogue, includes metadata, both formal and user-created. Both the community repository and the enriched catalogue are participatory. Yet to realise the dream of a seamless system of functionality, these two systems must be merged allowing users to find resources and, much more importantly, conversations.

Furthermore the users must be able to add to both metadata and content. The result may be conceived of as a single integrated information resource, which, for the purposes of this conversation, is called the Participatory Library. Users may access the Participatory Library directly through the library, or they may access it as a series of services in Google, MySpace, or their own homepages. The point is that the access to the library takes place at the point of conversation, not at the point the user realises he or she needs information from the library.

CONVERSATIONS AND PRESERVATION

The conversation model highlights the need for preservation. Aside from simply providing systems that facilitate conversation, libraries serve as the vital community memory. Conversations construct knowledge, but someone must remember what has already been said, and know how to access that dialog. Scientific conversations, for example, are built on previous conversations. Capturing conversations and 'playing them back' at the right time is essential.

This might mean the preservation of artifacts but it also means the increasingly important tasks of capturing the digital dialogs. This highlights the need for institutional repositories. Specifically, Web sites, lectures, courseware, articles must be kept. Further, they must be kept in true conversational repositories that capture the artifacts the methods and the process. They must be kept in information structures that make them readily available as conversations: in other words, users must be able to search for materials, and be able to reconstruct a conversation in its entirety from one fragment.

BEING WHERE THE CONVERSATION IS

Imagine the conversations that are going on in your local library as you read this. Imagine the physicist chatting with the gardener, and the trustee talking with the volunteer who is reading the latest best seller. What knowledge can be gleaned from these novel interactions? Can you measure it? Can you enhance it? Can you capture it? Can you recall it when it would be precisely what a user needs to meet an information need? Note also that these conversations do not belong solely to the library. The library is only part of the conversation. Faced with the daunting variety of resources available on the Web, many organisations try to become the single point of entry into it. Remember that conversations are varied in their mode, places and players, and, more importantly, that they are intensely personal.

This means that participants need to have ownership in them, and often in their locations as well. This also means that the library, as facilitator, needs to be varied in its modes and access points. In many cases, it is better to either create a personal space in which users may converse, or, increasingly, to be part of someone else's space. What we can learn from Web 2.0's Mashups is that smaller sets of limited functionalities lead to greater incorporation of tools into people's lives.

In the ChicagoCrime Google Maps Mashup, combining maps from Google and Chicago crime statistics, it was important for the host of the site to brand the space and shape the interface for his conversation on crime. Can your library functions be as easily incorporated into these types of conversations? Can a user search your catalogue and present the results on his or her Web site? The point is that libraries need to be proactive in a new way. Instead of the mantra, 'Be where the user is', we need to, 'Be where the conversation is. 'It is not enough to be at the users' desktops; you need to be in their e-mail programme, in their MySpace pages, in their IM lists, and in their RSS feed readers. All of these examples point to a significant mental shift that librarians will need to make in moving from delivering information from a centralised location to delivering information in a decentralised manner where the conversations of users are taking place.

The catalogue example presented earlier is an example of a centralised place for conversations. What if, Instead of only being in a catalogue, the same data were split into smaller components and embedded in the user's browser and e-mail programmes? Just as Google's mail system embeds advertising based upon the content of a message, The Library could also provide links to its resources based upon what a user is working on. By disaggregating the information within its system, The Library can deliver just what is needed to a user, provide connections into Mashups, and can live in the space of the user instead of forcing the user to come to the space of the library.

CHALLENGES AND OPPORTUNITIES

There is clearly a host of challenges in incorporating participatory networks and a participatory model into the library. This is to be expected when we are dealing with something as fundamental as knowledge and as personal as conversations. We consider four major challenges that must be met by libraries before they can truly get into the business of participatory librarianship.

Technical

There is a rich suite of participatory networking software that libraries can incorporate into their daily operations. Implementing a blog, a Wiki, or RSS feeds these days is not a hard task, and they can easily be used to deliver information about library services and conversations to the user's space. Furthermore, these systems are often tested in very large-scale environments and are, in some cases, the same tools used in large participatory networking sites such as Wikipedia and Blogger. Some of these packages are commercial, but others are open source software. Open source software is cheaper, easier to adapt, and, in some cases, more advanced.

The downside to open source is that it requires a considerable amount of technical knowledge by the library and does not come with a technical support hotline. The largest technological impediment, however, may be the currently installed base of software within libraries. Integrated library systems have a long history, and include a broad range of library functions. Legacy code and near monolithic systems have restricted the easy exchange of a diverse set of information. Were these systems written today they would use modular code and loosely coupled APIs and allow customers much more customizability of interface.

These changes may come to integrated library systems but it may take years. Several libraries are currently attempting to pick apart these integrated systems themselves. Often, libraries go to the underlying databases that hold the library metadata or create their own data structures, such as the University of Pennsylvania Data Farm project. Once components of this system are exposed, the catalogue simply becomes another database that can be federated into new and unified interfaces. However, such integration requires a great deal of technological expertise.

There is an opportunity for ILS vendors or large consortial groups such as OCLC to move quickly into this space. In the meantime, there is an opportunity for the larger library community. This technology brief was created in response to a perceived need. Whether evidenced in the Library 2.0 community or in conversations at LITA, libraries are now interested in incorporating new Web technologies into their offerings and operations.

The technologies under consideration here present platforms for experimentation. Rather than setting up thousands of separated experiments, however, the library community should create a participatory network of its own.

The technology certainly exists to create a test bed for libraries to set up various combinations of communication technologies to test new Web services against pooled data and even to incorporate new services into the current library offerings. By combining resources in a single, large-scale test bed, libraries cannot only get greater impact for the their investments, but can also directly experience life as a connected conversation. These connections, if built at the ground level, will then make it easier for The Library to come into existence. Terminology can be clarified, claims tested, and best practices collaboratively developed, greatly accelerating innovation and dissemination.

Operational

In addition to being in the conversation business, libraries are in the infrastructure business. One of the most powerful aspects of a library is its ability not only to develop a collection of some type of information but to maintain it over time. Sometimes infrastructure can be problematic but more often than not, it provides a stable foundation from which to operate. There are many conversations going on that need infrastructure but have none. Think of the opportunities in your community for using the Web to facilitate a conversation. It might be a researcher wanting to disseminate the results of his or her latest study. It might be a community organisation seeking funding. It might be a business trying to manage its basic operational knowledge.

The point is that such individuals and community organisations are not in the infrastructure business and could use a partner who is. Imagine a local organisation coming to the library, and within a few minutes setting up a Web site with an RSS feed, a blog and bulletin boards. The library facilitates, but does not own, that individual's or organisation's conversation. It does form a strong partnership, however, that can be leveraged into resources and support.

The true power of participatory networking in libraries is not to give every librarian a blog; it is in giving every community member a blog. In addition, the library can play the role of connecting these conversations to other users when appropriate. Participatory libraries allow the concept of community centre to be extended to the Web. Many public libraries have no problem providing meeting space to local non-profits. Why not provide Web meeting space in the form of a Web site or Web conferencing? Many academic libraries attempt to capture the scholarly output of their faculties, why not help generate the output with research data stores? The answers to these questions inevitably come back to time and money.

However, there is nothing in this brief that says such services have to be free. In fact, the best partnerships are formed when all partners are invested in the process. The true problem is that libraries have no idea of how to charge for such services. Faculty would be glad to write library support into grants, but need a dollar figure to include and how long each task will take. Many libraries aren't used to positioning their services on a per item basis, and this makes it difficult to build partnerships. Sometimes it is not a lack of money, but a lack of structure to take in money that is the problem.

Policy

As always, it is policy that presents the greatest challenges. The idea of opening the library functions to a greater set of inputs is rife with potential pitfalls. How can libraries use the technologies and concepts of Facebook and MySpace without being plagued by their problems? How can users truly be made part of the collection without the library being liable for all of their actions? The answers may lie in a seemingly obscure concept: identity management. Conversations can range in their mode, topic, and duration. They can also vary in the conversants.

The library needs to know a conversant's status to determine policy; and requires a unique identifier like a library card, to uphold it. In traditional libraries, that is the extent of identity management. In a participatory model, distinctions among identities become complex and graduated, and require us to consider a new approach. This new model, of patrons adding information directly to library systems, is not as radical as it may first appear. We have become very used to the idea of roles and tiered levels of authority in many other settings. Most modern computer systems allow for some gradation in user abilities. Online communities have even introduced merit systems, by which continual high-quality contributions to a site equals greater power in the site.

Think about Amazon, Wikipedia, even eBay; as users contribute more to the community they gain status and recognition. From participants to editors, from readers to writers, these organisations have seen membership as a sliding scale of trust, and libraries need to adopt this approach in all of their basic systems.

We currently do, to a degree, in the form of librarians, paraprofessionals, and other staff. Yet even these distinctions tend to be rigid and often class based, with high walls between the strata. Some of this is imposed by outside organisations but a great deal is there by inertia of the field. Skillful use of identity management will help libraries avoid the baggage of MySpace and Facebook.

As users grain greater access, greater responsibility, and greater autonomy, libraries need to be more certain of their identities. That is, for a user to do more requires the library to know more. Knowing about a user may involve traditional identity verification, or tracking an activity trail whereby intentions can be judged in relation to actions. These concepts may be expressed as, 'The more we know you, the more control you can have in valuable services such as blogging, or the catalogue."

The concepts are illustrated in Blogger and LiveJournal, both of which require some level of identity information. In another example: to join LiveJournal you must be invited, thus the community confers identity. The common theme is that verifying identity is community based. The difference between the library and MySpace is that the library works in an established community with traditional norms of identity, whereas MySpace is seeking to create a community. Both the library and the services, however, base their functions and services on identity.

Ethical

As knowledge is developed through conversation, and libraries facilitate this process, libraries have a powerful impact on the knowledge generated. Can librarians interfere with and shape conversations? Absolutely. Should we? We can't help it. Our collections, our reference work, our mere presence will influence conversations. The question is, in what ways? By dedicating a library mission to directly align with the needs of a finite community, we are accepting the biases, norms and priorities of the community. While a library may seek to expand or change the community, it does so from within. When Internet filtering became a requirement for federal Internet funding, public and school libraries could not simply quit, or ignore the fact, because they are agents of their communities. School libraries had to accept filtering with federal funding because their parent organisations, the schools, accepted filtering.

We see, from this example, that libraries may shift from facilitating conversations to becoming active conversant, but they are always doing both. Thus, the question is not whether the library shapes conversations, but which ones, and how actively? These questions are hardly new to the underlying principles of librarianship. And nothing in the participatory model seeks to change those underlying principles. The participatory model does, however, highlight the fact that those principles shape conversations and have an impact on the community.

WIRELESS NETWORKS IN MEDIUM-SIZED ACADEMIC LIBRARIES

Wireless networking offers a way to meet the needs of an increasingly mobile, tech-savvy student population. While many research libraries offer wireless access to their patrons, academic libraries serving smaller populations must heavily weigh both the potential benefits and disadvantages of this new technology. Will wireless networks become essential components of the modern academic library, or is this new technology just a passing fad? Prompted by plans to implement a wireless network at the Houston Cole Library (HCL), which serves a student enrollment close to ten thousand, this study was conducted to gather information about whether libraries similar in size and mission to HCL have adopted wireless technology. The study also sought to find out what, if any, problems other libraries have encountered with wireless networks and how successful they have perceived those networks to be. Other questions addressed include level of technical support offered, planning, type of equipment used to access the network, and patron-use levels.

REVIEW OF LITERATURE

A review of the literature on wireless networks revealed a number of articles on wireless networks and checkout programmes for laptop computers at large research institutions. Seventy percent of major research libraries surveyed by Kwon and Soules in 2003 offered some degree of wireless access to their networks. No articles, however, specifically addressed the use of wireless networks in medium-sized academic libraries.

Many articles can also be found on wireless-network use in medical libraries and other institutions. Library instruction using wireless classrooms and laptops has been another subject of enquiry as well. Breeding wrote that there are a number of successful uses for wireless technology in libraries, and a wireless Local Area Network (WLAN) can be a natural extension of existing networks.

He added that since, it is sometimes difficult to install wiring in library buildings, wireless is more cost effective. A yearly survey conducted by the Campus Computing Project found that the number of schools planning for and deploying wireless networks rose dramatically from 2002 to 2003. "For example, the portion of campuses reporting strategic plans for wireless networks rose to 45.5 per cent in fall 2003, up from 34.7 per cent in 2002 and 24.3 per cent in 2001."

The use of wireless access in academia is expected to keep growing. According to a summary of a study conducted by the EDUCAUSE Centre for Applied Research (ECAR), the higher-education community will keep investing in the technology infrastructure, and institutions will continue to refine and update networks. The move towards wireless access "represents a user-centred shift, providing students and faculty with greater access than ever before." In an article on ubiquitous computing, Drew provides a straightforward look at how WLANs work, security issues, planning, and the uses and ramifications of wireless technology in libraries.

He suggests, "Perhaps one of the most important reasons for implementing wireless networking across an entire campus or in a library is the highly mobile lifestyle of students and faculty." The use of wireless will only increase with the advent of new portable devices, he added. Wireless networking is the best and least expensive way for students, faculty, and staff to take their office with them wherever they go. The circulation of laptop computers is a frequent topic in the available literature.

The 2003 study by Kwon and Soules primarily focussed on laptop-lending services in academic-research libraries. Fifty per cent of the institutions that responded to their survey provided laptops for checkout. The majority indicated moderate-to-high use of laptop services. Positive user response and improved 'public reputation, image, and relations" were the greatest advantages reported with laptop circulation. The major disadvantages associated with these services were related to labour and cost. A study of laptop checkout service at the Mildred F. Sawyer Library at Suffolk University in Boston revealed that laptop usage was popular during the fall semester of 1999. Students checked out the computers to work on group projects.

A laptop area was set aside on one library floor to provide wired Internet access for eight users. However, students wanted to use the laptops anywhere, not one designated place. The wired laptop areas were not popular, Dugan wrote, adding that "Few students used the wired area and the wires were repeatedly stolen or intentionally broken." An interim phase involved providing wireless network cards for checkout to encourage patrons to use their own laptops, and, when a wireless network was put into place in the fall of 2000, demand exceeded the number of available laptops for checkout.

METHOD

A survey was designed to find out how many libraries similar in size and mission to HCL have adopted wireless networks, the experiences they have encountered in offering wireless access, and, most importantly, whether they felt the investment in wireless technology has been worth the effort. The National Centre for Education Statistic's Academic Library Peer Comparison Tool, a database composed of statistical information on libraries throughout the United States, was used to select institutions for this study.

A search on this database retrieved eighty-eight academic libraries that met two criteria: full-time enrollments of between five thousand and ten thousand, and classification by the Carnegie Classification of Higher Education as Master's Colleges and Universities I. The survey was administered to those thought most likely to be responsible for systems in the library; they were selected from staff listings on library Web sites. If such a person could not be identified, the survey was sent to the head of library systems or to the library director.

The survey was divided into the following sections:

- Implementation of wireless network
- Planning and installation stages
- User services
- Technical problems
- Benefits specific to use of network

Surveys were mailed out in March 2004. An Internet address was provided in the cover letter if participants wished to take the survey online rather than return it by mail. An e-mail reminder with a link to the online survey was sent out three weeks after the initial survey was mailed. All letters and e-mails were personalised, and a self-addressed stamped envelope and a ballpoint pen with the JSU logo were included with the mail surveys. In the e-mail reminder, the authors offered to share the results of the project with anyone who was interested, and received several enthusiastic responses.

RESULTS

A total of fifty-three completed surveys were returned, resulting in a response rate of 60 per cent. The overwhelming majority responded that their library offered wireless-network access. Even if the thirty-five surveys that were not returned had reported that wireless networks were not available, more than 50 per cent would still have offered wireless networks. Survey results also pointed to the newness of the technology. Only four of the fifty-three institutions have had wireless networks for more than three years. The majority has implemented wireless networks just within the last two years.

When asked to identify the major reasons for offering wireless networks to their patrons, the three responses most chosen were:

- To provide greater access to users;
- The flexibility of a network unfettered by the limitations of tedious wiring; and
- To keep up with technological innovation.

Least significant factors in the decision to implement wireless networks were cost; use by library faculty and staff; to aid in bibliographic instruction; and use for carrying out technical services. Somewhat to the authors' surprise, wireless use in bibliographic instruction was not high on the list of reasons for installing a wireless network, identified by only 9 percent of respondents. The benefits of wireless for library instruction was stressed in the litreature by Mathias and Heser and Patton. In addition to obtaining an instrument for gauging how many libraries similar in scope and size to HCL have implemented wireless networks and why they chose to do so, questions on the survey were also designed to gather information on planning and implementation, user services, technical problems, and perceived benefits.

PLANNING AND IMPLEMENTATION

Although Tolson mentions that some schools have used committees composed of faculty, staff, and students to look into the adoption of wireless technology, responses from this survey indicated that the majority of the libraries did not form committees specifically for the planning of their wireless networks.

In addition, 49 per cent of the libraries took fewer than six months to plan for implementation of a network, 37 per cent required six months to one year, and 15 per cent reported more than one to two years. Actual time spent on installation and configuration of wireless networks was relatively short, 98 per cent indicating less than one year. One of the most important issues to consider when planning to implement a wireless network is extent of coverage—where wireless access will be available. Survey responses revealed varying degrees of wireless coverage among institutions. 20 per cent had campus-wide access, 55 per cent had some level of coverage throughout the entire library, 37 per cent provided a limited range of coverage outside the building, and 20 per cent offered access only in certain areas within the library.

Institutions vary in their approaches to networking depending on enrollment. Smaller colleges and universities with fewer than ten thousand students are "more likely to implement campuswide wireless networks from the start. Larger institutions are more likely to implement wireless technology in specific buildings, consistent with a desire to move forward at a modest pace, as resources and comfort with the technology grow." Questions on the survey also queried respondents about the popularity of spaces in the library where users access the library's wireless network. Answers revealed that the most popular areas for wireless access are study carrels, tables, and study rooms. 19 per cent indicated that accessing wireless networks in the stacks is popular. Of particular concern to HCL, a thirteen-story building, was how the environment of the library would accommodate a wireless network.

A thorough site survey is important to locate the best spots within the library to install access points and to determine whether there are architectural barriers in the building that might interfere with access. The majority of survey respondents indicated that the site survey conducted in their library for a wireless network was carried out by their academic institution's IT staff. While library staff conducted 35 percent of site surveys, only 17 per cent were conducted by outside companies.

USER SERVICES

An issue to be addressed by libraries deciding to go wireless is whether laptop computers should also be provided for checkout in the library. After all, it might be hard to justify the usefulness of a wireless network if users do not have access to laptops or other hardware with wireless capabilities. While one individual reported working at a 'laptop university' in which campuswide wireless networking exists and all students are required to own laptops, not all college students will have that luxury.

In order to provide more equal access to students, checking out laptops has become an increasingly common service in academic libraries. Seventy percent of this survey's respondents whose institutions offered wireless access also made laptops available for checkout. Comments made throughout the survey seemed to imply that while checking out laptops to patrons is an invaluable complement to offering wireless access, librarians should be prepared for a myriad of hassles that accompany laptop checkout. Wear and tear of laptops, massive battery use, cost of laptops, and maintenance were some of the biggest problems reported. One participant, whose institution decided to stop offering laptops for checkout to patrons in the library, wrote, "It required too much staff time to maintain and we decided the money was better spent elsewhere.

The college now encourages students to purchase a laptop [instead of] a full-sized PC." One participant worried that the rising use of laptops in his library would lead to the obsolescence of its more than one hundred wired desktops, writing, "Our desktops are very popular and we think having them is one of the reasons our gate count has increased in recent years. What happens when everyone has a laptop?" The number of laptops checked out in the libraries varied. The majority of libraries had purchased between one and thirty laptops available for checkout.

Three institutions had more than forty-one laptops available for checkout. One library could boast that it had sixty laptops available for checkout with twelve pagers to notify students waiting in line to use laptops. When asked about the use of laptops in libraries, 46 percent observed moderate use, while 32 per cent reported heavy use of laptops. Only 3 percent indicated that they hardly ever noticed use of laptops in the library. For those students who chose to bring their own laptop to access the library's wireless network, half of the institutions surveyed required students to purchase their own network-interface cards for their laptops, while 19 per cent allowed students to check them out from the library.

In addition to laptops, personal digital assistants, (PDAs) were listed by 37 per cent of respondents as devices that may access wireless networks. One librarian indicated that cell phones could access the wireless network in his library. 56 per cent of respondents indicated that users are able to print to a central printer in the library from their wireless device. An important consideration for implementing a wireless network is how users will authenticate. Authentication protocol is defined by the Microsoft Encyclopaedia of Networking as "any protocol used for validating the identity of a user to determine whether to grant the user access to resources over a network." Authentication methods listed by the institutions surveyed varied greatly and the authors could not identify all of them.

Methods mentioned were Lightweight Directory Access Protocol (LDAP), virtual private network (VPN), and Media Access Control (MAC) addresses, Bluesocket, Remote Authentication Dial in User Service (RADIUS), pluggable Graphical Identification and Authentication (pGINA), Protected Extensive Authentication Protocol (PEAP), and e-mail logins. Out of the thirty-nine responses to this question, seven individuals indicated that they do not require any type of authentication at the present. Although some individuals noted that they are planning to enable some type of authentication in the future, one participant suggested that there were ethical issues involved in requiring users to authenticate. This person argued that "anonymous access to information is valued" and praised his institution's current policy of allowing "anyone who can find the network" to use it.

A concern about offering wireless network access in the library is how library staff will be prepared to handle the flood of technical questions that are likely to ensue. The level of technical support offered to users varied among the institutions surveyed. More than half of the respondents indicated that users receive help specifically from IT staff or from the campus computer centre. 39 per cent of users received help from the reference desk, while 19 per cent received help from circulation staff. 33 per cent of the responding institutions offered technical help from a Web site, while 7 per cent indicated that they did not offer any type of technical support to users.

Technical Problems

The technical problems most often encountered with wireless networks centered on architectural barriers that cause black-outs or slow-spots where wireless access fails. This confirms the importance of carrying out thorough site surveys and testing prior to installation of access points. Site surveys may be carried out by companies specially equipped and trained to determine where access points should be installed, the most appropriate type of antennae and how many access points are needed to provide the greatest amount of coverage. Configuration of the network was the second most highly reported problem associated with installing wireless networks, seeming to suggest the need for librarians to coordinate their efforts and rely on the knowledge provided by the IT coordinator within their institution.

Lack of technical support available to users, slow speed, and authentication were also indicated as technical problems most encountered. Integrating the wireless network with the existing wired network was the least-mentioned problem associated with wireless networks. Although security problems, particularly concerning Wired Equivalency Protocol (WEP) vulnerabilities, have been pointed out as one of the major drawbacks of a wireless network, the majority of users had not as yet experienced security problems. Although one participant wrote, "Don't be too casual about the security risks," another individual wrote, "Talk to your networking department," as many of them are overly worried about security.

Perceived Benefits

Respondents reported that the number-one benefit of offering wireless access was user satisfaction. Giving patrons the ability to use their laptops anywhere in the library and do multiple tasks from one machine is simply becoming what more and more users expect. The second largest benefit revolved around flexibility and ease of use due to the lack of wires. 35 per cent indicated that allowing students to roam the stacks while accessing the network was a significant benefit. Although a few studies have suggested the promise of wireless networks for aiding bibliographic instruction, only 9 per cent of respondents indicated this as a benefit of wireless technology. Use of wireless technology for instruction, it might be recalled, was not a significant factor noted by respondents in the decision to implement a wireless network.

Likewise, use of this type of network to carry out technical services was also low on the scale of benefits. 73 per cent of users claimed that wireless networks have thus far been worth the cost-benefit ratio. While 70 per cent indicated moderate to heavy use of the wireless network, 27 per cent reported low usage. When asked what advice they would give to others considering adopting wireless networks in their libraries, the overwhelming majority of responses were positive, recommending that HCL take the plunge.

As one individual wrote, "Offer it and they will come. It has really increased the usage of our library." Other individuals noted that it is simply necessary to offer wireless access to keep up with technological innovation, and that students expect it. The most significant warning, however, revolved around checkout and maintenance of laptops, which, from the results of this survey, seems be both a big advantage and a headache. Several individuals echoed the importance of doing site surveys to test bandwidth limitations and access.

One particularly energised participant, using multiple exclamations for emphasis, shared a plethora of advice. "Throttle connection speeds! Allow only http access! Block ports and unnecessary protocols! Secure your network and disallow unauthenticated users! Use access control lists! Establish policies that describe [wireless fidelity] Wi-Fi risks and liabilities on your part!".

Useful advice on wireless-access implementation gleaned from this survey fell under the following categories:

- Be aware of slower speed.
- Create a policy and guide for users.
- Do it because more users are going wireless, it is necessary to keep up with technological innovation, and because students love it.
- Provide plenty of access points.
- Install access points in appropriate places.
- Ensure continuous connectivity by allowing overlap between access points.
- Purchase battery chargers and heavy-duty laptops with extended warranties.
- Get support from IT staff for planning and maintenance.
- Offering wireless will increase library usage.
- Perform or have an expert perform a careful site survey and do lots of testing to locate dead or slow spots in the library due to architectural barriers.
- Enable some type of authorisation.
- Be aware of security concerns.
- Although the majority of participants' networks support 802.11b, a few participants suggest using the 802.11g standard because it is 'the fastest' and 'backwards compatible to 802.11b'.

6

Internet

Internet is the network of networks, *i.e.*, a global network which make WWW.

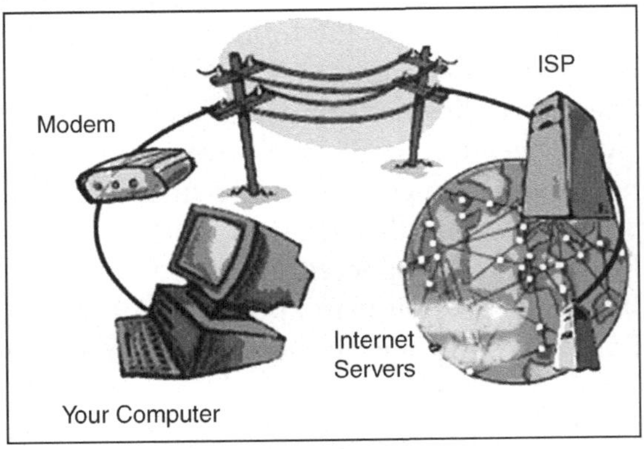

BIRTH OF THE NET

The Internet grew out of an experiment in the 1960s by the U.S. Department of Defence. The DoD wanted to create a computer network that would continue to function in the event of a disaster, such as a nuclear war. If part of the network was damaged or destroyed, the rest of the system still had to work. That network was ARPANET, which linked U.S., scientific and academic researchers.

It was the forerunner of today's Internet. In 1985, the National Science Foundation (NSF), an American research organisation, created NSFNET, a series of networks for research and education communication. Based on ARPANET protocols, the NSFNET created a national backbone service, provided free to any American research and educational institution. At the same time, regional networks were created to link individual institutions with the national backbone service. NSFNET grew rapidly as people discovered its potential and as new software applications were created to make access easier. Corporations such as Sprint and MCI began to build their own networks that they then linked to NSFNET.

When commercial firms and other regional network providers took over the operation of the major Internet arteries, NSF withdrew from the backbone business. NSF also coordinated a service called InterNIC that registered all addresses on the Internet so that data could be routed to the right system. This service has now been taken over by Network Solutions, Inc. and other Internet registration services in cooperation with NSF

NET ANATOMY

The Web physically consists of your personal computer, web browser software, a connection to an Internet service provider, computers called servers that host digital data, and routers and switches to direct the flow of information.

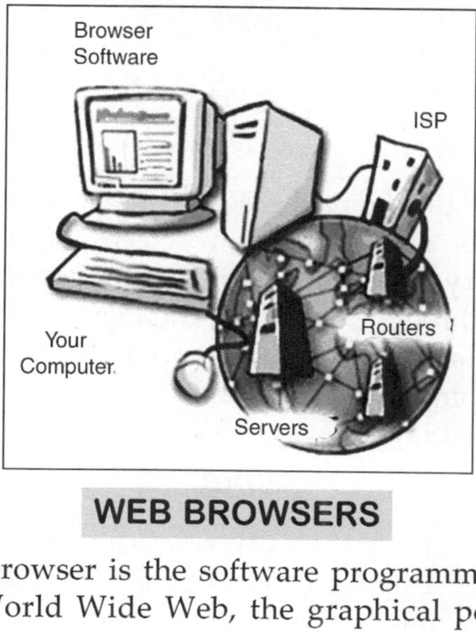

WEB BROWSERS

A web browser is the software programme you use to access the World Wide Web, the graphical portion of the

Internet. The first browser, called NCSA Mosaic, was developed at the National Centre for Supercomputing Applications in the early 1990s. The easy-to-use point-and-click interface helped popularise the Web. Microsoft Internet Explorer and Netscape Navigator are the two most popular ones.

NAVIGATING THE WEB

The Web is known as a client-server system. Your computer is the client; the remote computers that store electronic files are the servers. To visit the web site, enter the address or URL of the web site in your web browser. Browser requests the web page from the web server that hosts the requested site. The server sends the data over the Internet to your computer. Your web browser interprets the data, displaying it on your computer screen.

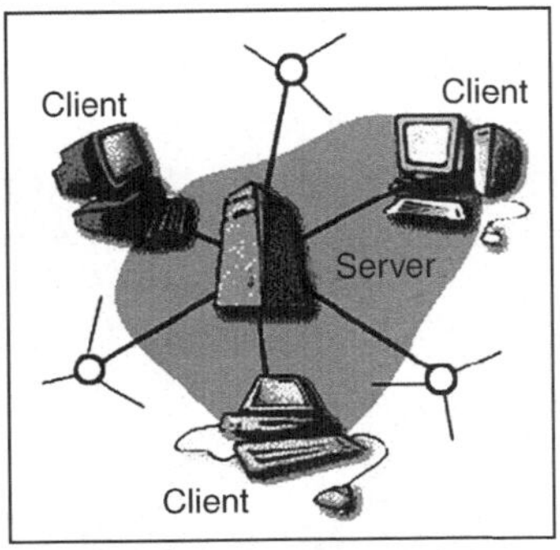

The 'glue' that holds the Web together is called hypertext and hyperlinks. This feature allows electronic files on the Web to be linked so you can jump easily between them. On the Web, you navigate through pages of information--commonly known as browsing or surfing-based on what interests you at that particular moment. Web pages are written in a computer language called Hypertext Markup Language or HTML

W3C

The World Wide Web was originally developed in 1990 at CERN, the European Laboratory for Particle Physics. The original idea came from a young computer scientist, Tim

Berners-Lee. It is now managed by The World Wide Web Consortium. The WWW Consortium is funded by a large number of corporate members, including AT&T, Adobe Systems, Inc., Microsoft Corporation and Sun Microsystems, Inc. Its purpose is to promote the growth of the Web by developing technical specifications and reference software that will be freely available to everyone.

WEB ADDRESSES

World Wide Web is a network of electronic files stored on millions of computers all around the world. Hypertext links these resources together. Uniform Resource Locators or URLs are the addresses used to locate the files. Every URL is unique and identifies one specific file.

DOMAIN NAMES

Every computer that hosts data on the Internet has a unique numerical address. For example, the numerical address for the White House is 198.137.240.100. But since, few people want to remember long strings of numbers, the Domain Name System (DNS) was invented. DNS, a critical part of the Internet's technical infrastructure, correlates a numerical address to a word. To access the White House web site, you could type its number into the address box of your web browser. But most people prefer to use 'www.whitehouse.gov.' In this case, the domain name is whitehouse.gov.

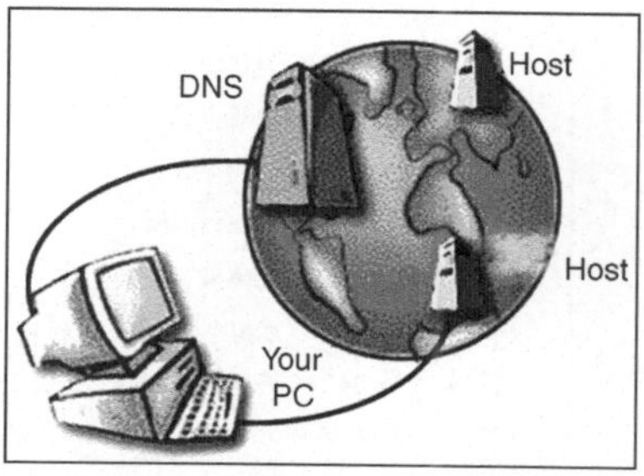

THE STRUCTURE OF A DOMAIN NAME

A domain name has two or more parts separated by dots and consists of some form of an organisation's name and a three letter or more suffix. For example, the domain name for IBM is 'ibm.com'; the United Nations is 'un.org.' The domain name suffix is known as a generic top-level domain (gTLD). It describes the type of organisation. Currently in use gTLDs:

```
.aero--For the air-transport industry
.biz--Reserved for businesses
.com--For businesses, commercial enterprises
.edu--For educational institutions and universities
.gov--Reserved for United States government agencies
.info--For all uses
.mil--For the United States military
.net--For networks; usually reserved for
organisations such as Internet
service providers
.org--For non-commercial organisations
```

BOOKMARKS AND FAVOURITES

Bookmarks and Favourites save Web addresses so you can return to them quickly. To save a web page, go to the Bookmarks or Favourites menu or click on its icon and select Add. When you click on the icon again, the title of the page you recorded will appear at the bottom of the list. To access the page, just double-click on the title.

To organise your Favourites, Click on the Favourites button on the toolbar to open the Favourites window. Now select Organise Favourites. Click on the folder icon to create a new folder, then name it. Now click on each Favourite once, hold down your left mouse button and drag the Favourite into the appropriate subject folder.

ABUSING INSECURE FEATURES OF INTERNET EXPLORER

INTERNET EXPLORER SECURITY MODEL

First, let us start with a description of the security framework used by Internet Explorer to classify resources and to enforce security policies when they are processed. Internet Explorer 4 introduced the concept of URL Security Zones as a means to classify web content according to its trustworthiness. Using this, framework security policies are configured for each of five pre-established Security Zones, then while it is running Internet Explorer dynamically assigns content received from the Web to a corresponding Security Zone based on the content's origin and the settings configured for that Security Zone are then used to enforce the security controls associated to its trust level. Thus, a web application executed by Internet Explorer will be granted authorisation to perform actions depending on the privileges set for the Security Zone to which it was assigned by Internet Explorer.

These are the five Security Zones of Internet Explorer listed by increasing level of trust:

- *Restricted Sites Zone*: Used for Web sites that contain content that can cause problems when downloaded. Use this zone to cause Internet Explorer to alert that potentially-unsafe content is about to download, or to prevent that content from downloading. The user explicitly adds the URLs of untrusted Web sites to this zone,
- *Internet Zone*: For Web sites on the Internet that do not belong to another zone. This default setting causes Internet Explorer to prompt the user whenever potentially unsafe content is about to download. Web sites that are not mapped into other zones automatically fall into this zone,
- *Local Intranet Zone*: For content located on an

organisation's intranet. Because the servers and information are within an organisation's firewall, it is reasonable to assign a higher trust level to content on the intranet,

- *Trusted Sites Zone*: For content located on Web sites that are considered more reputable or trustworthy than other sites on the Internet. Assigning a higher trust level to these sites minimizes the number of authentication requests. The user explicitly adds the URLs of these trusted Web sites to this zone.
- *Local Machine Zone*: The Local Machine zone is an implicit zone for content that exists on the local computer. The content found on the user's computer is treated with a high level of trust.

Although the default settings for each Security Zone have varied over time since, their introduction in Internet Explorer 4, the number of Security Zones and their implied level of trust have not changed.

For the purpose of this chapter there are two generic types of attacks to the Security Zone framework that are relevant:

- Security Zone elevation attacks, in which web content that should normally be assigned to a Security Zone with trust level *X* ends up assigned to a Security Zone with trust level *Y* where *Y* > *X*; and
- Security Zone restrictions bypass attacks, in which web content that ended up correctly assigned to a Security Zone successfully performs actions that require privileges not granted to that Security Zone.

WHEN A DOOR CLOSES, A WINDOW IS OPENED

Bad design decisions or flawed design sometimes result in features that leave an open door for different kinds of attacks and under the eternal alibi of backward compatibility, it often seems that they will never be closed. In this section, as suggested, describe some of these weak Internet Explorer features. Keep in mind that, as minimal as the security implications of these features may seem at a first glance, they have proved to be key components of the exploitation scenarios exposed herein, where the attacker can compromise a user desktop system by abusing nothing but these features.

Hiding the Key Under the Doormat

HTTP cookies and web navigation history are stored by Internet Explorer in several files and folders in the local file system. Apparently as a security measure random names are used for both files and folders. However, since, they need to be accessed by Internet Explorer in an efficient manner the names and location of the randomly named files are kept inside different mapping files named index.dat. Here are some examples:

```
%USERPROFILE%\Localsettings\History\History.IE5\index.dat
%USERPROFILE%\Localsettings\IECompatCache\index.dat
%USERPROFILE%\Cookies\index.dat
```

Although the format of these index files is not entirely plain text, the security sensitive content is being stored in plain text. Since, these index files are used to reference content stored in randomly named files, obtaining them would result in obtaining the actual locations of the aforementioned files and folders. Hence, the increase in security gained by storing potentially sensitive information in file system objects with randomly select names is dependent on the ability to prevent read access of index files from an attacker. If an attacker is able to inspect the contents of these indexing files, she can easily determine the exact location of the sensitive content that was protected by storing it in hidden files.

A Chip off the Old Block

Internet Explorer and Windows Explorer use common underlying components and resemble each other in many aspects. They both support access to file systems object on SMB shares and use of UNC (Universal Naming Convention) paths to reference them. The use of common components and the idiosyncrasies of both programmes allow a user to do some tricks with Internet Explorer when accessing special files and folders that yield similar results when done using Windows Explorer. For example, when directly accessing the History folder with Windows Explorer, the actual files stored in there are not shown.

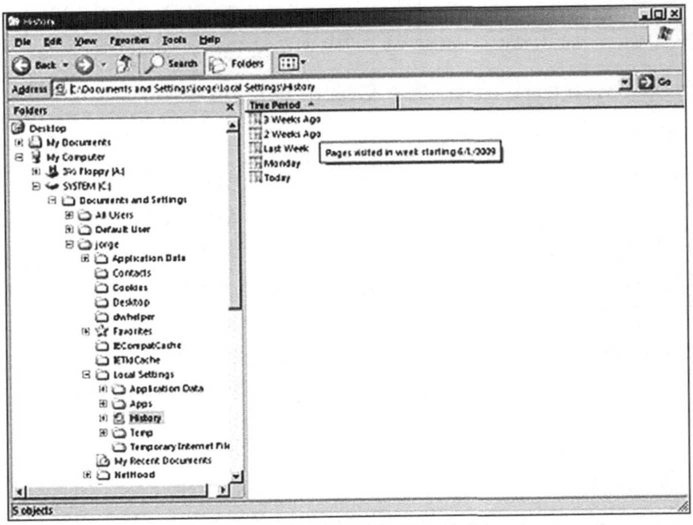

Fig 6.1 Internet Explorer History Folder Accessed Directly Tsing Windows Explorer

However, accessing the same folder as a network resource requested using an UNC path will show the actual contents of this folder.

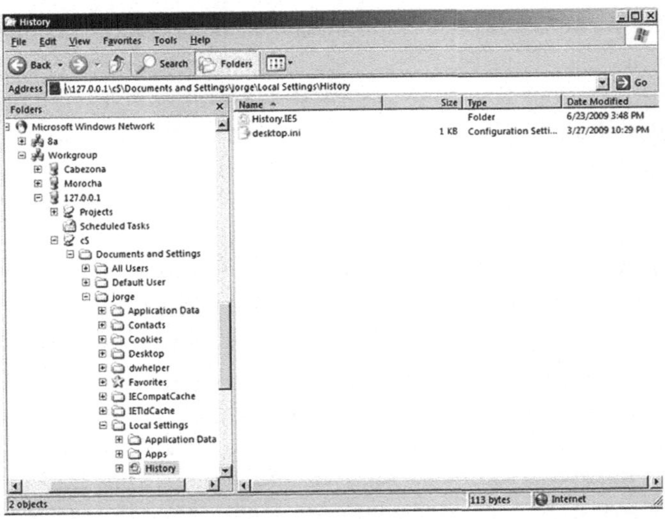

Fig 6.2 Internet Explorer History Folder Accessed with UNC Using Windows Explorer

As it was stated, Internet Explorer behaves alike when accessing these files and folders:

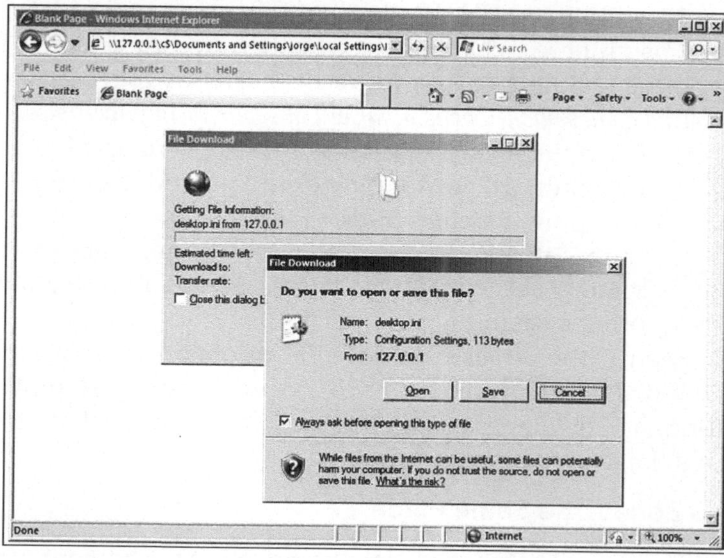

Fig 6.3 Internet Explorer History Folder Accessed with UNC Using Internet Explorer

Furthermore, the fact that Internet Explorer supports UNC and SMB has an important security implication. As this naming conventions and protocols can be used without restrictions inside web pages in the Internet zone or above, a web page in those zones can include an HTML tag such as the following:

```
<img src='\\[WEB SERVER IP ADDRESS]\image.jpg'>
```

When Internet Explorer renders this tag, it triggers an SMB request to a server at the IP address specified in the <img> tag. The NTLM authentication negotiation proceeds as follows: anonymous access is first tried and, if failed, the client starts the challenge-response negotiation. The server sends the client a challenge value and the client automatically responds back with the ciphered challenge.

Thus, as part of the challenge-response negotiation, the client sends to the server the following information about itself:

- Windows user name.
- Windows domain name.

- Windows computer name.
- A challenge value chosen by the web server ciphered with the LM/NTLM hash of this user's password.

This ciphered challenge could then be brute-forced to obtain the plaintext password for the currently logged user.

This achievement opens a variety of security implications:

- If the victim's computer is directly connected to the Internet, it could be compromised as easy as accessing it trough SMB.
- If the attacker knows something more about the victim, she could try this password for accessing other systems.

Even if the attacker is not able to obtain the plaintext password from that the SMB request, the rest of the information obtained can still be useful for other attack vectors as will be shown later on.

Two Zones, the Same Place

The Security Zones model mentioned at the beginning of this article requires Internet Explorer to determine to which zone it will assign a web resource based on its origin.

The Security Zone assigned to a given object referenced using the UNC convention is:

- The Internet Security Zone if the UNC path contains the IP address to specify the target machine.
- The Local Intranet Security Zone if the UNC path contains a NetBIOS name to specify the target machine.

So far this does not sound bad. It makes sense as NetBIOS names can only be resolved within the scope of the local network segment if not mapped explicitly in the lmhosts file. But what happens with IP address 127.0.0.1? As trivial as it may sound, it is not.

In fact, this is one of the root causes of the problems that Microsoft staff has mentioned for closing the attack scenarios described afterwards in this document. After several discussions with MSRC team members, they agreed that the issue is a kind of dead end, given that due to expected functionality and design decisions forcing this address to belong to one zone or another cannot be done without high impact on either security or backward compatibility with existing applications.

Since, Internet Explorer makes extensive use of cached files enforcing access control to them is not a minor issue. The assumptions and constrains of the Security Zones model make things become more complicated. Consider, for example, an Internet web site redirecting the navigation flow towards the following URL:

```
\\127.0.0.1\PATH_TO_RESOURCE
```

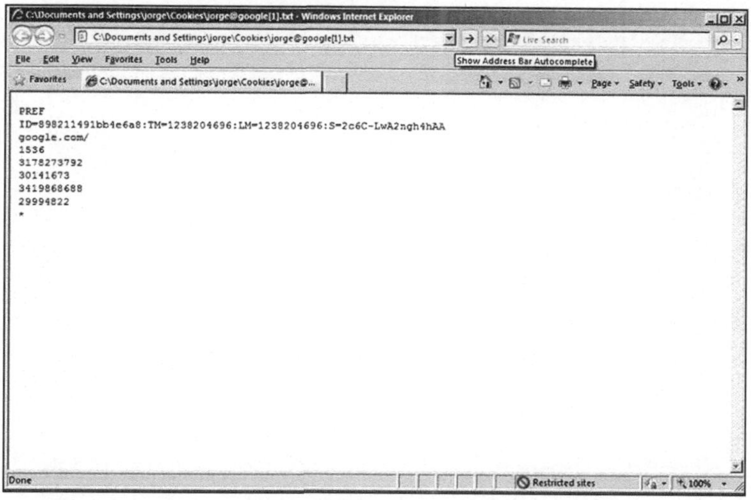

Fig 6.4 Internet Explorer Cookie Folder Accessed Directly Using Internet Explorer. As can be seen in the Status Bar, the Folder is Treated as a Restricted Site

The Security Zones scheme, a web site located in a less trusted zone could never provide content for and redirect its navigation flow towards a web site in a more trusted zone. This behaviour is known as Zone Elevation. However, in the case above Internet Explorer will erroneously apply Zone Elevation restrictions and the redirection will effectively occur. Content will be treated as belonging to the Internet zone, in spite of being stored in the local machine. Let us consider a different way to bypass Security Zones restrictions: suppose that example.com was explicitly added to the Restricted Sites Security Zone. Then the following URI will be treated with the privileges of that zone:

```
http://example.com/index.html
```

However, if the same resource is requested using the UNC notation:

```
\\10.1.1.1\index.html
```

it will be treated as belonging to the Internet Security Zone. As can be seen Internet Explorer fails to apply zone restrictions to a given resource if it is accessed using a different protocol.

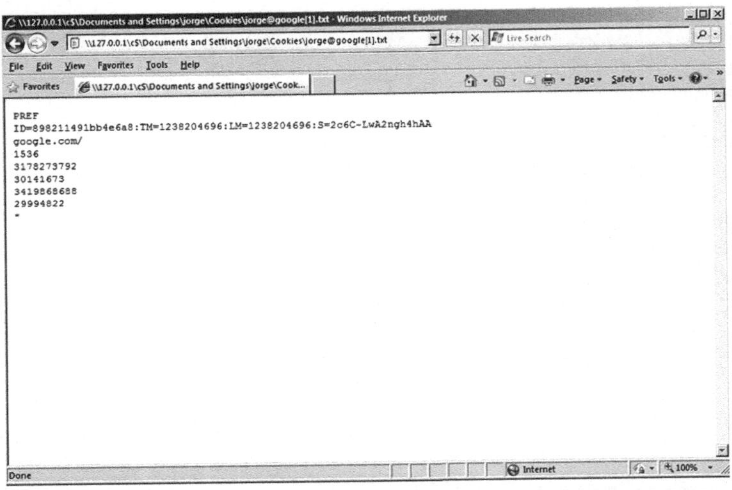

Fig 6.5 Internet Explorer Cookie Folder Accessed with UNC Using Internet Explorer. As can be seen in the Status Bar, this Time the Folder is Treated as if it Belongs to the Internet Zone

Ways to Put Arbitrary HTML/Script Code in the Victim's Computer

While not straightforward there are at least three different ways for remote servers to write arbitrary HTML/script code in the local file system of clients running Internet Explorer:

- Navigation history files;
- Cookies; and
- History tracking files.

Even though these features are common to every modern web browser, the problem is not in the features themselves but in the way they are implemented:

- The content that a remote server sends to the client is written to various files on the local file system as they are received with little or no transformations/overhead;
- Internet Explorer allows rendering of HTML content read from local files that are not pure HTML. The non-HTML portions that cannot be rendered are simply ignored.

Due to this a remote server that managed to write arbitrary but partially controlled HTML/script code inside these files could eventually force Internet Explorer to treat them as such.

Everything That Glitters is Not Gold

The way Internet Explorer determines how to process the contents of a given file is based on what is known as MIME type detection. This is basically a best-effort heuristic used to determine the content type of a given resource and then launch the corresponding object server/application to process it. Security problems may arise if type detection fails. In some cases, unknown content type is defaulted to be treated as HTML which could, obviously, include scripting code also. Besides, this mechanism has been proved not to be consistent when accessing the same resource through different methods. For example, the proof of concept code for the vulnerability reported in the CORE-2008-0826 Security Advisory took advantage from the fact that Internet Explorer was reacting different when an unknown MIME format resource was directly accessed from an <object> tag than when it was invoked from a script.

OVERALL IMPACT

As can be seen from what has been discussed so far, by chaining the exploitation of a series of weak features an attacker is able to store HTML and scripting code in the victim's computer and then force the victim's browser to load and render it. Even though 127.0.0.1 is in the Internet Zone an attacker can still do some other interesting things: as code is actually stored in the victim's computer, it has enough privileges to access other files in the same origin allowing blind but full access to every file in the victim's local file systems. Thus, interesting files such as the SAM backup file, all of the user's HTTP cookies and history files or any other file on the local system may become available to the attacker.

For example: if the computer compromised has IIS running, an attacker could get the source code of files stored in the Inetpub\wwwroot folder. Even more, as many applications store sensitive information inside configuration files, an attacker could gain complete access to these files if they exist. These attack scenarios have been proven to work in the past in at least three different cases. In each of those cases the same generic approach was applied with the only variations in the way to use Internet Explorer to render internal tracking files as HTML.

For each new attack scenario Microsoft addressed the specific way in which Internet Explorer internal files can be used to deliver malicious HTML/script content but it is very likely that as long as all the other components of the attack scenario could be chained together using the other individual weaknesses of Internet Explorer, an attacker will be just a single step away from successfully compromising the victim's system.

CORRIGENDA

Contrary to what has been stated in the Common Vulnerabilities and Exposures database for the CVE-2009-1140, it is not just a cross-domain information disclosure vulnerability. That is just a subset of the information you could get.

In fact, CVE-2008-1448 description says something more precise: allows remote attackers to bypass intended access restrictions and read arbitrary files. And both of them are the same set of features abused by different means.

SOLUTIONS AND WORKAROUNDS

By the moment of the publication of this document official hot fixes will not be available for the latest variant of the attack exposed herein. Then, users could apply the following workarounds so to protect them from exploitation of these vulnerabilities in the wild.

Internet Explorer Network Protocol Lockdown

Internet Explorer can be configured to lock down HTML content from particular network protocols in additional zones besides the Local Machine zone. This feature allows an administrator to extend the same restrictions of the Local Machine Zone Lockdown to be applied to any content on any arbitrary protocol in any security zone. In this case, in order to prevent this attack from occur, an administrator can configure Internet Explorer to lock down HTML content hosted on the file: protocol if it is in the Internet zone. Since, the file: protocol's most common use is for either Local Machine or Local Intranet content and not Internet content, this mitigation should not imply huge compatibility issues.

Set the Security Level setting for the Internet and Intranet Zones to High

This setting will prevent Internet Explorer from running scripts or ActiveX controls in both Security Zones. Nonetheless, the impact on existing applications could render them unusable.

Disable Active Scripting for the Internet and Intranet Zone with a custom setting

This means to manually adjust the security level for that particular item instead of switching to an entirely different preset as in the previous workaround. Anyway, this could also have a considerable impact in multiple applications.

Only Run Internet Explorer in Protected Mode

If it is available on the operating system you should enable Protected Mode to mitigate this vector. However, as some applications stopped working properly when this working mode was introduced, many users have opted for disabling it.

Use a Different Web Browser to Navigate Untrusted Web Sites

As will be explained next, other browsers different than Internet Explorer can not be exploited the same way. Even so, using other browsers implies that users will be exposed to other risks those browsers are vulnerable to. It is up to the users to evaluate which is the best option.

SEARCH ENGINES

A web search engine is designed to search for information on the World Wide Web. The search results are generally presented in a list of results often referred to as search engine results pages (SERPs). The information may consist of web pages, images, information and other types of files. Some search engines also mine data available in databases or open directories. Unlike web directories, which are maintained only by human editors, search engines also maintain real-time information by running an algorithm on a web crawler. During the early development of the web, there was a list of webservers edited by Tim Berners-Lee and hosted on the CERN webserver.

One historical snapshot from 1992 remains. As more webservers went online the central list could not keep up. On the NCSA site new servers were announced under the title 'What's New!' The very first tool used for searching on the Internet was Archie. The name stands for 'archive' without the 'v'. It was created in 1990 by Alan Emtage, Bill Heelan and J. Peter Deutsch, computer science students at McGill University in Montreal.

The programme downloaded the directory listings of all the files located on public anonymous FTP sites, creating a searchable database of file names; however, Archie did not index the contents of these sites since, the amount of data was so limited it could be readily searched manually. The rise of

Gopher led to two new search programmes, Veronica and Jughead. Like Archie, they searched the file names and titles stored in Gopher index systems. Veronica provided a keyword search of most Gopher menu titles in the entire Gopher listings. Jughead was a tool for obtaining menu information from specific Gopher servers.

While the name of the search engine 'Archie' was not a reference to the Archie comic book series, 'Veronica' and 'Jughead' are characters in the series, thus referencing their predecessor. In the summer of 1993, no search engine existed yet for the web, though numerous specialised catalogues were maintained by hand. Oscar Nierstrasz at the University of Geneva wrote a series of Perl scripts that would periodically mirror these pages and rewrite them into a standard format which formed the basis for W3Catalog, the web's first primitive search engine, released on September 2, 1993. In June 1993, Matthew Gray, then at MIT, produced what was probably the first web robot, the Perl-based World Wide Web Wanderer, and used it to generate an index called 'Wandex'.

The purpose of the Wanderer was to measure the size of the World Wide Web, which it did until late 1995. The web's second search engine Aliweb appeared in November 1993. Aliweb did not use a web robot, but instead depended on being notified by web site administrators of the existence at each site of an index file in a particular format. JumpStation used a web robot to find web pages and to build its index, and used a web form as the interface to its query programme.

It was thus the first WWW resource-discovery tool to combine the three essential features of a web search engine. Because of the limited resources available on the platform on which it ran, its indexing and hence, searching were limited to the titles and headings found in the web pages the crawler encountered. One of the first 'full text' crawler-based search engines was WebCrawler, which came out in 1994.

Unlike its predecessors, it let users search for any word in any webpage, which has become the standard for all major search engines since. It was also the first one to be widely known by the public. Also in 1994, Lycos was launched and became a major commercial endeavour. Soon after, many search engines appeared and vied for popularity. These included Magellan, Excite, Infoseek, Inktomi, Northern Light, and AltaVista. Yahoo! was among the most popular ways for people to find web pages of interest, but its search function operated on its web directory, rather than full-text copies of web pages.

Information seekers could also browse the directory instead of doing a keyword-based search. In 1996, Netscape was looking to give a single search engine an exclusive deal to be the featured search engine on Netscape's web browser. There was so much interest that instead a deal was struck with Netscape by five of the major search engines, where for $5 million per year each search engine would be in rotation on the Netscape search engine page. The five engines were Yahoo!, Magellan, Lycos, Infoseek, and Excite. Search engines were also known as some of the brightest stars in the Internet investing frenzy that occurred in the late 1990s. Several companies entered the market spectacularly, receiving record gains during their initial public offerings.

Some have taken down their public search engine, and are marketing enterprise-only editions, such as Northern Light. Many search engine companies were caught up in the dot-com bubble, a speculation-driven market boom that peaked in 1999 and ended in 2001. Around 2000, Google's search engine rose to prominence. The company achieved better results for many searches with an innovation called PageRank. This iterative algorithm ranks web pages based on the number and PageRank of other web sites and pages that link there, on the premise that good or desirable pages are linked to more than others. Google also maintained a minimalist interface to its search engine.

In contrast, many of its competitors embedded a search engine in a web portal. By 2000, Yahoo! was providing search services based on Inktomi's search engine. Yahoo! acquired Inktomi in 2002, and Overture in 2003. Yahoo! switched to Google's search engine until 2004, when it launched its own search engine based on the combined technologies of its acquisitions. Microsoft first launched MSN Search in the fall of 1998 using search results from Inktomi. In early 1999 the site began to display listings from Looksmart blended with results from Inktomi except for a short time in 1999 when results from AltaVista were used instead.

In 2004, Microsoft began a transition to its own search technology, powered by its own web crawler. Microsoft's rebranded search engine, Bing, was launched on June 1, 2009. On July 29, 2009, Yahoo! and Microsoft finalised a deal in which Yahoo! Search would be powered by Microsoft Bing technology.

HOW WEB SEARCH ENGINES WORK

A search engine operates in the following order:

- Web crawling
- Indexing
- Searching

Web search engines work by storing information about many web pages, which they retrieve from the HTML itself. These pages are retrieved by a Web crawler— an automated Web browser which follows every link on the site. Exclusions can be made by the use of robots.txt. The contents of each page are then analysed to determine how it should be indexed. Data about web pages are stored in an index database for use in later queries. A query can be a single word.

The purpose of an index is to allow information to be found as quickly as possible. Some search engines, such as Google, store all or part of the source page as well as information about the web pages, whereas others, such as AltaVista, store every word of every page they find. This cached page always holds the actual search text since, it is the one that was actually indexed, so it can be very useful when the content of the current page has been updated and the search terms are no longer in it.

This problem might be considered to be a mild form of linkrot, and Google's handling of it increases usability by satisfying user expectations that the search terms will be on the returned webpage. This satisfies the principle of least astonishment since, the user normally expects the search terms to be on the returned pages. Increased search relevance makes these cached pages very useful, even beyond the fact that they may contain data that may no longer be available elsewhere. When a user enters a query into a search engine, the engine examines its index and provides a listing of best-matching web pages according to its criteria, usually with a short summary containing the document's title and sometimes parts of the text.

The index is built from the information stored with the data and the method by which the information is indexed. As early as 2007 the Google.com search engine has allowed one to search by date by clicking 'Show search tools' in the leftmost column of the initial search results page, and then selecting the desired date range. Most search engines support the use of the boolean operators AND, OR and NOT to further specify the search query. Boolean operators are for litreal searches that allow the user to refine and extend the terms of the search. The engine looks for the words or phrases exactly as entered. Some search engines provide an advanced feature called proximity search which allows users to define the distance between keywords.

There is also concept-based searching where the research involves using statistical analysis on pages containing the words or phrases you search for. As well, natural language queries allow the user to type a question in the same form one would ask it to a human. A site like this would be ask.com. The usefulness of a search engine depends on the relevance of the result set it gives back. While there may be millions of web pages that include a particular word or phrase, some pages may be more relevant, popular, or authoritative than others. Most search engines employ methods to rank the results to provide the 'best' results first.

How a search engine decides which pages are the best matches, and what order the results should be shown in, varies widely from one engine to another. The methods also change over time as Internet usage changes and new techniques evolve. There are two main types of search engine that have evolved: one is a system of predefined and hierarchically ordered keywords that humans have programmed extensively. The other is a system that generates an 'inverted index' by analysing texts it locates. This second form relies much more heavily on the computer itself to do the bulk of the work. Most Web search engines are commercial ventures supported by advertising revenue and, as a result, some employ the practice of allowing advertisers to pay money to have their listings ranked higher in search results.

Those search engines which do not accept money for their search engine results make money by running search related ads alongside the regular search engine results. The search engines make money every time someone clicks on one of these ads.

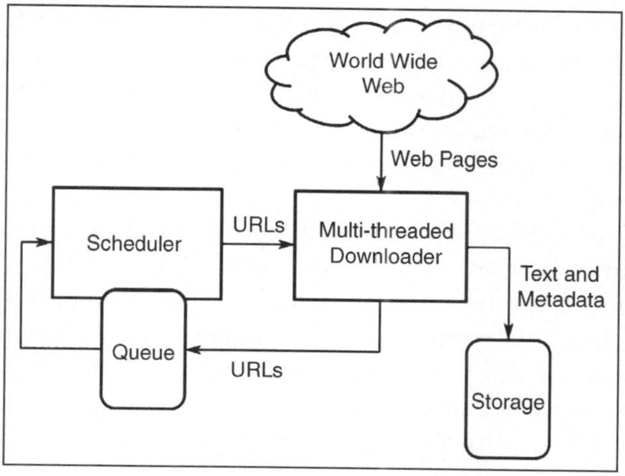

Fig 6.6 High-level Architecture of a Standard Web Crawler

SEARCH ENGINE BIAS

Although search engines are programmed to rank web sites based on their popularity and relevancy, empirical studies indicate various political, economic, and social biases in the information they provide. These biases could be a direct result of economic and commercial processes, and political processes.Google Bombing is one example of an attempt to manipulate search results for political, social or commercial reasons.

CUSTOMISED RESULTS AND FILTER BUBBLES

Many search engines such as Google and Bing provide customised results based on the user's activity history. This leads to an effect that has been called a filter bubble. The term describes a phenomenon in which web sites use algorithms to selectively guess what information a user would like to see, based on information about the user. As a result, web sites tend to show only information which agrees with the user's past viewpoint, effectively isolating the user in a bubble that tends to exclude contrary information. Prime examples are Google's personalised search results and Facebook's personalised news stream. Eli Pariser, who coined the term, users get less exposure to conflicting viewpoints and are isolated intellectually in their own informational bubble. Pariser related an example in which one user searched Google for 'BP' and got investment news about British Petroleum while another searcher got information about the Deepwater Horizon oil spill and that the two search results pages were 'strikingly different.'

The bubble effect may have negative implications for civic discourse, Pariser, but there are contrasting views suggesting the effect is minimal and addressable. Since, this problem has been identified, competing search engines have emerged that seek to avoid this problem by not tracking or 'bubbling' users. One example is DuckDuckGo.

INTERNET SEARCHING

In 300 B.C., the Library of Alexandria held some half million scrolls and served as a cultural centre for the world, uniting the thoughts of Greek, Egyptian, Macedonian and Babylonian culture. The Letter of Aristeas, the library had "a large budget in order to collect, if possible, all the books in the world." Whole fields of study such as geometry and grammar grew from the scholars who had the fortune to travel to and study at Alexandria.

In 2003 A.D., the Internet forms a distributed library of billions of pages, one that is accessible to anyone, anywhere in the world, at the click of a mouse. Every day hundreds of millions of 'trips' to the library start with a query to an Internet search engine. If I want to research a topic such as 'Library of Alexandria,' I can type those words to a search engine and in less than a second have access to a list of 14,000 pages, sorted by their usefulness to the query. This unprecedented ease of access to information has revolutionised the way research is done by students, scientists, journalists, shoppers, and others. It opens up an online marketplace of products, services, and ideas that benefits both information providers and seekers; sellers and buyers; consumers and advertisers.

How is it that an Internet Search engine can find the answers to a query so quickly? It is a four-step process:

- Crawling the Web, following links to find pages;
- Indexing the pages to create an index from every word to every place it occurs;
- Ranking the pages so the best ones show up first; and
- Displaying the results in a way that is easy for the user to understand.

Crawling is conceptually quite simple: starting at some well-known sites on the web, recursively follow every hypertext link, recording the pages encountered along the way. In computer science this is called the transitive closure of the link relation. However, the conceptual simplicity hides a large number of practical complications: sites may be busy or down at one point, and come back to life later; pages may be duplicated at multiple sites and must be dealt with accordingly; many pages have text that does not conform to the standards for HTML, HTTP redirection, robot exclusion, or other protocols; some information is hard to access because it is hidden behind a form, Flash animation or Javascript programme.

Finally, the necessity of crawling 100 million pages a day means that building a crawler is an exercise in distributed computing, requiring many computers that must work together and schedule their actions so as to get to all the pages without overwhelming any one site with too many requests at once. A search engine's index is similar to the index in the back of a book: it is used to find the pages on which a word occurs. There are two main differences: the search engine's index lists every occurrence of every word, not just the important concepts, and the number of pages is in the billions, not hundreds. Various techniques of compression and clever representation are used to keep the index 'small,' but it is still measured in terabytes, which again means that distributed computing is required. Most modern search engines index link data as well as word data.

It is useful to know how many pages link to a given page, and what are the quality of those pages. This kind of analysis is similar to citation analysis in bibliographic work, and helps establish which pages are authoritative. Algorithms such as PageRank and HITS are used to assign a numeric measure of authority to each page. For example, the PageRank algorithm says that the rank of a page is a function of the sum of the ranks of the pages that link to the page. If we let PR(p) be the PageRank of page p, Out(p) be the number of outgoing links from page p, Links(p) be the set of pages that link to page p and N be the total number of pages in the index, then we can define PageRank by

$$PR(p) = r / N + (1 -_{r}) \sum_{i} \subset Links(p)^{PR(i)/Out(i)}$$

where r is a parameter that indicates the probability that a user will choose not to follow a link, but will instead restart at some other page. The r/N term means that each of the N pages is equally likely to be the restart point, although it is also possible to use a smaller subset of well-known pages as the restart candidates. Note that the formula for PageRank is recursive—PR appears on both the right-and left-hand sides of the equation.

The equation can be solved by iterating several times, or by standard linear algebra techniques for computing the Eigen values of a matrix. The two steps are query independent—they do not depend on the user's query, and thus can be done before a query is issued with the cost shared among all users. This is why a search takes a second or less, rather than the days it would take if a search engine had to crawl the web anew for each query. We now consider what happens when a user types a query. Consider the query, where the square brackets denote the beginning and end of the query, and the quotation marks indicate that the enclosed words must be found as an exact phrase match.

The first step in responding to this query is to look in the index for the hit lists corresponding to each of the four words 'National,' 'Academies,' 'computer' and 'science.' These four lists are then intersected to yield the set of pages that mention all four words. Because 'National Academies' was entered as a phrase, only hits where these two words appear adjacent and in that order are counted. The result is a list of 19,000 or so pages. The next step is ranking these 19,000 pages to decide which ones are most relevant. In traditional information retrieval this is done by counting the number of occurrences of each word, weighing rare words more heavily than frequent words, and normalising for the length of the page.

A number of refinements on this scheme have been developed, so it is common to give more credit for pages where the words occur near each other, where the words are in bold or large font, or in a title, or where the words occur in the anchor text of a link that points to the page. In addition the query-independent authority of each page is factored in. The result is a numeric score for each page that can be used to sort them best-first. Traditionally this is done by listing a short description of each result in rank-sorted order. The description will include the title of the page and may include additional information such as a short abstract or excerpt from the page.

Some search engines generate query-independent abstracts while others customise each excerpt to show at least some of the words from the query. Displaying this kind of query-dependent excerpt means that the search engine must keep a copy of the full text of the pages at a cost of several more terabytes. Some search engines attempt to cluster the result pages into coherent categories or folders, although this technology is not yet mature. Studies have shown that the most popular uses of computers are e-mail, word processing and Internet searching. Of the three, Internet searching is by far the most sophisticated example of computer science technology. Building a high-quality search engine requires extensive knowledge and experience in information retrieval, data structure design, user interfaces, and distributed systems implementation.

Future advances in searching will increasingly depend on statistical natural language processing and machine learning techniques. With so much data—billions of pages, tens of billions of links, and hundreds of millions of queries per day—it makes sense to use data mining approaches to automatically improve the system. For example, several search engines now do spelling correction of user queries.

It turns out that the vast amount of correctly and incorrectly spelled text available to a search engine makes it easier to create a good spelling corrector than traditional techniques based on dictionaries. It is likely that there will be other examples of text understanding that can be done better with a data-oriented approach; this is an area that search engines are just beginning to explore.

7

Assessing Needs and Priorities: *Case Study of Washington Libraries*

INTRODUCTION

The University of Washington Libraries has utilised a number of approaches during the past decade to assess the effectiveness of service programmes and library support of faculty and student research, teaching, and learning. Among the most valuable methods employed have been large-scale surveys of faculty and students conducted every three years beginning in 1992. Focus groups, usability and observational studies, targeted surveys, and interviews are also used to assess library programmes and services as well as user needs. Results from the triennial surveys have played a critical role in supporting the transition to a user-centred library and in creating a culture of assessment.

The large representative data sets generated by these surveys have also proven to be powerful information sources in the campus political environment. These surveys, though quite valuable, are expensive and time-consuming to design, administer, and analyse. Participation in the ARL-sponsored SERVQUAL pilot provided an opportunity to use a well-established survey tool with a different methodology, design, content, and delivery mechanism. It also afforded the chance for inter-institutional comparisons using a standardised survey instrument. Another attractive feature was the ability to gain experience with a Web based survey that might reduce survey costs associated with printing, mailing, and data entry. This chapter will compare the UW Libraries' surveys with LibQUAL+ results from the University of Washington in such areas as response and representativeness of survey population, similarities and differences in results, and whether the right questions are being asked.

USER SURVEYS

Library user surveys have become widespread in academic libraries during the past twenty years. Surveys have often been used as a tool to assess service quality and user satisfaction. The Association of Research Libraries issued four Systems and Procedures Exchange Centre (SPEC) kits on user surveys and studies between 1981 and 1994. A substantial body of litreature has been developed on surveys and service quality, led by studies and reviews from such library educators/professionals as Hernon and McClure; Van House, Weil and McClure; Hernon and Altman; Nitecki and Franklin; and Hernon and Whitman. Library applications of the SERVQUAL instrument have been covered by Nitecki, and Cook and Heath, among others. Rapid changes in library services and operations, demands for internal institutional accountability, and assessment expectations by external accrediting agencies have contributed to further development and application of user surveys within academic libraries during the past decade.

User surveys can be designed and administered in a number of ways. Self-administered surveys are often employed to reach a large number of potential respondents with a minimum of direct contact and cost. Individuals are given or sent surveys to complete and return and the responses turned into data that can be analysed. Surveys can range from broad and comprehensive to those narrowly focused on specific services or activities. When properly designed and administered, user surveys can provide both quantitative and qualitative data directly from the target population.

UNIVERSITY LIBRARIES' SURVEY OF WASHINGTON METHODOLOGY AND DESIGN

The University of Washington Libraries began an active programme of assessing user needs, satisfaction, and the impact of library services and resources in 1992. Prior to this time, user input to the UW Libraries was generally informal and unsolicited through such channels as suggestion boxes and anecdotal comments from service desks. Other opportunities for user comment came through the Faculty Senate Council on University Libraries, a biennial meeting between subject selectors and faculty liaisons on collections-related issues and some earlier in-library surveys that focussed on specific activities within the library unit.

The catalyst for the development of a broad-based survey of faculty and students came from the UW Libraries' first strategic plan in 1991 that called for a user-centered approach to services. Specifically, the strategic plan recommended that the libraries: "Develop and implement a study to identify user populations, their information needs and how well they are being met".

The Task Force on Library Services was appointed by the Director of Libraries in late 1991 to design and implement a user survey that would provide information on the following:

- Determine who users and potential users are;
- How and why the library is used;
- What sources are used for library-related information;
- What faculty and students' library-related needs are;
- How satisfied faculty and students are with the libraries.

The litreature on academic library user surveys available at the time of the early 1990s revealed a wide spectrum of applications and uses.

Some common characteristics of these surveys were:

- Distribution within the library to users was more prevalent than mailed surveys;
- Focus on physical use of the library;
- Concentration on specific services;
- Interest in user satisfaction.

The task force designed the initial survey in 1992 in consultation with library staff and the University's Office of Educational Assessment (OM). The decision was made early in the design process to survey all user groups, distribute the survey through the mail in order to reach potential non-users, and provide similar survey content for each group to enable comparisons.

The survey would be sent to all faculty and a random sample of graduate and undergraduate students. While distributing the survey to all faculty would increase costs, it would also facilitate survey promotion and publicity, obtain sufficient number of responses to do analysis by academic subject areas, and foster positive political outcomes. Survey questions were similar for faculty and graduate students, with about 75 per cent consistency between faculty and undergraduates. Adequate space was provided for survey respondents to write comments. Content evolved with each subsequent survey in 1995 and 1998, and some aspects of survey design changed. Rapid changes in library services and programmes during the 1990s and usefulness of the data provided by some questions were prime factors in survey revision.

However, there was a core group of questions in each survey that dealt with:

- Information sources needed for research, teaching, and learning;
- Reasons and frequency of library use;
- Campus computer network connectivity;
- Use of electronic resources;
- Instructional needs and effectiveness;
- Library unit use;
- Satisfaction;
- Services availability or satisfaction.

The initial survey in 1992 was pilot tested in March with a group of faculty and students, revised, and then mailed mid-way through the Spring quarter to 3,900 faculty and a random, non-stratified, sample of 1,000 graduate and 1,000 undergraduate students. An incentive was offered to students who returned completed survey forms. Two weeks after the initial surveys were mailed, students were sent a second survey form, while faculty were sent a reminder notice. Completed surveys were returned to the Office of Educational Assessment (OEA) who arranged for data entry. Data were made available in SPSS format and results were available in early September 1992. Subsequent surveys in 1995 and 1998 generally employed a similar methodology and design. Survey design work began in January of each year, pilot testing took place in March, and surveys were mailed in late April to early May.

The undergraduate sample was increased to 2,000 for 1995 and 1998, and the 1998 survey also included a specialised set of questions for faculty and graduate students in the biological and health sciences, and one for faculty and students in the fine arts. Focus groups were also held prior to the 1998 survey to provide input from users on their perception of issues and concerns.

The bookstore gift certificate drawing was extended to all groups beginning with the 1995 survey. Reminder notices were sent in 1995 but not a follow-up survey form. In 1998, a survey accompanied the reminder letter. Both the cover letter and survey form included the name, phone number, and e-mail address of a librarian as a contact person for questions or clarification.

The few questions received generally requested another survey be sent to replace a lost one. Sending this type of survey to nearly 7,000 faculty and students is not inexpensive. Direct survey costs in 1998 totaled $19,000, about $7 per returned survey. Survey costs in 1992 and 1995 were about $12,000.

The 1998 costs were distributed in the following manner:

- Printing 30 per cent
- Mailing 30 per cent.
- Data entry 30 per cent
- Other 10 per cent

Staff time for the 1998 survey was estimated at approximately 500 hours, including analysis and reporting.

LIBQUAL+

The UW Libraries was one of twelve libraries that participated in the ARL-sponsored LibQUAL+ pilot administered in Spring 2000. Survey design and methodology were handled primarily by a team from Texas A&M where a SERVQUAL based library survey had been used several times. In addition to the twenty-two basic SERVQUAL questions which covered the standard dimensions of accountability, assurance, reliability, responsiveness, and tangibles, nineteen additional questions were added to test two additional dimensions: access to collections and the library as place.

Thus, there were forty one questions that used the SERVQUAL three-column response format of minimum, perceived, and desired. Another fourteen behavioural questions, two on frequency of library use, and an overall service quality question were also added which used just one response column. The survey also collected demographic data. The survey team at Texas A&M determined that the survey be administered to a random sample of 600 faculty, 600 graduate students, and 900 undergraduates at each institution based on an anticipated return of 200 surveys from each group. The UW Office of Educational Assessment extracted the sample from the faculty and student databases, and e-mail address lists created for each group were sent to the UW Libraries.

The UW Libraries systems office created separate mailing lists for each group. A cover letter from the director of the UW Libraries was sent by e-mail to each participant. The letter included information about the survey and the university's reasons for participation, and also provided a URL address where respondents could complete the survey. The initial message was sent May 2 and a reminder notice was sent on May 11.Almost immediately after the initial e-mail notification was sent, there was a steady stream of messages back to the director and the local survey coordinator.

LibQUAL+ implementation at the University of Washington ultimately generated more than fifty e-mail messages, most coming from faculty members. The messages fell into two basic groups: technical problems trying to complete the survey, and comments, usually negative, on survey design and content. Direct expenses were $2,000 for the UW Libraries paid as a participant in the ARL project. This worked out to be about $5 per completed survey. Library staff contributed about 150 hours to the project, including responding to e-mail messages, analysis, and report writing.

SURVEY RESPONSE AND REPRESENTATIVES

Survey return rates for the 1992, 1995, and 1998 UW Libraries' surveys and the 2000 LibQUAL+ survey are shown in table.

Table 7.1 Surveys Distributed and Returned

Survey		Faculty		Graduate Students			Undergraduates		
Year	Sent	Returned	Rate	Sent	Returned	Rate	Sent	Returned	Rate
2000	600	128	21.3 %	600	131	21.8 %	900	137	15.2 %
1998	3750	1503	40.1 %	1000	457	45.7 %	2000	787	39.4 %
1995	4400	1359	28.4 %	1000	409	40.9 %	2000	489	24.5 %
1992	3900	1108	28.4 %	1000	561	56.1 %	1000	422	42.2 %

A second survey mailing appeared effective in raising the response rate as seen in the 1992 return rates for students and for all groups in 1998. The number of faculty surveyed varied according to criteria used to define the faculty pool, but all surveys included tenure track and research faculty as well as full-time lecturers.

The overall response rate as shown is slightly understated as undeliverable surveys were not subtracted from the total sent out. Undeliverable survey rates ranged from approximately.5 per cent of faculty to 2 per cent of undergraduate students. Response rates to the LibQUALt survey were substantially lower.

The definition of faculty was the same as used in the UW Libraries' 1998 survey. LibQUALt response rates were calculated by matching the number of completed surveys against the number of e-mail addresses to which the survey message was sent. Approximately 1percent of these messages were undeliverable.

REPRESENTATIUENESS OF SURVEY RESPONDENTS

The large number of responses to the UW Libraries' surveys generated correspondingly large data sets, especially for the faculty survey.

Table 7.2 Faculty Population and Respondents by Academic Area, 1998 and 2000 In Percentage

Academic Area	2000 LibQUAL+ Respondents n=128	1998 Faculty Population n=3750	1998 Survey Respondents n=1503
Health Sciences	43.0	48.6	44.7
Sciences/Engineering	25.8	26.2	27.1
Humanities/Arts/ Social Sciences	31.2	21.0	24.4
Other (non- Health Sciences)		4.2	3.8

As table 7.2 shows, the faculty survey respondent population in 1998 was reasonably representative of the population as a whole when grouped by broad subject areas. Faculty in the Health Sciences were slightly underrepresented, while those in the Humanities/Social Sciences/Fine Arts group were somewhat over-represented compared to the actual population. Response rates by academic schools ranged from 31 per cent in Business to 54 per cent in the Social Science departments within the College of Arts and Sciences. Graduate student responses were similar to the faculty with Health Sciences respondents again lower than their percentage of the actual population while those from Humanities/Arts/Social Sciences were slightly higher.

Response rates by academic schools ranged from 24 per cent in Dentistry and 28 per cent in Education to 62 per cent in Nursing and '72 per cent in Social Sciences. Health Sciences does have a larger proportion of faculty and graduate/ professional students located away from the main UW campus, and this may be a factor in the under representation of respondents from those areas.

Table 7.3 Graduate/Professional Student Population and Survey Respondents by Academic Area In Percentage

Academic Area	2000LibQUAL+ n=131	1998 Graduate Population n=8183*	1998 Survey Respondents n=457
Health Sciences	22.1	30.4	26.0
Sciences/Engineering	28.20	29.4	30.2
Humanities/Arts/ Social Sciences	45.0	40.3	43.8
Other (non-Health Sciences)	4.6		

*Law was not included in the 1998 survey, 1998 graduate population with Law is 8,785, Law is 69. per cent to total.

Determining how representative undergraduate respondents are is more complicated. Undergraduates in earlier UW Libraries' surveys appeared to identify with certain academic majors before they were actually accepted into those programmes, thus skewing responses by academic areas. Year in school appeared to be a more reliable measure. Table shows undergraduate population and respondent population by year in school. Again, the respondent population is reasonably similar to the entire population. Freshmen were somewhat underrepresented in the 1998 survey and sophomores underrepresented in the LibQUAL+ survey.

Table 7.4 Undergraduate Student Population and Survey Respondents by Year In Percentage

Class	2000LibQUAL+ n=137	1998 Undergraduate Population n=23413	1998 Undergraduate Respondents n=787
Freshman	22.6	19.0	14.4
Sophomore	13.9	18.3	17.0
Junior	27.7	26.3	26.9
Senior	35.8	32.9	33.9
Other (including 5th Year		3.4	7.8

Compared to the population as a whole, and UW survey respondents in 1998, the LibQUALt respondent pools, although significantly smaller than those generated by UW surveys, appear reasonably representative when grouped by broad academic areas for faculty and graduate students, and by class for undergraduates.

The under representation of Health Sciences and overrepresentation by those in the Social Sciences mirrors the respondent population achieved in the large-scale UW Libraries' surveys. This is probably reflective of the way faculty and students in these areas use libraries as well as the larger proportion of the Health Sciences population located away from the main Seattle campus.

SURVEY RESULTS

Results from the UW Libraries' surveys provide an effective record of changes in the way that students and faculty used library and information resources during the 1990s. These results also documented significant variations within groups and between groups in some areas. Information from these surveys has been used extensively by the University of Washington Libraries to revise existing programmes and services and promote new ones.

Survey results showed:

- High satisfaction levels;
- A shift towards remote use and increased importance of electronic re- sources;
- Continuing importance of libraries as place for students;
- Increased complexity of finding and using information for teaching, learning, and research.

Although the University of Washington Libraries' surveys and the LibQUAL+ survey differs substantially in design and content, it is interesting to compare results where questions were similar.

The large respondent pool for the 1998 UW Libraries survey can serve as a benchmark for viewing the LibQUALt results based on a much smaller sample. For example, UW

Libraries' surveys results revealed that faculty generally viewed the libraries through a collections-related focus, while undergraduate students placed a high value on the library as a place.

Even though the questions and design in these surveys differ, would LibQUAL+ results also show similar responses? Results from the UW Libraries' survey in 1998 and the LibQUALt survey in 2000 will be compared in the areas of overall satisfaction, opening hours, collections importance, the library as a place, and remote use of library services and resources. These areas are often barometers of service quality.

OVERALL SATISFACTION

Responses to overall library satisfaction questions on the 1998 survey showed faculty had the highest satisfaction while undergraduate students the lowest.

Table 7.5 Overall Satisfaction: UW Libraries 1998 Survey and Libqual+ 2000 Survey by Group In Percentage

Level	Libqual+ Faculty	1998 Faculty	Libqual+ Grad Students	1998 Grad Students	Libqual+ Undergrads	1998 Undergrads
Very satisfied	78.0	91.3	80.9	84.9	72.9	78.5
Satisfied	21.2	7.8	18.3	13.5	24.0	19.9
Not satisfied	0.8	0.9	0.8	1.6	3.1	1.6
Mean Score	7.17	4.33	7.13	4.11	6.88	3.99

The LibQUAL+ survey phrased the questions as overall quality of services but still produced similar results although the difference in Likert scales can lead to a different type of response. For LibQUALt, the differences between undergraduate scores and graduate and faculty ones were significant at the.10 level using t-tests.

LIBRARY HOURS

The 1998 survey asked whether libraries were open when needed on evenings, weekends, summer, and interim periods. Graduate students had the lowest satisfaction with hours while faculty had the highest, as shown in figure. Undergraduate student satisfaction had slipped from 1995 when it was similar to faculty satisfaction.

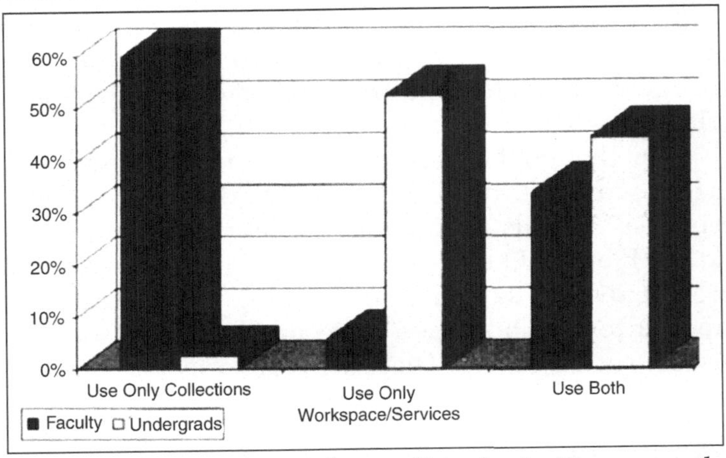

When asked to choose from a list of priorities, more than 37 per cent of graduate students and 42 per cent of undergraduates chose increased library hours as a priority compared to 17 per cent of faculty. Graduate students also wrote more comments about hours than any other group. The LibQUAL+ question was concerned about expectations and perceived level of service related to whether the library had convenient business hours.

Table 7.6 LibQUAL+ Convenient Business Hours

	Faculty Minimum	Faculty Perceived	Grad Minimum	Grad Perceived	Undergrad Minimum	Undergrad Perceived
Convenient Business Hours	6.45	6.56 (.11)	6.68	6.63 (-.05)	6.50	7.13 (.63)

As table shows, graduate student minimum expectations for convenient business hours exceeded their perception of library performance. Faculty minimum expectations were lower, and the gap between expectations and performance, while small, was positive. Undergraduate students had both the highest perceived value and most positive gap. One likely reason for this positive response in LibQUAL+ was the Undergraduate Library's move to 24 hour opening in autumn 1998.

COLLECTIONS

A valuable part of each one of the UW Libraries' surveys is asking users to identify their library priorities from a list of ten to twelve choices. The list of potential priorities is compiled from comments provided on the pretests as well as areas the libraries are interested in. The first survey in 1992 showed that all three groups had the same priorities in their top three choices, while in 1998 the top three priorities for undergraduates were different than those for graduate students and faculty. Faculty, in particular, showed an almost exclusive focus on collections/information resources-related areas as shown in table.

Table 7.7 1998 Survey: Library Priorities by Group In Percentage

	Faculty	Graduate Students	Under-graduates
Maintain quality of print collections	69.6	52.3	28.2
Deliver full-text to your computer	60.4	55.8	34.4
Deliver bib databases through the web	52.1	40.0	17.7
Provide reserves electronically	18.8	36.6	50.8
Add more computers in the library	8.6	20.1	54.5
Provide training in use of web/ library resources	28.3	27.4	47.5
Increase library hours	17.0	37.5	41.9
Preserve library materials	40.0	34.9	24.7
Add group study/seminar rooms			35.5
Provide consulation on how to do library research		13.3	39.8

The LibQUAL+ survey reinforced the primacy of collections and in- formation resources for faculty. This was the only area where faculty had negative gap scores. Faculty minimum expectations were generally higher as well. Graduate student results also showed high expectations for collections-related questions and negative gaps for full-text delivered electronically and complete journal runs. Undergraduate students had lower expectations and positive gaps in all collections related areas. Reviewing mean scores for six collections-related questions on LibQUAL+ showed higher mean scores for faculty and graduate students in minimum expectations.

Table 7.8 LibQUAL+ Collections Expectations/Perceptions

Question		Faculty Minimum	Faculty Perceived	Grad Minimum	Grad Perceived	Undergrad Minimum	Undergrad Perceived
10.	Resources added on request	4.23	6.10 (-.13)	6.04	6.27 (.23)	5.97	6.37 (.40)
17.	Timely document delivery/IIL,	6.41	6.82 (.41)	6.61	7.22 (.61)	6.31	6.88 (.57)
23.	Full text delivered electronically	6.32	5.84 (-.48)	6.20	6.16 (.04)	5.96	6.24 (.28)
27.	Comprehensive print collections	6.30	6.64 (.34)	6.65	6.65 (.02)	6.14	6.98 (.84)
36.	Interdisciplinary needs addressed	6.89	6.44 (.55)	6.24	6.55 (.31)	6.05	6.65 (.60)
37.	Complete journal	6.52	6.40 (-.12)	6.77	6.58 (-.19)	6.22	6.61 (.39)

However, the differences between undergrads and faculty were not significant at the.05 or.10 level according to t-tests. There were differences at the.05 level between grad students and undergraduates in complete runs of journal titles and comprehensive print collections, and at the.10 level for timely document delivery and interlibrary loan.

LIBRARY AS PLACE

A consistent theme revealed through each of the UW Libraries' surveys has been the different perspectives of faculty and students on the library as a place. Faculty use of the library is primarily collections driven, while students view the library as a place to do work, including finding and using information resources.

This difference shows up dramatically in responses to a 1998 survey question on reasons for visiting the library as well as other questions dealing with priorities and needed services. LibQUAL, clearly showed similar differences between faculty and students on the library as a place.

Table 7.9 LibQUAL+ Library as Place

Question		Faculty Minimum	Faculty Perceived	Grad Minimum	Grad Perceived	Undergrad Minimum	Undergrad Perceived
14.	Comfortable and inviting location	6.08	6.12 (1.04)	5.72	6.12 (.40)	5.98	6.73 (.75)
21.	Secure and safe place	6.77	7.51 (.74)	6.81	7.26 (.45)	6.80	7.23 (.43)
22.	Center for intellectual interaction	5.61	5.31 (1.15)	5.20	5.97 (.59)	5.75	6.24 (.49)
29.	Space for group/individual study	5.57	5.94 (1.34)	5.90	6.07 (.17)	6.20	6.78 (.58)
30.	Haven for quiet and solitude	4.74	6.02 (1.28)	6.12	6.08 (-.04)	6.53	6.46 (-.07)
40.	Space that facilitates quiet study	4.69	5.75 (1.06)	6.23	6.30 (.07)	6.52	6.62 (.10)

On seven questions related to the library as place, the differences in minimum expectations were significant at the 0.01 level except for 'safe and secure space.' With the exception of 'secure and safe space," faculty minimum expectations were generally below 5 and gaps between minimum and perceived were larger than 1.O. While graduate student expectations were higher than those of faculty, they were still lower than those of undergraduates. Both student groups were concerned about quiet study areas.

REMOTE USE

The 1995 UW Libraries' survey revealed for the first time that more were' going so remotely than physically visiting the library. This trend continued in 1998, and table shows degrees of remote use among all groups both in the 1998 survey and LibQUAL+.

Table 7.10 Type and Frequency of Library Use among Faculty and Students who Use Library at Least Weekly In Percentage

Type of Library Use	Visit in Person	Visit Remotely Using Computer
LibQUAL+ Faculty	54.5%	81.1%
1998 Faculty	47.3%	73.4%
LibQUAL+ 1998 Grad	77.0%	80.2%
1998 Grad	77.9%	66.1%
LibQUAL+ Undergrad	66.7%	48.8%
1998 Undergrad	70.3%	45.5%

Responses to other survey questions in 1998 revealed that more than 97 percent of faculty had access to the Web through a desktop computer. While remote use is not itself a measure of service quality, this information is critical for planning and delivering electronic services and resources. In general, LibQUAL+ results tended to correlate with results from the libraries' surveys which had a much larger number of respondents for each group, especially faculty. Differences between groups, especially faculty and undergraduates, that were evident in earlier UW Libraries' surveys, were also found in the LibQUAL+ results.

SUB-GROUP ANALYSIS

One of the benefits of a large respondent pool is the ability to do analysis on differences within the group. While there may be a set of similar characteristics that define a group, there may also be significant variation within that group. Academic user communities are not homogeneous in the way they use libraries nor in their needs for library resources and services. In addition to differences between faculty and students, there may also be significant differences between those in different academic areas or by gender or some other demographic component.

These have important implications for identifying user needs, concerns, and issues that may be missed in analysing aggregate results. The number of respondents to the UW Libraries' 1998 survey, especially for faculty, was sufficiently large to examine the degree of variation within the group and between subject areas. The sample size and response rates of the LibQUAL+ survey generally precluded analysis by academic area and made it difficult to find differences among demographic characteristics. Increasing the LibQUAL+ sample size and the response rate would provide larger data sets that could be used to examine variation within and between groups.

Factors related to the low response rate for LibQUALt include survey length, complexity, perceived redundancy, technical problems, behavioural issues associated with Web-based surveys, and how related survey content is to actual library use and issues of the respondent. While the LibQUAL+ sample appears representative of each group as a whole, it is not large enough to perform sub- group analysis. How important is it to have a respondent pool large enough to do analysis at the subgroup level? UW Libraries' surveys have consistently shown significant differences in how faculty from different academic areas use libraries and in their needs for library resources and services.

They also show surprising uniformity in areas such as connectivity arid remote use where differences might be expected based on traditional use pat- terns. Although graduate student response numbers are lower, they were similar to faculty in the same academic areas. Satisfaction responses, while showing some variation, generally do not differ significantly by academic area. Priorities, on the other hand, clearly do as shown in figure.

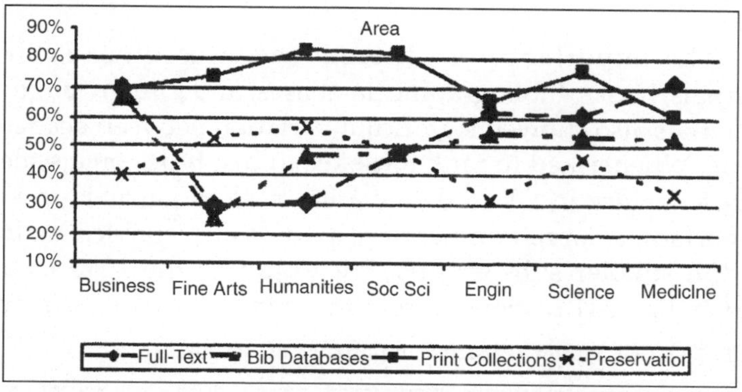

Fig 7.1 1998 Survey. Faculty Top Priorities by Academic Area

The 1998 results showed significant variation among academic areas in the top four overall priorities, especially for de- livery of full text to the desktop and preservation. Variation within undergraduate responses to the UW Libraries' 1998 survey were more difficult to determine. There were some gender differences, especially in areas related to computer access and library instruction as well as differences by class year.

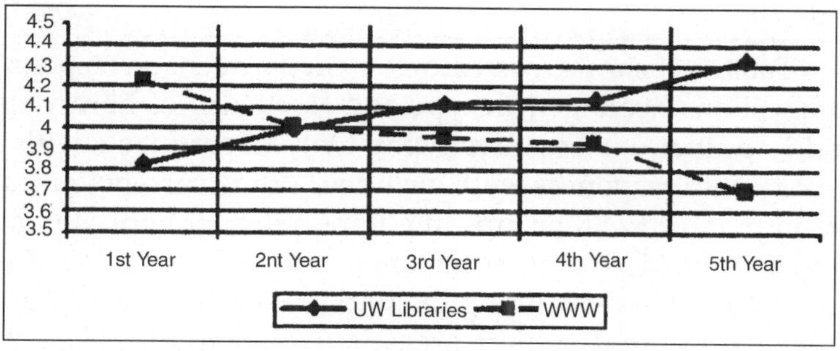

Fig 7.2 1998 Survey. Importance of World Wide Web and UW Libraries by Undergraduate Class (Scale of 1 not important to very important)

Figure shows the importance of UW Libraries and the World Wide Web to the work of undergraduates by year in school. The differences between first year and upper division students were significant at the.05 level using a simple t-test. However, LibQUALt survey results did not show any statistical differences in responses either by gender or class year.

The importance of different resource types such as journals, books, bibliographic databases, and foreign language materials also showed significant variation between academic areas. When asked to rank these re- source types on a scale of 1 to 5, faculty in all academic areas ranked journals as very important. A large number of responses also enables analysis within smaller sub- groups. For example, the 1998 faculty survey had 241 responses from those in science departments.

Table 7.11 1998 Survey (Faculty). Importance of Resource Types

Department (Responses)	Books	Journals > 1980	Journals < 1980	Bibliographic Databases
Chemistry (36)*	4.28	4.83	3.92	4.39
Geology-Geophysics* (22)	4.54	4.91	4.27	4.18
Math-Stat (37)**	4.89	4.89	4.57	3.51
Physics (39)*	4.21	4.56	4.08	3.69
Psychology (24)	4.13	5.00	3.75	4.42
Zoology (27)	4.11	5.00	4.30	4.63
All Science (241)	4.26	4.76	4.09	4.05

Table 7.11 shows mean scores by department on responses to questions dealing with type and frequency of library use and importance of resource types. Only departments with at least twenty responses were included. While current journals are important to all groups, the importance of books, earlier journals, and bibliographic databases showed variation within each group. Understanding the importance of these resource types to different subject areas is useful in allocating the collection-development budget as well as making decisions on what materials to house on-site or in storage. There were also

significant differences in the frequency of physical visits to the library by science faculty. Perhaps it is not surprising that distance from the library appeared to play an important role. Not only did the departments located closest to their primary library visit those libraries more often, the frequency of their physical visits exceeded the frequency of library use from an office computer.

A comparison between large-scale user surveys done by the UW Libraries and the LibQUALt survey administered to UW faculty and students shows good agreement in population representation and in broad result categories at the group level. However, the ability to do subgroup and intra group analysis can provide valuable results and efforts to increase the number of responses if the Web based LibQUAL+ survey should continue.

ASKING THE RIGHT QUESTIONS

Whether the survey results are statistically reliable, representative, valid, or significant, doesn't necessarily mean that they provide information that can be used to assess and improve library service quality. It is also important to examine whether these surveys are asking the right questions in the right way to the right group. Survey design is a complex and evolving process that requires substantial interaction between the surveying group and the surveyed population. At many large academic research institutions, user communities are diverse and differ in their needs for library resources and services.

It is essential to recognise that these differences exist when designing and administering surveys. Undergraduate students, based on their understanding or experience, may respond quite differently from faculty to some questions, making it difficult to do cross group comparisons. It is also important to remember that surveys are just one method of acquiring user input. While surveys offer the prospect of obtaining quantifiable data from large populations at reasonable costs, they need to be employed in the right situation. Surveys should be de- signed from the user perspective. Questions should be short, simple, and clear to the user. Complex issues may be better addressed using other techniques.

There should be sufficient motivation for faculty and students to take the time to complete a survey. The evolution of SERVQUAL to LibQUALt is a positive step. The ability to move away from the twenty-two question SEKVQUAL core pack- age to a design that provides a library focus, and perhaps a simpler format, is welcome. Grounding the survey based on user-provided information on library needs and use is critical to maintain currency and relevancy. Such qualitative data obtained at regular intervals enables the library to keep on top of user issues and concerns.

The library and information environment is changing rapidly. The continued growth in remote use of library services and resources and in user self-sufficiency calls for new ways to measure user needs and library performance that can be done quickly, inexpensively, and flexibly enough to catch environ- mental changes. The ARL New Measures Initiative plans to provide libraries with tested tools that can help provide information that will assist in meeting these challenges. The underlying concept of developing a standard instrument to mea- sure service quality across libraries is a powerful one and certainly one deserving institutional support.

However, it cannot supplant local efforts to work closely with faculty and students to assess user needs and library collections and services. There are local issues at each institution that probably cannot be effectively addressed in a standardised survey tool. The University of Washington Libraries expects to continue both its participation in LibQUALt as well as utilising a variety of ways to assess user needs and library performance, including the deployment of locally based large-scale user surveys.

8

Describing Existing Library Services and Technology

INTRODUCTION

Libraries across India, as in other parts of the world, are facing sweeping changes on account of the media in which information is generated, transmitted, disseminated and archived due to the increasing presence of electronic formats. There is no doubt that information in electronic form is a potential asset, and that it can be vigourously applied in any environment.

The advent and spread of electronic formats has made a major difference in the information processing and service environments in libraries, especially after the emergence of the Internet and Web as the dominant pathway and repository of electronic information resources.

In an increasingly networked world, it is possible that universities may be able to take back control of scholarly information, and libraries may risk being cut out of the author-publisher-dissemination loop. Libraries act as facilitators to provide the right information to the right user at the right time. Users visit libraries to borrow identified documents, or to take photocopies/printouts of those documents from reference collections or journals not issued out normally.

The advent of Web-enabled information resources, such as e-journals, e-books and e-reference sources, and their access through networks has taken the library to the users and a significant amount of information access is now taking place beyond the four walls of the library. In many cases users want a 'pinpointed precision' in the information search process whereas the library attempts for an 'exhaustive recall' to comply with the various ways in which an information source is approached and to satisfy each user's diverse interests.

This information overload may cause doubts in the users regarding the relevance of information services as perceived from a professional angle. Along with quantifying use, it is equally important to assess the qualitative attributes of implicit and explicit use and examine the difficulties of users in properly framing their requests for information. The limitation on the part of library professionals to perceive and represent what is demanded by users in information systems, and the dilemmas of information organisation and retrieval to handle these demands must be effectively addressed. Libraries and professionals are equally concerned about the emergence of Internet as an information repository beyond the library's walls, as amply demonstrated by enhanced citations of Web resources.

As library acquisitions are falling, information sources are increasing, and a single site library satisfying the user's needs is a doubtful proposition; users are forced to look beyond the library for their information needs. Thus the only option for the libraries is to enter into collaborations, networking and consortia and to reorient their roles as information services and access centres from their previous roles as information warehouses.

At the same time, the technical advances resulting from enhanced research in science and technology have made it possible to reduce drastically the time involved in information collection and identification. Also the extra time required in adapting printed information to client service through cumbersome manual routines of classification and cataloguing is considerably reduced by the availability of electronic information, leaving the professionals to concentrate more on tasks to support the extensive teaching and intensive research environment.

ACADEMIC AND RESEARCH LIBRARIES

The application of computing to library work in India has a history of at least three decades because since, the time the computer entered premier academic institutions and selected R & D facilities, it has been explored for improving information processing and management routines. Information technology (IT) enriched library services arrived initially for science and technology (S&T) information handling and for the special libraries attached to research and development (R&D) centres and academic libraries in higher education institutions. In comparison to other libraries, academic and research libraries have better infrastructure and skilled manpower in greater numbers, making them able to offer information services comparable to advanced countries. Like qualified teaching and research personnel and well-equipped laboratories, the right information service is another vital element in the trinity which completes a fruitful academic or research environment.

MARKET-DRIVEN COLLABORATION

Academic and research libraries, especially in developing countries, are passing through a very challenging phase in their existence due to unfriendly trends in the emerging information market. On the one hand, these libraries are still left with many of the old problems such as poor budgetary support and weak infrastructure, as well as staff in fewer numbers and often with less expertise. But the new information marketing techniques, like the possibilities of delivering and accessing electronic information in diverse channels, force these libraries to be very vigilant and cautious in their approach towards information acquisition and services. Libraries and professionals in India were quick to understand the emerging information environment was forcing their users to depend largely on those resources, which are becoming more expensive day by day due to the rise in production costs, fall in subscriptions and inflationary trends of Indian currency.

When individual libraries found that alone they are not in a position to satisfy the information requirements of their clients, they formulated various collaborative arrangements with other libraries such as, interlibrary loan (ILL) services, document delivery services (DDS), resource-sharing, and consortia-based subscriptions.

PRESENT PRACTICES AND EMERGING GOALS

The special libraries attached to research and higher education were lucky enough to garner resources to automate their in-house routine operations and for hosting online public access catalogues (OPACs); some of them also set up facilities to search electronic databases. A few of them evolved the desired infrastructure for Internet surfing, for hosting of full-text database access, and for setting up digital libraries. The major advantage of the progress in computerisation is a considerable increase in the amount of information available online.

We have experienced that at the start of computer applications only the surrogates existed online, but some full-text content has been made accessible online in recent years. These libraries are experiencing the virtues of electronic information in different forms such as e-journals, e-books, bibliographic/full-text electronic databases on CD-ROMs and through Web access. Due to publishers' 'electronic plus' policies, libraries are able to access electronic versions of printed sources such as journals either for free or by paying an additional fee. However the goal these libraries in specialised research and academic centres should have set for themselves is to enhance their information facilities to fully functional digital libraries, comparable with similar facilities in the developed countries.

CULTURES AND CONFLICTS FACED BY LIBRARIES

The fixed roles suggested by Levy for researchers, publishers and libraries are either overlapping or changing in the electronic scene. There are cases where an author or a library is acting as electronic publisher, and there are publishers providing a wide variety of information packages beyond the contents of printed journals. The real question is: has the library really lost ground in the emerging information scene? Even the critics will not say so.

The concerns expressed are only to revitalise the professional skills of librarians, rejuvenate the style of working and reorient the library towards its rightful place in effective dissemination of information. Maybe the common feeling that the library is a central place in the institution visited everyday by large numbers of users, like any public utility, has lost some ground in the electronic scene. Nonetheless, apart the continuing provision of information services for print sources, the electronic revolution has reaffirmed the library more as an information service and access centre than as an information storehouse.

TECHNOLOGY-ENHANCED LIBRARY SERVICES

TECHNOLOGY ADVANCES

The major technology breakthroughs in the context of libraries include:

- Advent of printing press and mass production of printed documents enabled democratisation of information. Libraries had a major role in the print era, as no one can own a large number of books on a particular subject whereas libraries by their very purpose concentrated on doing so.
- Microforms helped to preserve less used information in a compact space and as a smoother delivery option for voluminous sources. Libraries had their unchallenged role even in the microform era as the special purpose readers for microfilms and microfiche were costly and exclusively housed in the library.
- The economical and affordable copying technology revolutionised the concept of information use as it spearheaded the trend of owning copies of relevant portions of library resources. The copying technology

freed the user from sitting in the library for long duration for reading, since, one can simply get a copy quickly and leave.

- Computing is the biggest technology revolution so far, as it is a major enabler in the information dissemination chain; also it is not a stand-alone technology unlike earlier technologies and can be networked and integrated with a whole lot of other devices and technologies. It not only revolutionised the production of books and microforms but also brought the arrival of online and CD-ROM databases, electronic information resources, Internet and the digital revolution.

PRODUCTS AND SERVICES

Adapting IT for library applications is an ongoing process, right from procuring or developing IT enabled information products through computer aided processing and management to delivering IT-enriched services. Library professionals in India are already exposed to the different offshoots of IT for library organisation and information services.

LIBRARY AUTOMATION PACKAGES

The availability of a wide variety of library automation software to suit the varied needs of libraries themselves is a reflection of the progress libraries have made in automating the operations of procuring, processing and providing information sources. Procurement is the end of the story for many other software/databases used in a library, whereas library automation systems will open a floodgate of issues. What the vendor provides is a structure to build information concerning the collection and users, to conduct various aspects of organising the collection and offering information services.

Thus software needs to be evaluated for its suitability for the target library before purchase. This may include case studies from other libraries using the software, evaluation of hardware and operating system required, computer awareness among staff and users, network as well as computer infrastructure in the institution, and all estimation of cost and charges for after-sales support. Using suitable software for library automation will significantly reduce manual operations and enable professionals to dedicate more time for professional jobs.

CD-ROM AND ELECTRONIC DATABASES

Due to the poor communication infrastructure prevalent in India and to the immense costs involved, online database services were used only by few institutions. The distribution of the same content of online data repositories subsequently in CD-ROMs made it affordable to a larger number of institutions. While the library automation package gave search-and access facility to information sources present in the local collection, CD-ROM databases attempted consolidated access irrespective of holdings to the bibliographic data of publications in a discipline. CD-ROM databases have also freed library professionals from conducting searches and allowed the end user to conduct the searches. CD-ROM is so common nowadays that a library holds a good number of them not only for bibliographic, numeric and full-text databases, but also those received along with printed books and other reference sources. Managing and serving these high capacity discs was a problem earlier due to the stand-alone software required, whereas the onset of networking and hard-disk cached solutions provides an effective and functional way to enable access to them through the intranet.

WEB

Since, the 1990s, the Internet has changed the dissemination of information, such as electronic copies of traditional paper-based journals and conference proceedings, free electronic-only refereed journals, haphazard copies of all kinds of material on home pages and a handful of electronic preprints archives. Most libraries in India now have a web site and they use the site to present the basic strengths of the library and to host services such as the OPAC and Web access to electronic information. The 'size of the catalogue card' and the field lengths of primitive database technology are surpassed in the Web era. Types of information resources on the Web also vary from authentic primary information about the latest research results to ephemeral product catalogues. Issues worth consideration are often the content of the sites that are deleted, modified or changed to new machines without proper redirection and the extraction mechanism through search engines, when a flood of sources is retrieved against a query, of which few are relevant.

The Internet and Web demonstrate that a large amount of electronic information can be hosted in a decentralised fashion in a cost-effective manner. The Web has also freed the user's dependence on library resources for finding information related to address and contact details of a person/institution, contents pages of books, journals, etc. As far as possible, especially for reference and information services, looking at the Web has become an innovative trend in the reference service to complement dated print sources.

Many publishers visibly feel the benefits and reach of the Web, and have considered it as an alternate medium for delivering information sources; some publishers even permit unrestricted access of tables of contents and abstracts of their primary journals. As a result of these initiatives, the 'print and distribute' paradigm is challenged by 'distribute and print' paradigm.

CONSORTIAL LICENCES

The term 'consortial licences' designates library groupings to negotiate access rights to (print and) electronic information with publishers and vendors aiming at enhanced access to more resources at better pricing. "Consortia can be a means to introduce products to a previously untapped market" for vendors and "consortia provide shared expertise, access to new electronic and print resources, professional development, new sources of funds, and safety in numbers" for libraries. In contrast to earlier library collaborative arrangements such as ILL and resource sharing, the publisher and trade community are parties in the consortial agreements. In resource-sharing, libraries concentrate on collaborative subscriptions by avoiding duplication, where as in consortial licences, the emphasis is to strike the 'best deals' even if the library suffers some duplication.

The publisher community experience is that increased subscription costs lead to a reduction in the total number of subscriptions, further raising the subscription cost every year. Publishers also found it difficult to enforce ownership rights with electronic sources, even after adopting the latest technology tools and forcing libraries to sign the toughest of the legal clauses. The good marketing wisdom of the publisher and trade community prevailed to open up information access rights through consortial licences for a large part of the product spectrum to at least those libraries or groups of libraries which procure products beyond a certain threshold value.

The Indian National Digital Library in Engineering Science and Technology (INDEST) is the first and the major consortium in India. It is under the aegis of the Ministry of Human Resource Development (MHRD). Before the creation of the consortium, access to electronic journals in these institutions remained at 60 per cent of subscribed titles, but the number of online journals has increased 10 times after the establishment of the consortium.

The rates for access offered to the consortium are lower by 50 per cent to 90 per cent depending upon the category of institution and the consortium paid only 11 per cent of the list price to access these resources. Info net, another consortium, floated by the University Grants Commission (UGC) for Universities, is also gaining strength. Similar consortia are also operational for research institutions under the Council of Scientific and Industrial Research (CSIR) and the Department of Atomic Energy (DAE).

DIGITAL LIBRARIES

Libraries in India are engaged in the development of prototypes of digital information resources, as influenced by developments in other countries. There are certain types of content which lie inaccessible or less used in their present physical forms that can be put to more visible and enhanced use through digitisation. Also heavily used content presently available in limited numbers of copies can be identified for conversion to electronic format.

The linear text in many of the print sources presents difficulties for providing a hypertext approach or a multimedia feeling, for simulating learning by doing; sustaining attention and interest for long duration calls for using electronic technologies to enable content to be more functional. The static content in printed sources fails to attract users who are increasingly exposed to the widely appealing features of broadcasting and IT-intensive presentation tools. Multimedia-enabled digital information will be useful to a large percentage of illitreate and older population also. There are cases such as papers in journals and conferences in print form that never get their deserved visibility and often end up with out reaching the target population.

The digital dissemination of this content may lead to very effective teaching and more focused research in most areas. To demonstrate the efficacy of digital libraries and collections, libraries must be able to identify materials in the public domain, sources generated in-house, and similar materials to overcome the constraints of copyright. Digital library (DL) development needs a two pronged strategy to digitise local content as well as to devise options for providing access to external resources obtained as free or as part of existing subscriptions or access licences.

The typical academic or research library in-house digital library on an Intranet must include the following components:

- Consortial access to electronic journals and electronic databases.
- Free/paid Web access to journals subscribed in print format.
- Subject gateways and virtual libraries.
- Free/paid e-books from publishers and portals.
- Intranet access to bibliographic and full-text databases, and CD-ROM publications.

- Local archiving of free and paid e-books.
- LAN serving of e-supplements of purchased books.
- In-house digitisation of copyright-owned and copyright-free printed books in the collection.
- Born-digital in-house publications such as research reports, annual reports, convocation reports, teaching materials, theses and dissertations, in-house journals, proceedings of conferences, seminars, workshops, etc., conducted by the institution.
- Preprints and post-prints of research papers sent for publication to journals, conferences, and books, especially with respect to the Open Archives Initiative gaining ground to provide further access to research published in toll journals and to make the results of publicly funded research available to those who need them.
- Publications in the public domain, such as government publications, publications from non-profit institutions, etc.

But many libraries are unable to provide these components due to lack of awareness or due to the hurdles invariably faced by libraries in India. The lack of interest on the part of parent institutions and the absence of action plans or priorities is the major hindrance. Though computer and communication infrastructure is improving, their availability for information work is not appreciated in many organisations. Paschoud commented how several of the speakers and many of the delegates at the International Conference on Digital Libraries (ICDL) 2004 conference in New Delhi focussed on addressing what most European libraries would consider very basic issues such as network/Internet connectivity and management.

Even in places where infrastructure is available, there is an acute shortage of competent labor to take up the task of digitising local content and evolving digital information repositories. The students, faculty, curriculum and training methodology at the disposal of library schools have to be improved visibly to meet this challenge. Coupled with this is the need for continuing education for retraining the working professionals. Institutions, individuals, or private publishers have rights over content, and motivating them to ease these rights when they are not inclined towards digitisation is not a simple task. Levying charges for access is a distant proposition; instead sponsorships from institutions, government bodies and library suppliers can be explored.

Even when hosted as a free facility, enough security mechanisms must be evolved to prevent any trespassing by hackers. Selecting useful content requires careful review and evaluation by subject experts, as digitisation will only help to preserve the record, and not its enhanced and continued access. Internet bandwidth in India has to be sufficiently augmented to allow faster access to Web content as more content is being hosted on the Web. The different funding agencies, research councils and institutions are not currently offering monetary support to the desired extent for digital library development.

CULTURE AND CONFLICTS FACED BY USERS

MANUAL AND ELECTRONIC SEARCH

Searching for manual sources required scanning catalogue cards or indexing and abstracting sources. As cross-references often increase the number of cards or pages, there was a difficulty in being very exhaustive. Conducting selective dissemination of information (SDI) services had been extremely difficult as the document profiles must be matched with user profiles with the aid of semi-mechanical systems. Most of these limitations are easily eliminated in the electronic environment due to the very nature of information processing and organisation in electronic form.

The inherent advantages of indexing electronic information help the user to search for any or all the fields in a timesaving manner. Since, document profiles are already stored in the database and search software supports creation of user profiles, current awareness services (CAS) and SDI services are achieved more easily. The concern for end-user searching was dominant right from the beginning of early CD-

ROM database systems since, the time spent for searching does not involve communication costs as is the case with online searching. Also with the universe of knowledge getting increasingly complex as a result of continuing advances in research in intra and inter-disciplinary areas, vitiating the search conducted by a generalist like a librarian may not be effective in amassing the user's information requirements completely or not achieving the desired results expected by the user.

The convoluted information requirements of present day researchers require sufficient knowledge of their disciplines and since, the users are increasingly exposed to the computerised work environment, they feel very confident to conduct information searching on electronic systems. The professional ethos and egos also plays a part as users find more satisfactory results from electronic systems than manual systems, and in a relatively easy and convenient way. The librarians should recognise the confidence and maturity of users to conduct searches on their own as they have better knowledge of their disciplines, more exposure to the different keywords and their relationships and because of the inherent advantages of locating related sources serendipitously while scanning the retrieved results.

There should be closer interaction and effective communication between library professionals and users to understand each other's views about information needs and use. Library user meetings, orientation sessions for new users, special help for research scholars, training programmes about usage of print and electronic resources, a help desk at reference counter, holdings locator services, interacting with users through phone and e-mail, encouraging users to approach the librarian, ask a librarian, and user friendly web sites are some options practiced in libraries in India.

INFORMATION USE

Information services provided by a library are primarily based on subjective input from users and hence, justify users commenting about misses or noise in electronic information service outputs. An information need is what an individual ought to have; an information want is what an individual would like to have; an information demand is what an individual asks for; an information use is what an individual actually uses; and an information requirement denotes what is needed, what is wanted or what is demanded.

Information needs are affected by a variety of factors such as the range of sources available, the uses to which information will be put, individual characteristics of the user, social, political and economic systems surrounding the user, and the consequences of information use. Accessibility of information resources is usually assumed to depend on a range of cognitive, social, and physical factors, such as whether a person is aware of a resource, has the knowledge and skills needed to access it, and has the resource close at hand. Scientists spend 50–60 per cent of their time communicating. The computerised environment has increased the quantum of information available nearby, but it has not enhanced a person's information consumption skills.

There is a burden of effort in information storage and retrieval that may be shifted from author to indexer to index language designer to searcher to user. Though the user is exposed to more microfilms, Xerox copies, and electronic information on desktop/ Intranet/Web, ready to display at the touch of a button, the more time one spends in searching and collecting information, the less time s/he gets to use the information. Scholarly articles are identified for reading in five basic ways: browsing, automated searches, citations found in the litreature, mentions by other people, and current-awareness tools. How much information one requires to work on a particular problem is also subjective as human beings observe the 'principle of least effort'. Perhaps one may easily deal with an information crisis by identifying a part of the total references and by using few of what is identified.

USER BYPASSING

Though libraries in India are progressing well on the automation and information access front, there is a definite case of fewer users present in the library due to different reasons. The real question is whether electronic services of libraries have in any way affected the user interests or have the users found more confidence in an information superhighway beyond the library. The same proportions of scientists still browse to identify scholarly articles to read, but more are using online searches and the proportion of readings identified through online searches appears to be increasing. Library acquisitions suffered a serious setback in recent years unable to withstand the price rise and these budgetary constraints forced users to look beyond the library for their varied information requirements.

Hence, research publications in some disciplines now cite more Web resources. Librarians are not yet acting as true consumers and hence, cannot blame predatory publishers for taking advantage of the situation. Another issue involves the very large and rapidly increasing number of articles obtained through photocopying, interlibrary loan, document delivery, preprints, and reprints. The right step in assessing whether there is a depleted user interest in libraries is to study use patterns over the years and, in a populous country like India, just going by the numbers will not address the qualitative aspects.

There has not been much reduction in book issues in an academic library, but are the new acquisitions being used to the same extent? But what is seen is the fall in library attendance, as observed and reported by many library managers. It is evident that fewer users actually visit the library, and very few still spend more time, a lot of others use the library through lending, photocopies, electronic access through networks, etc. It becomes difficult to quantify use as the library has statistics only about explicit use, but there are also implicit uses through browsing or reading inside the library, which are difficult to quantify.

There are also vital questions about whether mere issuing a book or taking a photocopy of a journal article attribute to use and hence, comes the need for a qualitative assessment of use. Perhaps professionals are afraid to look at these issues as the results of such assessment may force the authorities to examine critically the investments in a service institution like the library. Like Reenen's comment about false consumers, it seems that librarians fear self-assessment of library usage or to undergo a performance audit.

THE LIBRARIAN'S IDENTITY CRISIS

EDUCATION AND TRAINING

The students, faculty, curriculum and training methodology at the library schools have to be visibly improved to meet the challenges posed by electronic information and impatient, highly demanding users. There are also problems of infrastructure and a directionless attitude in the teaching and research sector often forgetting the interdisciplinary aspect of the subject. Working librarians have good exposure to new databases, their acquisition and use, pragmatic implementation of various routines, etc., which are not accessible to library schools. Thus apart from teaching faculty, expert practitioners in the discipline would also be involved in education programmes to bridge the gap between preaching and practice.

The existing courses must always look at the sweeping changes in the library workplace and adapt well to enable the students to face the challenges with confidence, giving ample opportunities for improving reasoning, communication skills, general awareness, and other characteristics identified for a multi-tasking service organisation. The age-old teacher-centric teaching has to be circumvented by student oriented and professional (job)-centric teaching.

JOB OPPORTUNITIES

Though the major employer, the government, is not recruiting many, more and more universities/institutions are offering library courses in the regular and distance modes. And this upheaval in quantity does not contribute in any way to the quality of these courses. For a prospective student/parent, the job advertisements provide an impression of plenty of jobs in the field, as library jobs at different levels in different institutions do not follow standard designations. But only when one finishes the course and looks for job openings, does the actual state of affairs come to light. Actually the increase in library-related jobs is merely additive, and not multiplicative, like computers, management or engineering, and should not show an exponential rise at any point of time.

CONTINUING EDUCATION

Since, the mode and rate at which information is generated, organised and used is witnessing sweeping changes in the perfectly wired information age, a continuously evolving discipline like LIS is meant to tackle the intricacies of information for societal development; thus it shall not be learned effectively and practiced perfectly by exposing students to a framed curriculum in formal education only. The discipline has changed drastically from being based totally on print sources; aware of the increasing richness of information in electronic forms and available over networks thus is leading to embracing vigourously other disciplines like computers, management, and information and communication technology.

It is imperative for the information practitioners to continuously monitor and augment their professional skills through continuing education (CE) to discharge their duties to users, employer and profession. The present initiatives on CE are generally being made by national institutions and suffer limitations such as: they are of short duration, generally infrequent, claiming comparatively high fees, working professionals finding it difficult to get sponsorship from their institutions, involve travelling to far off destinations hampering their regular work, etc.

CULTURES AND CONFLICTS FACED BY LIBRARIANS

Gone are the days of close-minded librarians and the quality of candidates entering the profession is continuously improving. As technology-intensive librarianship is gaining ground in the country, working librarians are getting much exposure to new technology tools for providing better information products and improved information services. Working librarians in at least the major academic and research institutions have better computer infrastructure and possess better expertise on the latest information products and services.

It is quite natural in the emerging print plus electronic hybrid library scenario that a library professional right from first job is expected to be conversant with the electronic apart from the manual means of information collection, processing, management and servicing. But there are also apprehensions about the level of technology appropriate to conducting well in the challenging and demanding academic and research setup.

A library professional must be distinct from a computer professional due to the very nature of their profession and the expected deliverables. But the acute emphasis on technology has created a situation that a professional can hide many of his/her professional ignorance by a little computer knowledge which is not going to be good either for the profession or for the libraries. Google cannot and will not be replacing libraries because both can co-exist with their diverse functionalities catching the attention of users at different occasions.

The professional nature of the librarian's job always motivates him or her to help the users unlike administrative staff in the institution who are always rule-based; sometimes this may lead to not so proper upkeep of administrative procedures and records, and in some cases cause unnecessary rivalry with the administrative staff. There are also personnel problems as the librarians fail to command a leadership role in many institutions thereby eclipsing their role in strategic planning.

Institutions attach prime importance to libraries but are they doing the same towards the personnel in their libraries? It is a strange case of all the virtues are of the system and the problems are due to the staff. Largely a service wing in many institutions, not enjoying the power, visibility, service conditions, and career prospects of the research and teaching staff, the status of library professionals in many of these institutions is not a morale booster, leaving many of them underperforming. It is not uncommon to see non-professionals heading many libraries, maybe just because they are senior teachers or good administrators or researchers and not because they are good as librarians.

There are also problems of the lack of a peer group in the profession resisting such attacks on the profession as many senior professionals have become self-centred, and professional associations compete for minor issues. The professional staff members working in many libraries in developing countries are totally engrossed in administrative and routine jobs related to library operation and administration. Many institutions do not demand their library professionals to pursue an offensive role. The users always need quick services and they never respond to any of the reasonable operational or managerial delays.

The real situation is that the libraries have very little control over their suppliers whereas their consumers have too much control over them. Users are not patient enough to interact constantly with the library staff to tune their profiles to improve the relevance of information services, maybe due to time constraints on their parts. Again by a rough assessment, it seems that less than 10 per cent of the users usually respond to SDI results and the remaining are either using it as it is or rejecting it straightaway. Out of those responding, only a few show their willingness to give feedback to modify their keywords to improve the utility of such services. Users may sometimes get so arrogant with the helpful nature of library staff and doubt it as their weakness.

CONCLUSION

Like building collection and providing services, improving access to information should be the guiding criteria for libraries in the electronic era. Apart from hosting external information, they should also evolve local digitisation ventures to give more visibility to internal information. We have to design a new set of parameters to judge operational efficiency and performance effectiveness of libraries. Traditional libraries boasted that they attracted a lot of users to stay inside their premises for comparatively longer duration whereas a modern librarian will be more concerned about carrying information to users' desktops.

No library, no matter how rich its budget allocation and collection may be, is in a position to satisfy all the information needs of its users. As a person well versed in the intricacies of the emerging information market, the librarian should be frank enough to admit that the information needs of all users are not met by the library alone. Collaboration with other libraries through consortia or networks increases the amount of resources available to users. Most academic and research libraries spend a lot of public money for information needs of a small percentage of the population and optimising that spending for the benefit of more number of users is the need of the hour. Library professionals have a major role in the emerging print plus digital hybrid information environment that is looming large in many academic and research libraries.

This role can be properly identified and refined only through constructive interaction of administrative heads of institutions, library professionals and professional associations. There is no doubt that we are passing through a severe phase and this is the right time to have a close introspective and critical look at collections developed, services offered and professional skills required in the light of complex user needs, hazy use patterns and the ever-increasing spread of Internet, electronic databases and digital libraries.

9

Strategic Planning

A DEFINITION OF STRATEGIC PLANNING

Strategic planning is a tool for organising the present on the basis of the projections of the desired future. That is, a strategic plan is a road map to lead an organisation from where it is now to where it would like to be in five or ten years. It is necessary to have a strategic plan for your chapter or division. In order to develop a comprehensive plan for your chapter or division which would include both long- range and strategic elements, we suggest the methods and mechanisms outlined in this manual.

The plan must be:

- Simple
- Written
- Clear
- Based on the real current situation
- Have enough time allowed to give it a time to settle. It should not be rushed. Rushing the plan will cause problems.

BENEFITS AND PITFALLS IN STRATEGIC PLANNING

Since, the beginning of Special Libraries Association in 1909, it has experienced phenomenal growth in membership and influence. In the past ten years, growth has been particularly significant. Changes in the fields of special librarianship and information science have been dramatic and fundamental to the very way of doing business. The advent of on line systems and the computer age rapidly changed the way librarians/information managers operate.

The Association recognises that it can no longer merely react to issues as they emerge. If it is to continue as a leader in improving the profession, it must begin to anticipate future change rather than merely react to change. The Association as well as each chapter and division needs to consider this long-term future. Drawing on the resources it has, both human and financial, it needs to continue to grow. These resources are limited, and careful thought must be given to the allocation of these resources.

To meet obligations to the profession, the public, and the membership, it is essential that the Association and its units use these resources in the most efficient manner by determining priority areas on which to concentrate. This means the identification of goals, pursuing those goals, and achieving them. Strategic planning will help build continuity in the Association's programmes, particularly in the areas of continuing education and publications. The Association has the gift of a great deal of diversity among the membership. The Association draws its strength from this diversity but at the same time, that diversity lessens the Association's impact in key areas because of a lack of cohesive focus by the organisation.

Therefore, it is necessary for each chapter and division to have a plan that is compatible with the overall strategic plan of SLA thus concentrating its efforts and greatly increasing its impact. There are several pitfalls associated with strategic planning. First, the plan may not turn out as well as expected because of changes in the environment in which the plan is supposed to operate. Also, strategic planning is worthless in getting an organisation out of a major crisis.

A crisis is a current problem not solved by a strategic plan. And, if the planning process itself is weak, the resulting plan may be weak and not satisfactory to the organisation. George Steiner in his Strategic Planning lists 50 major common pitfalls in starting, doing, and using strategic planning.

STRATEGIC PLANNING MODEL

In choosing the strategic planning model, two main things need to be considered. The first is whether you want the Association unit to plan as a not-for-profit, or as a profit organisation. Association planning is not the same as the planning for universities or businesses or government agencies. Associations need to be consistently receptive to the needs of the membership-at-large. The main purpose is to serve the members more than to make a profit or to increase the size of the organisation. The strategic plan needs to include a Mission Statement, Objectives, Goals, and an Action (or Implementation) Plan.

MISSION STATEMENT

This is the agreed-upon statement by the organisation and explains the reason for its existence. It is necessarily broad to encompass the diversity within the Association. The statement is not precise in its measurements nor does it need to be, but it does need to be periodically reviewed by the Association to see whether it still encompasses all of the relevant activities of the Association.

OBJECTIVES

The objectives are the areas of emphasis within the Association. Rather than specific statements with a specific goal, objectives state that the Association plans to continue to do quality work in the following areas. These objectives or areas of emphasis need to be attained by discussion and review of the organisation's current activities as well as activities in which it would like to participate.

GOALS

These need to be both long-term and short-term goals; six months, one-year, threeyears, and ten-year goals need to be set so that the strategy for reaching these goals can be outlined in the plan. Most organisations recommend setting the long-term goals first and then setting short-term goals: those goals which can be reached as steps to attaining the long-term goal.

ACTION PLAN

The Action Plan should be designed after the main goals and objectives have been set in order to attain the mission in a straightforward and measurable way. With an Action Plan, the goals themselves can be obtained. Without the Action Plan, and the measures it entails, it would be impossible to implement the plan and measure its success. Being able to measure success would certainly be important both for maintaining our tax status as a not-for-profit organisation as well as to explain the use of it to the membership-at-large.

STRATEGIC PLANNING PROCESSES AND MECHANISMS

The publications 'A Guide to Nominal Group and Delphi Processes' by Andre L. Blebecq, et al, and "Guide for Leaders Using Nominal Group Technique" by James G. Cope and Carl Moore, describe the combination of nominal group and Delphi processes. Using these techniques, an organisation that is geographically separate can communicate and develop the working document in fairly rapid fashion.

GATHERING OF BACKGROUND INFORMATION

Background information is used by your Strategic Planning Committee for its review. By shifting through that information, the Committee would be able to develop a sound basis to continue their work. After existing information has been gathered, another information gathering activity should take place.

Develop a survey questionnaire to poll all members for their viewpoints on the directions your chapter or division should take. After the information has been synthesised from the questionnaires as well as from information already gathered, move to the second step.

A PLANNING WORKSHOP

The title of the article is 'Strategic Planning: Lead Your Association With a Plan for Tomorrow'.

Based on this article, your chapter or division needs to gather information on five basic questions:

- Where are we now? (The Situation);
- How did we get there? (Our Momentum);
- Where are we going? (The Direction);
- Where should we be going? (Desired Direction);
- How will we get there? (The Strategic Plan).

Bailey recommends that after gathering the background information, the planning workshop should take place. The first session would assess the current situation and how you arrived at that present situation. The second activity of this first workshop is to try to figure out where you are going and where you want to be. This is a very hard-hitting and difficult time for any association or business given the economic conditions and the change within our profession itself.

DESIGNING A PLANNING WORKBOOK

The planning Workbook will bring together all of the information gathered during the Planning Workshop, sift through the ideas put forward, and organise them into a meaningful body for review by the Planning Workshop attendees and other interested parties in the organisation.

SECOND PLANNING WORKSHOP

After the Planning Workshop information has been gathered into a workbook, another workshop should be planned. At this workshop (which should not be held too long after the first one), several things need to be accomplished. In the first half-day a Mission Statement should be adopted for the Association. The Mission Statement will include what the Association intends to stand for; what it hopes to contribute to the world-at-large. It should set goals for the Association and then, having set the goals, fulfill the Mission Statement by translating each goal into a specific objective. This means that the Mission Statement will be carried forth into a strategic plan.

THE COMMITTEE STRUCTURE

The Strategic Planning Committee should be composed of people who understand the organisation of Special Libraries

Association, but also who have a constant feel for the Association and your chapter and division in general, and where it is moving. The Strategic Planning Committee should be made a permanent standing committee within the chapters and divisions with a rotating membership. This will encourage constant review and updating by the membership.

THOUGHTS REGARDING SHORT AND LONG RANGE PLANNING

In order to achieve a sound basis for the development of programmes and activities, systematic planning efforts must be undertaken. The following is a stream of ideas about planning which have been able to find their way to paper. They are presented merely for a point of departure and not meant for any other purpose--a 'Plan for Planning' so to speak.

PLANNING

Planning includes the ability to identify opportunities, analyse problems, establish priorities and needs, and allocate available resources. This also includes the establishment of priorities and needs, and allocate available resources.

This also includes the establishment of policies and procedures, objectives and standards of performance, forecasts and budgets, programmes and schedules:

- Planning is necessary:
  - Provides direction
  - Gives perspective
- Planning facilitates:
  - Involvement of concerned people and groups.
  - Communication
  - Coordination
- Steps in Planning:
  - Organising
    - *a.* Establish a structure
    - *b.* Group involvement
  - Setting objectives
    - *a.* Nature of objectives
    - *b.* Basis for objectives

- Establishing priorities—based on needs, opportunities, interrelationships between elements.
- Designing activities
- Dividing action into feasible steps
  a. Short range
  b. Long range
- Implementing action
- Disseminating information
- Evaluating—a continual process
- Revising—at least annually

PROGRAMME

- Conceptual—why the programme should be undertaken:
  - Problem statement
  - Objectives
  - Hypothesis
  - Review of existing information
- Methodological—what has to be done and how it will be done:
  - Design Programme
  - Sampling
  - Analysis
    a. Quantitative
    b. Qualitative
  - Instrumentation selection or development.

CONTENTS OF PLANNING DOCUMENT

- Statement of philosophy:
  - General philosophy of the organisation
  - Philosophy of special libraries
- Needs assessment
- Goal of the Association
- Objectives of the Association
  - Something we want
  - Output—end product
  - Means—end product
- Establish programme alternatives

- Fiscal—costs of conducting the programme:
  - *a.* Time
  - *b.* Resources
    - i. Human
    - ii. Non-human
  - c. Money
- Programme—set of activities which are combined into some structure and are carried out to achieve some previously stated objective.
- Limits and constraints:
  - *a.* An analysis of what we have to work with and work against
  - *b.* Specify time, money, programme requirements, people, and facilities within which the Association must operate
  - *c.* The statement of ground rules under which the Association must operate
- Types of constraints:
  - *a.* Social
  - *b.* Technological
  - *c.* Administrative
  - *d.* Political
  - *e.* Legal
  - *f.* Economic
- Forces affecting programme development:
  - *a.* Political
  - *b.* Outside interest groups
  - *c.* Administrative hierarchy
  - *d.* Users
  - *e.* Professional organisations
- Establish programme priorities
- Select best programme alternative
- Action plan
- Evaluation of programme

10

Barcode Technology

INTRODUCTION

The circulation work in an automated library involves keying in a large amount of data. Sometimes, the library staff at the counter has to retype the same information due to error in data entry. All this results in long queues at the circulation desk in our libraries. This voluminous work can be handled in a smooth manner in a much less time by the application of barcoding, one of the simplest coding technologies available in the market. The speed of data capture is three times faster than the speed at which a skilled data entry operator can input data' and also the error rate is negligibly small2. The barcode technology originated out of the need of retail stores and big industries to track down their inventory errors in a faster way. Due to the cheap human labour available in our country, the estimated barcoding market was a mere 12 crores in 1995-96', out of which libraries and miscellaneous services accounted for only 1 crore. Libraries need to adopt this technology as it helps retrieve and collect data quickly and efficiently.

BARCODE DATA TRANSFER

The information that can be encoded on the barcodes is rather limited and hence, it is up to the individual libraries to decide what information they need to barcode for efficient handling of collection and for better operation of services. Libraries can use accession numbers of books, the unique information that distinguish their collection, as the vital information entity to barcode their collection. Similarly, the identification number of a user stands distinct for each member, which can be used to barcode the user's cards. Accession number/borrower number exported from the library database/borrower database is converted to a series of black and white lines by the barcode software.

This can be printed by a dot-matrix/laser printer and pasted on all books and borrower cards. The light beam flashed from the barcode scanner on the barcode label undergoes reflection at the white lines and absorption on the dark bands. This reflected light is collected back and is converted into electric pulses by the photoelectric circuitry of the scanner. Further, these pulses are converted into binary information by the interface circuitry of the scanner before they are fed to the computer, for further processing. So, the information read from barcode acts as a substitute for the same information entered through keyboard, to handle circulation/other routines of the library database.

The barcode technology is essentially a data transfer device and hence, it works in perfect harmony with any of the computerised database systems. Any customisation needed at the user end can be done either by the in-house system personnel or by local solution providers. The barcoding setup includes the barcode scanner to read the barcoded information, its interfacing with the library computer, the software to convert the requisite information to barcodes, and the printer.

The barcode scanners may be classified into different groups like:

- As per design (handheld and fixed-mount).
- As per light source (infrared or visible).

Hand-held scanners contain no moving parts. They are compact, light and cheaper as compared to fixed-mount models. Hence, they are of interest to libraries desiring to optimise their budgetary resources. Infrared scanners can read mutilated labels; however, they need special printers. But recent times saw the dominant categorisation, as per technology, into CCD and laser scanners. In CCD scanners, light from the LEDs is used to read the barcode information, whereas laser light is used in the latter. Accordingly, laser scanners have increased scan width and range (distance from which the labels are scanned), but they are comparatively expensive. The vendors used to offer requisite software to generate barcodes from suggested fields of library database. Since, materials and readers are added only in prescribed number in a library, it will be better to avoid commercial printing of barcode labels.

All required lables can be printed either on normal paper or on purchased blank labels on a dot-matrixllaser printer, as per their availability in the library. While generating lables, provision may also be made to print some other fields like author/title/user riame in normal text to identify the labels easily, as one is more comfortable with text than numbers like accession/identification number. The user cards are normally laminated and to ensure long life of the labels on books (defective labels always lead to wrong/no reading of data), transparent cellotape can be pasted over these.

CODING FORMATS/ SYMBOLOGIES

The different code formats and how the information is encoded in bars is available in the litreature4. The same information can be encoded by different schemes; however, at the user and application level, it doesn't make much distinction and the user may use any of the schemes. The same information can be encoded to and satisfactorily decoded from more than one scheme without hampering efficiency or time. Limitations are imposed by the barcoding software one uses, and it is better to consult the individual operational manual for such information.

Some of the common formats are:

- *Universal Product Code (UPC)*: US standard to encode only digits, UPC-A to encode 12 digits or UPC-E to encode 6 digits.
- *European Article Number (EAN)*: European code to encode digits, available in two variations:. EAN-8 to encode 8 digits and EAN-13 to encode 13 digits.
- *Interleaved 2 of 5. (ITF)*: Supports only numeric characters but can be used for variable length.

- *Code-39*: Encodes capital alphabets, numerical and few special characters like $, +, per cent. Asterisk (*) must be used as the start and stop character. Lowercase alphabets cannot be encoded.
- *Code-1 28*: Encodes both the lower and the upper case letters, numeric and special characters found on the keyboard.
- *Codabar*: Encodes only numeric and few special characters and is the most widely used coding format. Generally, libraries use this symbology to encode books and borrower cards.

BARCODING AT THE IIT KHARAGPUR CENTRAL LIBRARY

The Central Library of the Indian Institute of Technology, Kharagpur, is one of the few libraries in the country to have a huge database of their entire collections. Initially, the computerised issue return of books6 was done by keying in the accession number of books and identification number of borrower, but this mechanism was prone to errors and. also resulted in long queues at the circulation grant desk. Out of the project of ₹ 10 lakh received from AICTE in 1994 for the conversion of the conventional central library into the electronic library, the Library procured 5 CCD barcode scanners and one HP-5Si Mx Laser Printer. It was decided to barcode books and hence, the details of books brought for issue/return were exported from the library database for generating barcode labels with accession number as the key field and the labels were printed on the laser printer using 'Softbar vl' software supplied by the vendor.

The Library also received a consignment of 'Nashua Laser Labels' in 30 labels per page format as gift from one of its alumni settled in US. The system generates three labels for each book to be pasted on the back of title page, secret page and last page. To fasten the process, personnel were given honorarium and encouraged to work overtime/on holidays to barcode the entire book collection. Side by side, new books processed by the technical processing section were also barcoded before release. Out of a special operating fund of ₹ 1 lakh received from the Institute in 1998, all the pending old books were also barcoded.

Now, the entire collection of over 2 lakh books is barcoded. From the academic year 1998-99, all B.Tech and M.Tech students were given a laminated barcoded library identity card and the practice of issuing separate borrower cards as per the entitlement was discontinued.

This facility will be further extended to faculty, researchers, and other staff in near future. This practice not only resulted in saving a large amount of stationery for printing numerous borrower cards but also a total saving of staff time which would have otherwise been spent for filing those cards. The user can have a book in one third of the pre-barcode issue time. The faculty, students and the personnel manning the circulation desk find the barcode technology user-friendly, efficient and fast.

ADOPTION IN OTHER LIBRARIES IN INDIA

Few of the computerised libraries in the country like American Centre, British Council, other ITs, some R&D libraries have already started barcoded circulation. With an investment of less than a lakh, the computerised libraries can procure barcode related hardware and software. A CCD scanner can be purchased for ₹ 15,000 and a laser scanner for ₹ 25,000 with comparable costs for relevant software. It is always better to have a feedback from the nearby libraries who use this technology before procuring one. Also, the potential vendors may be called to give a demonstration of this technology.

The procurement may be carried out in one go or in stages, so that those required for barcoding active collection may be purchased first and on completion of that work, more scanners may be bought. The accrued savings for the first few years will be more than what has been invested. Further, it will also improve the status of the library which will move one step closer to realise the fourth law of library science.

APPLICATIONS OF BARCODING

Barcoding offers a lot of comfort and ease to handle bulk routine tasks efficiently. The application of this technology for issue/return of books is widely identified and practiced in the developed countries of the world. A few of the computerised libraries in our country have also started experiencing the fruits of this technology. It is important to emphasise that this technology is not limited to circulation work. Newnham describes the barcoding of DNA samples in Britain. It is not out of place to ponder over future barcoding applications in a library. With the help of a data gathering device, the barcodes can be used to verify stock, as libraries have to resort to stock verification, at intervals.

If the provision for multiple barcodes or multidimensional barcoding is incorporated to handle call number information also, wrong shelving of books can be autodetected which would help the staff to rectify the same. The individual journal volumes are handled in a library with lots of intricacies. Many a time these issues have to be taken out of the display area for Xerox work. There are also chances of their shelving in wrong cabinets.

These problems are tackled by using a control number for the current journal issues and barcoding them accordingly. A database of journal issues can thus be generated so that their management through cards can be avoided. If the parent institution also has a computerised accounting system, all the bills can be routed after barcoding so that their follow up and processing are done efficiently. Barcoding has come a long way and it is here to stay for faster and efficient library work.

AUTOMATED LIBRARY STOCK VERIFICATION WITH BARCODE AND LIBSYS

The modern technology has enabled automation and integration of the various processes of libraries and information centres to reduce or avoid human intervention and to increase the efficiency and speed. As the libraries provide open access service to make the holdings available to the users, the loss, damage, and misplacement of books are inevitable.

To know and replace the lost books, and to maintain balance between various subjects, and to take adequate precautionary measures, it is necessary to do periodical inventory and accounting of the library collection of the library.

The term stock verification thus came into existance with regard to libraries. It is also referred as stock taking, physical verification or checking, stock inspection, and inventory, taking meaning physical checkup of any article on record.

Libraries of Govt. of India and its other organisations has to do a mandatory physical verification of all their holdings as per the following guidelines:

- Complete annual physical verification of books should be done every year in the case of libraries having not more than 20,000 holdings and not fewer than one qualified library staff. In case there is only one qualified staff, the verification may be done as per sub-para.
- Complete physical verification at intervals of not more than three years should be done in the case of libraries having more than 20,000 but not more than 50,000 volumes.
- Sample physical verification at intervals of not more than five years may be done in the case of libraries having more than 50,000 volumes. If such sample verification reveals unusual or unreasonable shortage, complete verification shall be done.

Libraries traditionally perform the periodic stock verification by adopting any one of the following methods: Verification by accession register; using a separate register with accession numbers; slips containing accession numbers; numerical counting; and shelf register cards or shelf list cards. The methods are cumbersome, time-consuming, and error prone as these are done manually.

The automated stock verification procedure adopted at Raja Ramanna Centre for Advanced Technology (RRCAT) library by employing barcode and LibSys facilities library stock verification could be performed easily with less manpower; one person scanned the barcode label (accession number) of documents and other person marked the documents by putting month and year stamp at the inside back cover to ensure that the document was physically verified. Besides, identification of damaged and worn out documents for repair, binding of obsolete volumes, and rearrangement and cleaning can also be done simultaneously. During the stock verification period, the returned (check-in) documents were also verified before shelving. Once the data capturing was over, the verification and generation of report with LibSys could also be done in a short period of time.

IMPLEMENTATION OF BARCODE TECHNOLOGY AND LIBSYS AT RRCAT LIBRARY

To improve the library service and to have an efficient control over the entire operation, the LibSys, which is a commercially available integrated multi-user library automation package, was implemented at RRCAT in 1995. To improve the services further, the barcode technology (print-related automatic identification technology) was implemented in 2000. The hardware installed to implement these technologies at RRCAT are: Laser barcode scanner for reading labels (at circulation counter); portable data capturing terminal with build-in laser scanner for inventory (stock verification); and accessories such as cradle, cable, battery and other items. The softwares for interfacing the data capturing terminal with computer are: PowerGen, SysTools and Label Works for Windows for label designing.

BARCODE AND BARCODE SCANNER

The barcodes are being used effectively to speed up, avoid human error, and automate the processes in industry for production planning control, materials management, purchase/ sale, and inventory control. In libraries, barcode is being used to automate the data-capturing process, for stock verification, and in the circulation counter for issue/return of documents.

A barcode is a sequence of dark bars on a light background or the equivalent of this with respect to the light-reflecting properties of the surface. The coding comprises in the relative widths or spacing of the dark bars and light spaces. A barcode scanner is an optical device that reads the code by scanning a focussed beam of light, generally a laser beam, across the barcode and detecting the variations in reflected light. The scanner converts these light variations into electrical variations, which are subsequently digitised and fed into the decoding unit programmed to convert the relative widths of the digitised dark/light spacings into numbers and/or letters.

BARCODE LABELLING

Each document in a library should be uniquely identified for barcode labelling purpose. Most of the libraries in India use accession number for this purpose. RRCAT has also used the same for printing barcode labels. The labels designed using Label Works for Windows, which supports major barcode symbologies.

Code 128, a high density linear symbology that can encode text, numbers, several functions and the entire 128 ASCII character set was selected for designing the labels. Figure shows the barcode label design specifications.

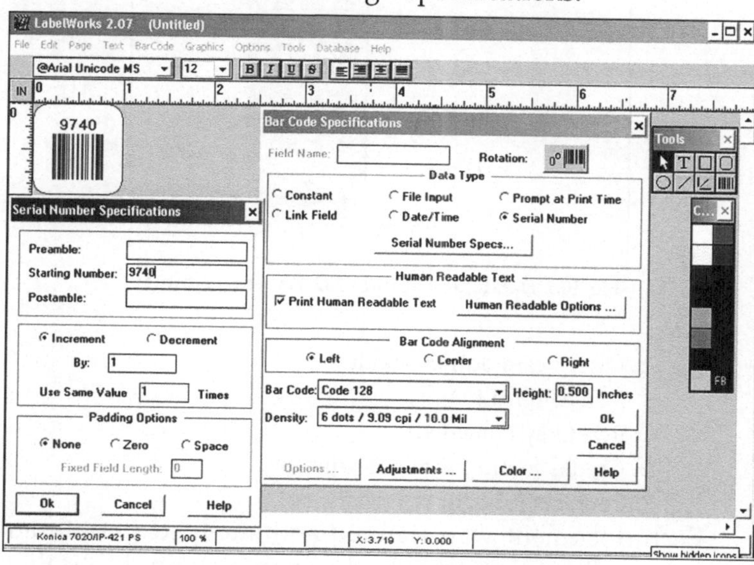

Fig 10.1 Barcode Label Design Specifications

DATA CAPTURING, MODIFICATION AND UPLOADING

The datalogic formula 732 wizard terminal was used to capture the data. The portable data collection laser scanner terminal scans the encoded data and automatically decodes and stores up to 128 KB of data in the memory. As the accession number differs from one to other, the terminal stores approx. 2500 accession numbers. The data was downloaded into the PC using Systool's (software utility for data exchange) and was saved in a data file (*.dat). Later downloads were also appended to the same file. The PowerGen was the other software utility used to build personalised settings as per the requirements.

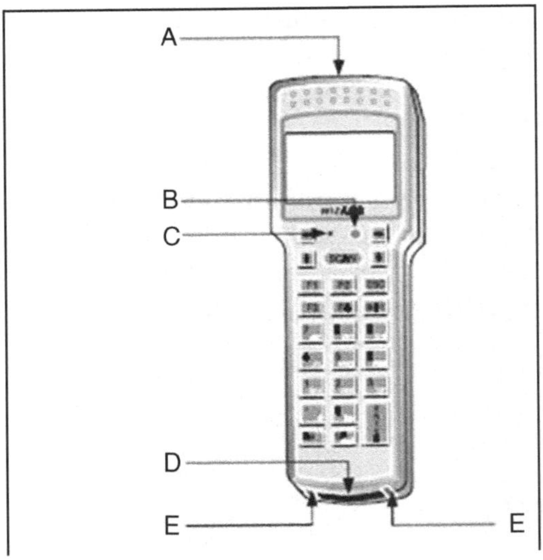

Fig 10.2 Datalogic Formula 732 Wizard Terminal

Notes:

A. Laser beam output window

B. Two colour LED

C. Reset key (shielded)

D. Cradle communications window

E. Contacts for battery recharging

Each document was scanned and stamped (month and year) manually at the inside back cover to avoid duplication.

During scanning, the terminal stores the accession number of each document and automatically displays the document number for a moment. If a data scanned is wrong, it can be manually updated or rescanned, and if a document has been inadvertantly scanned multiple times, the terminal simply stores the documents with duplicate accession numbers. The downloaded data in the PC shows a vertical bar '|' (pipe) character after each accession number. The '|' characters were manually removed from the file using the windows text editor. The comprehensive file was then moved to LibSys work file ('wfilexx' directory).

DATA PROCESSING

As the entire collection of RRCAT was catalogued in the LibSys, the data analyses and report generation was carried out through the LibSys cataloguing stock verification module. The initiation of stock verification function is executed at once. This operation sets the system for the big exercise on inventory entails.

Data Analysis

The LibSys provides data verification in two ways; accession numbers one by one, and list of accession numbers in a file. All accession numbers are stored in a file. The system registers accession numbers for verification in the database. After matching the accession number from the file, the LibSys automatically generates an exception case file with extension '*. exp' and saves it in the work file path, i.e., in the wfilexx directory. This file enlists the list of mis-matching accession numbers and wrongly scanned numbers.

Report Generation

As the term stock verification implies only on stock, a list of missing accession numbers is generated against the captured data file. After several cross checkings, the final verification report is prepared in a text (*.txt) file. The flow chart is presented in figure.

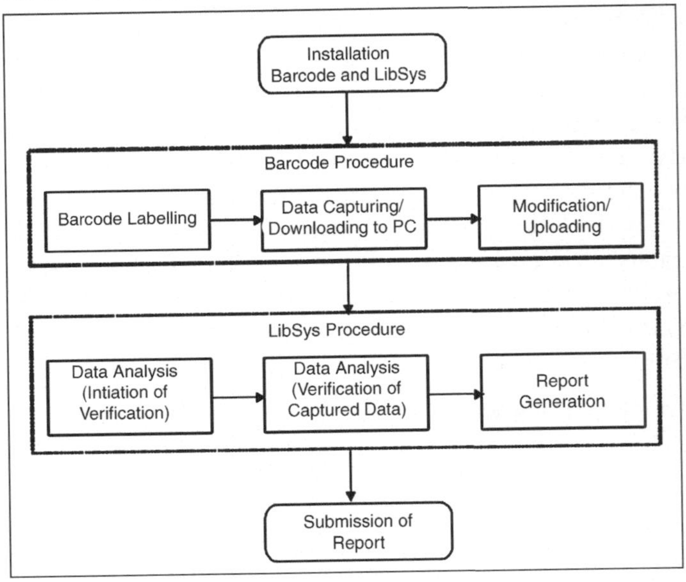

Fig 10.3 Flow Chart of Automated Stock Verification

CONCLUSION

Barcode technology is reliable and easy to use. It improves accuracy and accelerates the processing time, eliminates the typing errors, decreases the costs and improves the services. During the stock verification period, routine library activities can be carried out without any disturbance. Data-capturing terminal is handy and portable, and there is no problem of scanning the data multiple times. The only disadvantage being like libraries assign simple accession numbers 1 to n for books, R1 to Rn for reports, and S1 to Sn for standards (R and S are the accession series of specific publication type). If libraries carry out stock verification for books alone LibSys has no option to carry out stock verification by an accession series wise. It process as the data and generates a report for all records available in the cataloguing module. Overall, the technology is beneficial for carrying out stock verifications in libraries. Since, there is no human intervention, the verification report generated by the system is perfect and accurate.

11

Academic Library Automation
Case Studies

HRD ASPECTS OF LIBRARY AUTOMATION IN COLLEGE LIBRARIES OF GUWAHATI

Guwahati is the gateway of North East and capital city of Assam. It is an ancient city having mentioned in Mahabharata and Purans. Of course in those days it was known as Pragjyotishpur and Kamrup. It has been a glorious city since, old days. It was famous for astrological studies besides the regular studies in education and philosophy. It is covered by 340 sq km in area with a population of about 11 lakks. With the passage of time, the city is also trying to develop its educational scenario by adopting the latest techniques in this field as far as possible. However, due to different factors, such as geographical isolation, political situation, insurgency problem there has not been much improvement as compared to other cities of India.

COLLEGE OF GUWAHATI CITY

At present the city of Guwahati has a total number of 20 colleges including deficit and non-deficit colleges. Besides there are a good number of junior colleges, law colleges, B.Ed. colleges, technical colleges, which has not been taken into consideration in this study. The colleges under study are shown below which are arranged according to their year of establishment. From the table, it is seen that some colleges are very old while some are newly established. Cotton College established in 1901 is the oldest while West Guwahati Commerce College was established in the year 1992. Out of 20 colleges, 6 college libraries are named on the great legendary of Assam.

Table 11.1 Name of College Library with Year of Establishment

S. No.	Name of College	Year of Estd.	Name of Library
1.	Cotton College	1901	Dr Surya Kumar Bhuyan Library
2.	Handique Girls' College	1938	Handique Girls' College Library
3.	B.Borooah College	1943	Hem Barua Library
4.	Pragjyotish College	1954	Pandit Tirthanath Sarma Library
5.	Arya Vidyapith College	1958	Arya Vidyapith College Library
6.	K K Handiqui Sanskrit College	1960	K K Handiqui Sanskrit College Library
7.	Gauhati Commerce College	1962	Dr Brinchi Kumar Baruah Library
8.	Pandu College	1962	Pandu College Library
9.	North Guwahati College	1962	North Guwahati College Library
10.	Gauhati College	1964	Surabala Bardoloi Memorial Library
11.	Lalit Chandra Bharali College	1971	Lalit Chandra Bharali College Library
12.	KRB Girls' College	1971	KRB Girls' College Library
13.	Kanya Mahavidyalaya	1977	Kanya Mahavidyalaya Library
14.	R G Baruah College	1978	R G Baruah College Library
15.	Dispur College	1978	Dispur College Library
16.	K C Das Commerce College	1983	K C Das Commerce College Library
17.	S B Deorah College	1986	S B Deorah College Library
18.	Karmashree Hiteswar Saikia College	1988	Dandeswar Gogoi Memorial Library

(Contd...)

19.	Narengi Anchalik Mahavidyalaya	1991	Narengi Anchalik Mahavidyalaya Library
20.	West Guwahati Commerce College	1992	West Guwahati Commerce College Library

The colleges of Guwahati city are offering all the Stream of Gauhati University, *i.e.*, arts, science and commerce.

Collection of the Libraries

Collections of any type of library reflect the types of services offered by the library to its reader. A balance collection selected on a judicious basis is a must to offer the appropriate service by the library. The college libraries have to acquire a wide variety of learning materials both in printed and non-printed forms. The table shows the collection of different college libraries of Guwahati. It reveals that the collection of Cotton College has highest collection and Karmashree Hiteswar Saikia College has the least collection. The table further reveals that 5 colleges are having CD-ROMs, DVD-ROMs, VCD, etc.

Table 11.2 Collections

S. No.	Name of College	Collections		
		Printed	Non-Printed	Total
1.	Cotton College	119114	–	119114
2.	Handique Girls' College	38000	–	38000
3.	B.Borooah College	37000	20	37020
4.	Pragjyotish College	52100	–	52100
5.	Arya Vidyapith College	41065	45	41110
6.	K K Handiqui Sanskrit College	8680	–	8680
7.	Gauhati Commerce College	38499	–	38499
8.	Pandu College	35625	216	35841
9.	North Guwahati College	25897	–	25897
10.	Gauhati College	32000	–	32000
11.	L C B College	12800	–	12800
12.	KRB Girls' College	6935	–	6935
13.	Kanya Mahavidyalaya	16271	–	16271
14.	R G Baruah College	8684	–	8684
15.	Dispur College	10000	–	10000

(Contd...)

16.	K C Das Commerce College	11500	120	11620
17.	S B Deorah College	6500	25	6525
18.	Karmashree Hiteswar Saikia College	2540	–	2540
19.	Narengi Anchalik Mahavidyalaya	4200	–	4200
20.	West Guwahati Commerce College	3820	–	3820

LIBRARY SERVICES

The colleges under the studies are having library facilities of different levels. The traditional services such as issue and return and reference service being common to most of the colleges a few of them are initiating the library automation to provide different modern information services to the users. The table reveals the different services being offered by the colleges of Guwahati.

Table 11.3 Services of College Libraries

Sl No.	Name of College	User Education	Circulation service	Reference Service	Internet	Bibliography/Doc/ Book Bank	CAS	SDI	Reprography
1.	Arya Vidyapith College	Yes	Yes	Yes	–	–	–	–	Yes
2.	B. Borocah College	Yes	Yes	Yes	Yes	–	–	–	Yes
3.	Cotton College	Yes	Yes	Yes	Yes	Bibl	–	–	Yes
4.	Dispur College	Yes	Yes	Yes	–	–	–	–	Yes
5.	Guwahati College	–	Yes	Yes	Yes	–	–	–	Yes
6.	Guwahati Commece College	–	Yes	Yes	–	–	–	–	Yes
7.	Handique Girls' College	Yes	Yes	Yes	–	–	–	Yes	Yes
8.	K C Das Commerce College	Yes	Yes	Yes	Yes	Bibl, Ind, Abs, Book, Bk	–	–	–
9.	K K Handiqui Sanskrit College	Yes	Yes	Yes	–	–	–	–	Yes
10.	Kanya Mahavidyalaya	–	Yes	–	–	–	–	–	–
11.	Karmashree Hiteswar Saikia College	–	Yes	Yes	–	–	–	–	–
12.	KRB Girls' College	–	Yes	Yes	–	–	–	–	Yes
13.	Lalit Chandra Bharali College	–	Yes	Yes	–	–	–	–	Yes
14.	Narengi Anchalik Mahavidyalaya	–	Yes	Yes	–	–	–	–	–
15.	North Guwahati College	Yes	Yes	Yes	–	–	–	–	Yes
16.	Pandu College	Yes	Yes	Yes	Yes	Bibl	Yes	Yes	Yes
17.	Pragjyotish College	Yes	Yes	Yes	–	Book bk	–	–	Yes
18.	R G Baruah College	–	Yes	Yes	–	–	–	–	–
19.	S B Deorah College	Yes	Yes	Yes	Yes	–	Yes	Yes	Yes
20.	West Guwahati Commerce College	–	Yes	–	–	–	–	–	–

LIBRARY AUTOMATION

Library Automation may be defined in simple sense as a process of mechanisation of library operations, which are of routine and repetitive in nature. This covers usually all the housekeeping operations, acquisition, serial control, cataloguing, circulation, reference, etc. Library Automation is a process that brought and will continue to bring profound changes to the library world, in terms of both technology and the involvement of people. Library automation refers to the processing of routine clerical function of the library with the assistance of computer or other mechanised or automation equipments. Actually it is nothing but the application of computer to the library operation.

Table 11.4 Automation Status of Libraries

S. No.	Name of College	Fully Automated	Partiallty Automated	Not Automated	Year of Automation
1.	Arya Vidyapith College	–	Yes	–	2007
2.	B. Borooah College	Yes	–	–	2002
3.	Cotton College	–	Yes	–	2002
4.	Dispur College	–	Yes	–	–
5.	Guwahati College	–	–	Yes	–
6.	Guwahati Commerce College	–	Yes	–	2004
7.	Handique Girls' College	–	Yes	–	2004
8.	K C Das Commerce College	Yes	–	–	2004
9.	K K Handiqui Sanskrit College	–	–	Yes	–
10.	Kanya Mahavidyalaya	–	–	Yes	–
11.	Karmashree Hiteswar Saikia College	–	–	Yes	–
12.	KRB Girls' College	–	–	Yes	–
13.	Lalit Chandra Bharali College	–	Yes	–	2006
14.	Narengi Anchalik Mahavidyalaya	–	–	Yes	–
15.	North Guwahati College	–	–	Yes	–
16.	Pandu College	Yes	–	–	1999
17.	Pragjyotish College	–	Yes	–	2003
18.	R G Baruah College	–	–	Yes	–
19.	S B Deorah College	–	Yes	–	2003
20.	West Guwahati Commerce College	–	–	Yes	–

Automation of academic libraries in Assam is a recent phenomenon. Pandu College started the library automation in 1999, which was followed by B. Boarooah College in 2002.

In the same year Cotton College also initiated library automation followed by Pragjyotish College in 2003. The table gives a clear picture of automation status of college libraries of Guwahati. From the table it is clear that only 3 colleges have fully automated, 8 colleges have partially automated while 9 colleges are yet to start automation services.

Library Software

Table 11.5 Library Software

Sl No.	Name of College	Library software used
1.	Arya Vidyapith College	SOUL
2.	B.Borooah College	SOUL
3.	Cotton College	SOUL
4.	Dispur College	Third Eye Library Management
5.	Gauhati College	SOUL
6.	Gauhati Commerce College	SOUL
7.	Handique Girls' College	SOUL
8.	K C Das Commerce College	SOUL
9.	K K Handiqui Sanskrit College	–
10.	Kanya Mahavidyalaya	–
11.	Karmashree Hiteswar Saikia College	–
12.	KRB Girls' College	–
13.	Lalit Chandra Bharali College	SOUL
14.	Narengi Anchalik Mahavidyalaya	–
15.	North Guwahati College	–
16.	Pandu College	SOUL
17.	Pragjyotish College	Third Eye Library Management
18.	R G Baruah College	SOUL
19.	S B Deorah College	SOUL
20.	West Guwahati Commerce College	–

Software packages are brain of the hardware system, which runs the system as well as helps in particular assignment. In the field of Library and Information Science, though there is a good number of library software only Libsys, SOUL and CDS/ISIS are popular among the library professionals in Guwahati city. The table shows the availability of library software in college libraries.

From the table it is seen that out of 20 colleges under this study 11 colleges used SOUL software for library automation while 2 colleges used Third Eye Library Management software. The remaining seven doesn't have any library software. The study further reveals that the colleges without library software are not taking part in library automation.

Prerequisites for Library Automation

Library automation demands the following prerequisites:

- Willingness of the library committee and librarian.
- Adequate finance.
- Proper planning.
- Hardware requirement, such as PC, UPS, Scanner, Printer, Storage media, etc.
- Software requirement, such as operating system, system software, application software, etc.
- Human ware, such as trained staff or manpower.

Areas of Automation

Ranganathan's five law of library science stipulates that documents of the library should have the maximum number of users. With the application of ICT in the area of libraries there has been tremendous improvement in the library services offered to the users by the libraries.

Following are the main areas of library automation:

- Library management.
- Library house keeping operation.
- Information Retrieval System.

MANPOWER FOR LIBRARY AUTOMATION

Fully trained professional staff is a must for any type of library. The college libraries under the study are having a staff trends from 1-3 on average, however fully trained librarians in those colleges are not sufficient in relation to their work load arising out of number of users. The table shows the existing position of different professionals and non-professionals in the colleges.

Table 11.6 Library Staffs

S. No.	Name of College	Professional	Semi Professional	Non Professional	Total
1.	Arya Vidyapith College	1	–	2	3
2.	B. Borooah College	2	2	2	6
3.	Cotton College	3	3	5	11
4.	Dispur College	1	1	2	4
5.	Guwahati College	1	1	2	4
6.	Guwahati Commerce College	1	–	4	5
7.	Handique Girls' College	1	–	5	6
8.	K C Das Commerce College	2	–	2	4
9.	K K Handiqui Sanskrit College	1	–	2	3
10.	Kanya Mahavidyalaya	–	–	2	2
11.	Karmashree Hiteswar Saikia College	1	–	1	2
12.	KRB Girls' College	1	–	1	2
13.	Lalit Chandra Bharali College	2	1	4	7
14.	Narengi Anchlik Mahavidyalaya	1	–	2	3
15.	North Guwahati College	1	–	1	2
16.	Pandu College	1	1	4	6
17.	Pragjyotish College	–	1	2	3
18.	R G Baruah College	1	–	2	3
19.	S B Deorah College	1	–	2	3
20.	West Guwahati Commerce College	1	–	–	1

The table further reveals Cotton College has the maximum staff followed by LCB College, B. Borooah College, Handique Girls' College, Pandu College, etc., while West Guwahati Commerce College has the least number of library staff, *i.e.*, only one. From the observation it is found that out of the 20 colleges in 15 colleges the librarians besides being professionally qualified have acquired special skilled in library automation by attending different short-term courses, orientation, refresher course, etc.

However from the observation of the college library, it is found that the training skilled acquired by the librarians is reflected only in 5 colleges. It may be observed that simply acquiring library skill is not sufficient for ensuring library Automated services to the readers. The mindset of the librarians has to be changed in a positive way to make the benefit of library automation passed on to the users. Again the cooperation of college authorities also factors for which many college librarians are not in a position to reflect their library automation expertise in an effective manner.

USE AND USEFULNESS OF E-JOURNALS A CASE STUDY OF RESEARCH SCHOLARS

We present and collocate the findings of a recent investigation that have been conducted under the Research Starter Fund at University of Madras, a Project that seeks to bring e-journals use and utilisation of the research scholars of the University of Madras. The results of this study bring a comprehensive detailed picture of the use of e-journals by the research scholars. This investigation is probably one of the first of its kinds in the University after implementing the University Grants Commission's Infonet Programme. The main aim of this chapter is to present the outcome of the research project undertaken to examine the use and utilisation of the e-journals by the research scholars of the University of Madras. The increasing move from print collection to digital collections has generated much significant research on scholars' reading patterns and the take-up the use of e-journals.

This project examines about the kinds of people use e-journals and their information seeking behaviour of the sample population. To understand how e-journals forms and functions may evolve, study examines the current role that e-journals play in scholarly work. This may provide some insight as to how e-journals will establish their niche within a broader set of scholarly resources and how they will complement and challenge traditional paper journals. This investigation applied a standard survey method to analyse the use and utilisation of e-journals. This study restricted only to the research scholars and excluded the faculty members, post-graduate students and M.Phil degree students.

REVIEW OF RELATED STUDIES

Many studies tell us that using of e-journals articles has increased during the last decade and has been boosted by the application of Information and Communication Technologies (ICTs) in scholarly communication. More use of e-journals by the scientists than social scientists, however, enthusiasm for e-journals and patterns of use vary even among field of science. Chemists and physicists use them frequently, while earth scientists and mathematicians see few advantages in using ejournals. Tenopir and King also found these variations that physicists and astronomers to be among the most enthusiastic users of e-journals articles, because of the digital archives and e-journals available and designed specifically to facilitate their natural work patterns. Dillon and Hahn report the use of e-journals with study conducted at the University of Maryland. More faculty member used e-journals daily or weekly than they did print journals.

This corresponds to the decrease in physical visits to the library by graduate students and faculty, especially in health sciences, sciences and engineering. Business school faculty reported the highest use, while Palmer and Sandler found economics faculty to be the most enthusiastic users of e-journals. Speier and Hahn found that among business faculty, finance and management information systems faculty were more aware of e-journals than those in other fields.

Faculty members for history, education, and the arts have been slower to adopt e-journals. Among the corporate users, investment and banking companies or departments spend a higher percent of their budgets on electronic products than do other types of business such as pharmaceutical firms, legal services, food services, or telecommunications. Rudner, Miller-Whitehead and Gellamn found graduate students, particularly Ph.D. students are to be heavy users of e-journals, most likely in their role as researchers.

As found in the SuperJournal Project, graduate students may be 'binge' users consulting e-journals extensively for a short period when they are writing a thesis or dissertation. There are some exceptions—under graduates were the most frequent users in an experimental study conducted by American Chemical Society. Different workplaces or types of institutions have varying use patterns as well. Davis examined e-journals users logs in libraries of the Northeast Research Library Consortium and found that each institutions has a unique pattern of use - medical institutions users had higher use of a smaller number of journals, while users at large universities and smaller colleges downloaded articles from a greater variety of journals title. Differences in e-journals use may be attributed to age, status or rank. Speire and Hahn found that young ARL University Business faculty members reported that they use e-journals more often and were aware than were older faculty.

Another study reported that more than half of the faculty members under the age of 40 reported using e-journals as compared with only 14 per cent of those over 40, although more than 80 per cent of the total respondents indicated that would consider using e-journals in the future. Antoir found that older people preferred print articles; Monopoli found that user between age 21 and 34 used e-journals most frequently. Tenner and Yang found that assistant professors are most likely to have used e-journals (44.7 %), followed by professors (34.5 %) and followed by associate professors (34.2 %).

Researchers in other studies found no relationship between age and searching skills, although the researchers observed that younger users are more likely to browse on the computers, while older users prefer print journals for browsing. Tenopir and King also found no relationship between age and reading patterns among astronmers. Monopoli et al studied amongst the staff of the University of Patras, Greece, found that male staff has frequent use of electronic journals than female staff. Dilhon and Hahn found 70 per cent of the faculty wants core journals in both print and electronic form, but the some member wanted non-core journals only in electronic form. Worlock found that articles recommended by colleagues were more often in print than in electronic format.

Tenopir and King found contradictory results that e-mail and listerv make it easier to share recommended articles with colleagues. University faculty members opined that the ability to send articles to their colleagues instantly as being one of the major advantages of ejournals. Use of electronic books is also clearly course driven-books with the highest usage are those required in a class, and most users come to an electronic book collection to use a single title.

Most college students now are computer litreate and they use the web frequently. This does not necessarily correlate with effective use, however, an study found that professors performed newspapers and journal articles significantly better than graduates. The perceptions that e-journals are of lower quality than print is another problem that may be diminishing as a high percentage of peer-reviewed journals are digitised. Reported that they did not perceive e-journals to be of as high quality as paper counterparts.

While more than 70 per cent of the faculty members in a British University believe the quality of articles in electronic journals is the same as in print journals, this same group of respondents cited the top disadvantage of electronic journals as being the impression that electronic publication is not 'real' publication. Tenopir found that more undergraduate students used the web and web search engines frequently, students are mostly unaware of the distinction between materials on the web and peer reviewed journals.

A nationwide survey of students and academics in the Netherlands found that 60 per cent of respondents in the humanities, 78 per cent of respondents in the social sciences, and 82 per cent of respondents in the sciences used the Internet for study or work and nearly all believed they had Internet skills. Waldman found that 97 per cent of psychology students access the Internet at least weekly, about 44 per cent of the time for educational information.

Lack of awareness was one of the contributing factors for non-use of e-journals. Science, engineering and health sciences faculty at the University of Washington favoured cancelling print journals in favour of electronic only, while humanities and social sciences faculty opposed this idea and responded that maintaining the quality of the print collection is their higher priority.

MEANS AND METHODS

A whole range of different methods with different approaches and objectives have been employed to the use of e-journals. Questionnaire surveys and interviews are the common favourite methodologies amongst the researchers. Transactional log analysis studies are not so common, but they are more popular to study the e-journals as well as digital libraries. A survey method would be adopted to carry out this research project.

In the process of surveying, a predefined questionnaire has been used to collect the necessary data. The questionnaire having questions like personal information, computer education, computer use, Internet and World Wide Web aware and use, search engines, browser, skills search techniques, awareness of the e-journals, level of use, purpose of sue, problems of using e-journals, etc.

The University Departments are spread into four campuses and located in different places with group of Departments. Social sciences and humanities in Chepauk, languages in Marina, life sciences and physical and chemical sciences in Guindy and basic medical sciences in Taramani. Questionnaires have been distributed with equal proportion based on the number of departments available in that campus.

DATA ANALYSIS

The data collected through questionnaire have been analysed using statistical tool and presented. The total questionnaire admired this study is two hundred and distributed to the research scholars of all the campuses. Only 72 per cent of research scholars responded. Among the respondents, male representation was 69 per cent and female represent 31 per cent under this survey.

The respondents are grouped into two broad categories for sake of convenient into data analysis, *viz.*, arts and science. Science (53 %) arts (47 %) and disciplines research scholars having same proportion in the sample population. This indicated that questionnaire have been distributed with equal proportion based on the disciplines. Among the researchers, young researchers are more (45 %) than the second year (22 per cent), third year (11 %) and fourth year (17 %). Research scholars can be grouped into full-time and part-time students. Fulltime students are again divided into stipendiary and non-stipendiary candidates. Part-time candidates are also included in the sample. Full-time non-stipendiary candidates are higher (59 %) than the stipendiary candidates. Very small number of part-time candidates responded.

This may be due to the non-availability of researchers in the departments during the survey period. Almost all the respondents are below 35years old except 5 per cent of respondents are above 35 years old. This is because sample population belonging to only the research scholars. The basic qualification for pursuing Ph.D. degree also taken into consideration with view of, is there any factor affecting the pattern of use? Respondents with Post-graduation are higher (60 %) than with M. Phil as qualification for pursuing Ph.D. degree programme. While study the e-journals use, access to e-journals requires computer knowledge some extend. Whether the respondents had acquired any formal computer education or not have been asked to correlate with e-journal use.

The level of education was divided into four categories such as level of degree, postgraduate diploma, diploma and certificate course. Amongst certificate course level is more (36 per cent) followed by diploma holder (20 %), 7 and 9 percentages of respondents acquired degree and P.G. diploma levels respectively. The remaining 28 per cent of respondents are having any level of formal computer education. Almost all the research scholars are using computer for one or other purposes, very less number of respondents are not using computer. Nearly half of the respondents are viewed that the computer is being used for purpose of communicate with others.

More than half (55 %) of the respondents are using computer for their project work. Now-a-day, digital and electronic resources are playing vital role in satisfying the users' requirements. Researchers and students are depending mainly on electronic sources. But the survey shows that less than half of the respondents (45 %) opined that computer is using for preparing assignments. Twothird of the respondents (70 %) are using computer for their research purpose.

Apart from their academic and/ or research purposes the respondents were asked whether computing is being for entertainment purposes, very less segment of the sample population (24 %) is using computer for entertainment. Among the respondents, only 36 per cent are having either personal computer or laptop. Surprisingly 2 per cent of the research scholars respond that they are not aware of Internet and World Wide Web (WWW). Remaining respondents are aware and using Internet with varied years of experience. As far as years of experiences is concerned, more than five years of Internet using experience is more (27 %) than the other categories.

This was followed by very young users, *i.e.*, less than two years (21 %) and between 2-5 years experiences spread equally in three groups. Almost all the respondents are active users of Internet, either they are using daily (33 %) alternate days (22 %) or once in a week (22 %). A small percent of the respondents are occasional users. The possible places of using Internet are University's Internet Centre (34 per cent), cyber cafes (26 %) and home (5 %). More than half (52 %) of the respondents learnt Internet through self-learning method.

The second position occupy by the through friends (23 %), sixteen percent of the respondents are taken formal training course for Internet access and only 3 per cent of the respondents are through media/ newspapers. The respondents mainly preferred Internet Explorer for browsing web pages. More than 90 per sent of the respondents are preferred this browser and only 4 per sent of the respondents are using other than Internet Explorer.

Google search engine is most preferred search engine among the respondents. More than three fourth of the respondents are using the search engine either often or sometimes. Yahoo and MSN are not in a significant place among research scholars. Only negligible amount of respondents are preferred Alltheweb, Altavista, Askjeeves,

Excite, Hotbot, Lycosand and Infoseek. Alltehweb advanced, Altavista advanced, Google advanced, Hotbot advanced are taken into consideration for identify the usage of advanced search engines. Nearly 70 per cent of respondents are using Google advanced search either often, rare or sometimes.

One fourth of the respondents are not using advanced search, no significant numbers using other search engines. The preferred type of resources among the respondents were been questioned, nearly 20 per cent respondents are using databases often. Full-text publications often search by 42 per cent of respondents. In relation to library web sites, half of the respondents are often or sometimes visits to the library web sites. More than half of the respondents are not having interest to see health related web sites, others are visits rarely (6 %), sometimes (19 %) or often (17 %). Similar range of respondents engaged with job searching and newspaper reading areas.

However, recreational web sites gets high position among the researchers (73 %). The possible difficulties in Internet access have been identified, *viz.*, language barriers, broken links, instability of network, slow expansion, finding relevant, and information overload. The respondents opined in this survey that language is low degree of problem in searching the Internet. At the same time 16 per cent of respondents are opined that the language barrier is in moderate level. Broken link is also available in moderate level while searching the web. Regarding instability of network, high degree of responses occurs on that. Slow expansion is another problem among the respondents of the Internet users. High percentage of respondents opined that it occurs in moderate level.

Among the respondents, 30 per cent respondents are strongly agreed that Internet resources are up-to-date information. Very negligible number of respondents disagrees or strongly disagrees this and majority of the respondents are opined that that Internet has lot of information. Good accessibility was scored high (60 %) from the opinion about the accessibility of the Internet resources. Similarly optioned on accuracy of the resources available in the Internet, but very limited number of the respondents said that sources are

(26 %) are using e-journals through consortium, remaining respondents are using open sources. Majority of the respondents (82 %) felt that the e-journals are useful sources of information. Regarding the substitution of e-journals, two third of the respondents (61 %) felt that e-journals are considered as a substitute to the print journals.

The remaining of them opined reverse. The e-journals characteristics such as accessibility, authenticity, availability and usefulness are asked and the results are: half of the respondents (51 %) are 'agree' about the accessibility. Nearly 30 per cent of respondents 'somewhat agree' on accessibility of e-journals. At the same time very few of them opined 'strongly agree'. Only 2 per cent of the respondents have opinion of 'disagree' and 'strongly disagree'. While asking the authenticity of the e-journals, the result is reflecting the same as in the accessibility. Nearly half of the respondents (47 %) of the respondents 'agree' about the authenticity of the e-journals.

One-third of the respondents are 'somewhat agree'. Similar result one could see from the results on availability of the e-journals. Majority of them (75 %) either 'agree' or 'somewhat agree'. The opinion of the usefulness of the e-journals slightly differs from the other characteristics. Majority of the respondents (82 %) are 'strongly agree' and 'agree' and 13 per cent respondents 'somewhat agree'.

INFERENCES

The following inferences have been arrived and summarised as follows:

- *Sex*: Male respondents are more than female in the sample population.
- *Department*: More or less equal number of distributions of respondents in both Arts and Science disciplines.
- Fresh-hand researchers are more than senior researchers among the sample population.
- Full-time non-stipendiary candidates are more than stipendiary candidates; very less number of respondents belongs to part-time researchers.

- *Age*: Majority of respondents are youngster rather old persons.
- *Qualification*: Post-Graduation qualified research scholars are more than with M.Phil qualified respondents in the sample population.
- *Computer Education*: Two third of the respondents are having formal computer education.
- *Computer Use*: Almost all the researchers are using computer one or other purposes.
- *Purpose of using Computer*: The research scholars are using computer for preparing assignment, project, research and some extend to entertainment rather business purpose.
- One-third of researchers under survey are having own computer system. Others dependent outside resources.
- *Internet and World Wide Web*: Almost all the respondents are aware of Internet and World Wide Web and one third of them having good experiences in using Internet and World Wide Web.
- All the respondents are active users of Internet and World Wide Web. They spent reasonable time in browsing the net.
- The research scholars are not only depending upon the University's Internet Centre's but also Cyber cafes. Only minimum number are using in their home.
- *Internet use Learning*: The researchers are learnt Internet browsing by themselves and through friends. This indicates that the syllabus does not have any course on Internet study area.
- *E-mail*: E-mail communication exists as one of the communication channels among the research scholars of the University of Madras.
- *Internet Browser*: Internet Explorer is popular Internet browser among the respondents. Mozilla Firefax occupies the second position. No other became popular to the research scholars.
- *Search Engines*: Google, Yahoo, MSN are the most

popular search engines among the research scholars. Other search engines are rarely using by the respondents. No much use of the advanced search engines, except some respondents are using Google's advanced search engine.

- *Type of sites using*: The researchers mostly preferred full-text publications, Education and Job sites. Recreational, Health, etc are visiting by the researchers sometimes. Newspapers/ Magazine, Travel and Tourism related web sites are least preferred.
- Internet Access Difficulties:
  - *Language Barriers*: Language is not at all considered as barriers in Internet access.
  - *Broken Links*: Broken/ dead link problem affect the researchers in the moderate level.
  - *Instability of Network*: The instability of network also not affects the use of Internet.
  - *Slow Expansion of site*: Researchers opined that it is in moderate level.
  - *Relevant Information*: The research scholars are found relevant information while searching the Internet.
  - *Information overload*: The same opinion of the above could find this case also.
  - *Internet Resources*: The researchers are strongly felt that the Internet resources are up-to-date and enormous information is available. But somewhat agree on ideal way of communication.
- The University research scholars felt that the attributes such as accessibility, accuracy, availability, consistency, flexibility and usefulness are good rather excellent or poor.
- *Impact of Internet*: The Internet had positive impact on research and academic activities of the research scholars.
- *Search Skills*: Keyword search is preferred search methods adopted by the majority of the researchers rather content/ topical search. The moderate level of

satisfaction they acquired through keyword search.

- *Search techniques*: Boolean operators, phrase searching are some of search techniques rarely being used by the researchers. The other techniques such as nesting, truncation, controls, wildcard, etc never being used by the almost all the research scholars.
- Advanced search by restricting type of resources, file format and period never being used by the University of Madras research scholars.
- Type of Resources browsing:
  - *Bibliographic databases*: It is not a preferred resource for browsing by the research scholars.
  - *E-books*: Almost all the researchers are not having the habit of using e-books.
  - *Audio-Video*: Rarely it being used by the researchers.
  - *Full-text databases*: Full-texts databases are preferred areas of interest of most of the scholars.
  - *E-journals*: The majority of the research scholars often use e-journals.
- *Open Sources*: The researches are aware of 'open sources' in the Internet and World Wide Web.
- *Virtual and Electronic Libraries*: They have knowledge about 'virtual library' and 'electronic library'.
- Consortia:
  - University of Madras is one of the member institutions in the UGC's InfoNet Programme. The researchers are aware of it. But the other major consortia such as AICTE's INDEST and CSIR's Consortia are not aware of by the researchers.
  - The researchers of the University do not often use UGC's InfoNet. Science discipline research scholars fully aware about the programme and using, whereas Arts discipline researchers are not aware and used.
- E-journals:
  - E-journals are using by the research scholars of the University. Among the researchers, Science

discipline researchers are using open sources as well as consortia.

- Generally the e-journals are useful sources of scholarly communication
- Both the opinions are found that Ejournals are considered as substitution to the print journals and not.

- E-journals characteristics:
  - Accessibility of the e-journals is easy than printed journals.
  - Though authenticity is one of the criticisms when the 'open sources', e-journals are considered as one of the authentic sources of information. Lot of e-journals is available in an electronic form, which made available through open sources and consortium.
  - Digital information has an attribute of manifestation. e-journals are considered as useful resources.

OPEN ACCESS JOURNAL PUBLISHING IN INDIA A STUDY WITH OJS SOFTWARE

Open-access (OA) litreature is digital, online, free of charge, and free of most copyright and licensing restrictions. Providing open access to the research work will help the researchers, especially in the developing world, to have access to the research litreature from across the world. Also, studies have shown that the citations for the open access scholarly litreature is higher than the subscription based scholarly litreature.

Open Access to scholarly information can be achieved by two methods:

- Open Access Journals;
- Open Archives.

Open Access Journals publish articles like conventional journal but are accessible in full without any fee or subscription charges. Open Archives are publicly accessible online repositories where the authors or their representatives or other right holders upload their pre-print or post-print articles.

OPEN ACCESS PUBLISHING

Open access publishing is the publication of material in such a way that it is available to all potential users without financial or other barriers. An open access publisher is a publisher producing such material. Many types of material can be published in this manner scholarly journals, known specifically as open access journals. Open access journals are scholarly journals that are available to the reader "without financial or other barrier other than access to the Internet itself."

Some are subsidised, and some require payment on behalf of the author. Subsidised journals are financed by an academic institution or a government information centre; those requiring payment are typically financed by money made available to researchers for the purpose from a public or private funding agency, as part of a research grant.

In 2002, the Budapest Open Access Initiative (BOAI) was launched to encourage science to be freely available on the Internet. To support this nowadays a scientific community can use different open source electronic publishing systems for the e-journals.

Some of the popular ones are Digital Publishing System (DPubs), ePublishing toolkit (ePubTk), Open Journal System (OJS). With its features, functionalities such as easy to use, modest system requirements, extensive documentation, user manuals, support, customisation and biggest user community Open Journal System (OJS) has become popular journal management system.

OPEN JOURNAL SYSTEM (OJS)

Open Journal Systems (OJS) is a journal management and publishing system that has been developed by the Public Knowledge Project (PKP) through its federally funded efforts to expand and improve access to research.

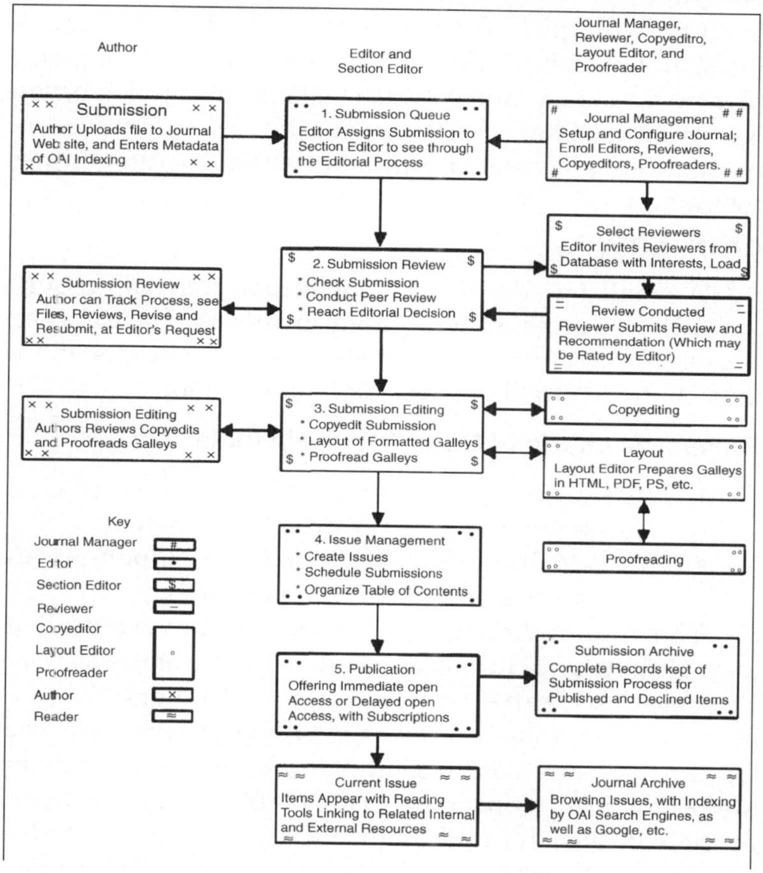

Fig 11.1 OJS Editorial and Publishing Process

OJS has a 'plugin' architecture, similar to other community-based projects such as WordPress, allowing new features to be easily integrated into the system without the need to change the entire core code base.

Some of the plugins contributed to OJS include tools to facilitate indexing in Google Scholar and PubMed Central, a feed plugin providing RSS/Atom web syndication feeds, a COUNTER plugin, allowing COUNTER-compliant statistics and reporting, and more. OJS is also LOCKSS-compliant, helping to ensure permanent archiving for ongoing access to the content of the journal. OJS has been translated into eight languages (English, French, German, Italian, Portuguese, Russian, Spanish, Turkish), with an additional languages (Arabic, Catalan, Chinese, Croatian, Persian, Hindi, Japanese, Norwegian, Thai, Vietnamese) in development. All translations are created and maintained by the OJS user community

OA IN INDIA

A small but the number of Indian journals moving towards open access is significantly increasing. There is a need to create a great deal of awareness of OA concepts and its impact on the visibility of scholarly information.

Present Scenario of Open Access in India

- 107 Journals found at DOAJ—Directory of Open Access Journals when searched with India.
- Browse India ROAR Registry of Open Access Repositories resulted in 39 repositories.

The Indian Academy of Sciences converted all its journals into OA. The Indian Medlars Centre at the National Informatics Centre brings out the OA version of 40 biomedical journals under its medIND programme. Four OA journals are from Indian National Science Academy. MedKnow brings out more than 70 OA journals on behalf of their publishers (although not all of them are Indian journals), Calicut Medical College brings out 3 OA medical journals.

It is also noted that inspite of their online presence the articles in some of these journals are less used because some of these journals do not comply with indexing standard of OA, *i.e.* OAI-PMH (Open Access Initiative—Protocol for Metadata Harvesting) protocol. Hence, the articles in these journals are not easily 'discoverable' due to poor metadata and poor indexing.

As OJS is OAI-PMH compliant, it makes the content of the journal's metadata OAI–PMH compliant which will significantly increase the accessibility of content.

PRESENT ISSUES FACING SCHOLARLY PUBLISHING IN INDIA

- Fear that revenue loss from print subscriptions if journal becomes OA, even as it increases readership and circulation of knowledge.
- Lack of IT infrastructure or the funds to develop it for using far more efficient online means of managing and publishing journals.
- Other obstacles include uncertainty around copyright issues and a lack of management support and clerical support.

OJS INITIATIVES IN INDIA

SJPI

Project in partnership with PKP demonstrated electronic publishing through a prototype and disseminated the knowledge by conducting two workshops in which participants from different parts of India who are involved in publishing attended.

Open Knowledge Society (OKS)

OKS a non-profit organisation working for the dissemination of all forms of Open Access to the Knowledge. OKS as PKP partner in India supports publication of Open Access Journals through OJS and conversion of print journals into online versions. With the support of OKS Medicinal and Aromatic Plant Association of India the newly formed scientific society at National Research Centre for Medicinal and Aromatic Plants (NRCMAP) a constituent establishment of ICAR has launched an Open Access Journal on Medicinal and Aromatic Plants (OJAMP). Open Knowledge Society aims to facilitate all forms of Open Access to Knowledge.

It includes:

- Supporting publication of Open Access Journals;
- Supporting conversion of print journals into online versions;

- Supporting making online journals OAI-PMH complaint;
- Supporting creation of Institutional Repositories;
- Supporting automation of libraries;
- Supporting Digital Libraries;
- Other activities that promotes open access to knowledge.

Following are some of the test journals setup:

- Mysore Journal of Agricultural Sciences;
- Journal of Spices and Plantation crop;
- Journal of soil Science and management;
- Journal of Pest Management. etc...

SKILL ENHANCEMENT OF LIBRARY PROFESSIONALS AND USERS OF SHERUBTSE COLLEGE, KANGLUNG, BHUTAN

Bhutan is one of the Asia's smallest country located in the eastern Himalayas. The total population is 6.35 lakhs. Historically the education in Bhutan started with the early Monastic bodies. The monastic system of education has sustained the Bhutanese society in its spiritual fold for many centuries.

The monastic education system was practised through informal relationship between the master and the disciples. In total 4971 monks have registered with the Deratshang Lhentshog (Central Monastic Body). The development of a comprehensive modern education system in Bhutan was initiated in 1961.

In Bhutan two kinds of modern education system exits namely, Formal and Non-formal system. Education is free for all which is applicable to all types of educational system in Bhutan. Sherubtse College was first inaugurated in 1968 as a public school. It became a University College in 1983. It is the apex institution of higher education for Arts and Science of the country.

The total number of admission at the higher education level is 4373. Out of which, Sherubtse College alone occupies 1009 which is approximately one fourth of the total admission of the country for higher education. It is a residential college where 90 per cent of the students stay in hostels. The college library has over 30,000 volumes of books and hundreds of journals, magazines and ebooks. It also subscribes a good number of online journals. The annual budget for the library is over 10 lakhs per year and also receives some UNFPA fund. It is fully computerised.

The library has ten computers, two allotted for Online Public Access Catalogue (OPAC). The OPAC is also available on intranet. Recently a data security gate has been installed for security purpose. The Library is kept open from 7.30 a.m. to 10.30 p.m. on all days. The average visitors of the library per day will be around 350-400 patrons. There are two librarians and nine other staff members working in the library. Two simple types of questionnaire have been distributed, first one is for library staff and the second one is for the users.

The questionnaire for Library staff is distributed to all the ten library staff with their respective responses. The random selection method has been adopted to distribute the questionnaire to the users and 150 questionnaires have been distributed which is about 12.5 per cent of the total users (both Students and Staff).

ANALYSIS OF LIBRARY STAFF

Table 11.7 Library Staff Details.

Design	Libn	SAL	AL-1	AL-2	LA-1	LA-2	LA-3	LA-4	LA-5	LA-6
Qin	PG	10	12	10	10	8	12	10	10	10
Yrs of Exp	1	19	10	10	2	7	14	3	2	1
Nature of Duty	Overall Mgt	Jrs Sec	Tbk Sec	Data Entry	Barcoding	Bk Process	Counter Service	Stacking	Stacking	Security

There is no Library Science programme in the country. Except the Librarians, all the Library staff are non-professionals. But they have good experience. As the library staff were sent to various countries to attend training programmes, they have good working knowledge in the library.

Except the temporary staff, almost all are familiar with the Dewey Decimal Classification System, processing of

Library books and all other routines of the Library services. The library staff are user-friendly with computers and internet. They are independently working in their own sections of the library like journal section, internet section, reference section and so on. The following table will show the details of training programmes attended by the Sherubtse library staff:

Table 11.8 Training Programmes Attended by the Library Staff

Designation of Library Staff	No. of Progs.	Duration	Countries Visited	Funding Agency
Librarian (1)	1	Two years (PG)	UK	UNFPA - 1
Sr. Asst. Libn (1)	6	8 Months	Bhutan – 4 Philippines – 1 India - 1	SAARC – 1 UNFPA – 1 RUB - 4
Asst. Libns (2)	6	Each 4 Months	Bhutan – 3, India – 2, Thailand – 1	RUB – 2 UNFPA – 1 SAARC - 2
Library Assts (3)	8	2 Months – 1 4 Months – 2	Bhutan – 5, India – 2, Thailand – 1	RUB – 5 SAARC – 2 UNFPA - 1

To evaluate the feasibilities to work in the library and scope for the skill enhancement, the library staff were asked some relevant queries, and their responses are in the table. It says that library staff are getting good support from the management and there is good scope for self enhancement.

Table 11.9 Feasibilities to Work in the Library

	Best	Good	Normal	Poor	Worst
Work Eny	2	6	2		
Job Sat	1	7	1	1	
Rel lib	6	3	1		
Rel Users	1	5	3	1	
Self Dev	3	5	2		
Mgt Support	1	4	5		

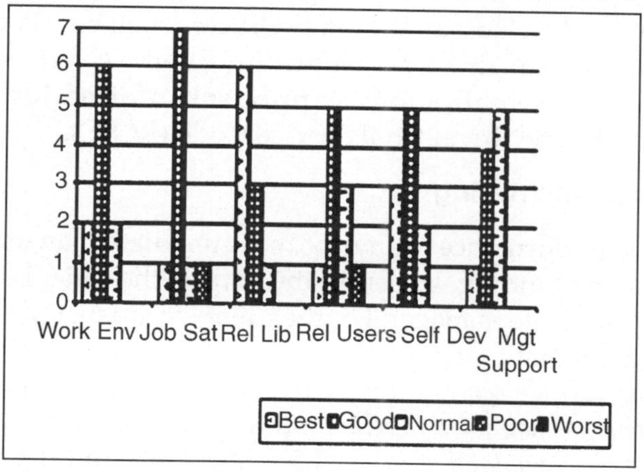

Fig 11.2 Feasibilities to Work in the Library

PERFORMANCE MANAGEMENT SYSTEM

The performance management system is being in practice to evaluate the performance skills of all civil servants.

This is to:

- Enable fairness in career advancement and promote competence, meritocracy, productivity and self-esteem.
- Enhance both organisational and individual development and effectiveness by introducing objective performance management mechanism.
- Enhance professionalism and accountability.

Every beginning of the academic year, each and every one of the staff will be asked to submit their goals to work for the year. At the middle of the year, the performance of individual staff against the goals will be checked and reviewed, and the same will be analysed thoroughly and the grades will be awarded.

Appraisal Cycle

All performance information, including the ratings shall be analysed and archived accordingly, and shall be computed through the use of appropriate software which shall be used to generate quantitative data as well as document of critical incidences. The Human Resource Officers shall be responsible for managing this information. Every Civil Service Organisation shall submit appraisal information when required by the Royal Civil Service Code (RCSC).

Performance Rating

The performance ratings of the immediate manager shall be final and binding. In case of the library, the Chief Librarian is the immediate manager. For the Chief Librarian, the Director is the immediate manager.

The average scores across both performance outputs and core competencies shall form the final rating of the employee as follows:

- *Average total scores of 3.5—4.00*: Outstanding.
- *Average total scores of 2.5—3.49*: Very Good.
- *Average total scores of 1.5—2.49*: Good.
- *Average total scores of 0—1.49*: Improvement Needed.

Use of the Performance Appraisal Results shall be used to:

- Identify and address development needs of employees.
- Determine appropriate performance increment.
- Recognise good performers and provide appropriate incentives and rewards.
- Promote an employee to a higher position available in Civil Service.
- Take other personnel actions like, transfer, confirmation of services for the probationers and assigning special tasks.
- Identifying non-performance.

Managing Non-performance

Analysis of Users

For this purpose 150 questionnaires have randomly been distributed to assess the skill enhancement of library users, out of which 30 were for staff and 120 were for students. Out 30 staff members, 9 are doctorates, 17 are PG and M.Phil degree holders of which 8 are research scholars, 4 are PG degree holders and in this group 3 are doing research.

To give an account of their experience, two staff has more than twenty years of experience, four are in between 16 and 20, six are in between 11 and 15, eleven in between 6 and 10, lastly 7 falls in the group of five and less than that. The staff members were to answer the queries regarding the articles they have published in the last five years. For this query, seven persons answered no as they have not published any such articles, nine members have mentioned 1-2 articles, 6 members have published 3-4 articles, 5 members have published 5-10 articles and 3 members have published more than ten articles in the last five years. Again the staff members were asked whether they have published any books in the last five years and if so how many.

Table 11.10 Time Spent in the Library.

Time Spent in Library	No. of Respondents
Less than 1 hr a day	16
1-2 hrs a day	48
2-3 hrs a day	36
More than 3 hrs a day	28
1-2 hrs in a week	14
Occasionally	8

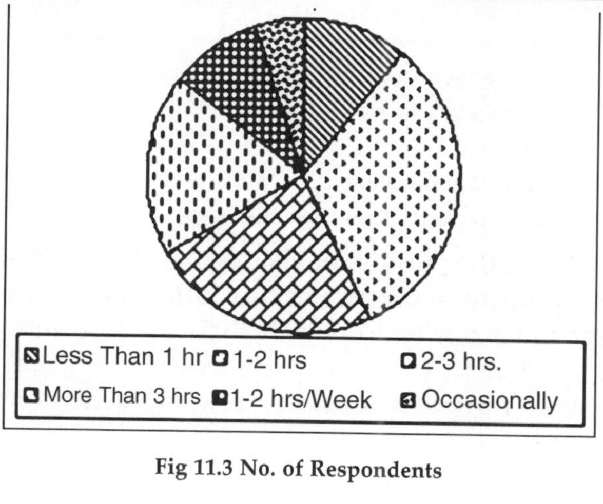

Fig 11.3 No. of Respondents

For this purpose, six members were told that they have published one or two books, two staff have responded for 3 to four books. In this survey of students group, 28 are first years, 45 are second years and 47 are final year students. All these basic information will notify the importance of Library for their skill enhancement.

In response to the query of time spending in the library, almost 75 per cent of the users responded that they are spending sufficient time for potential purposes. Out of 150 users only 8 have responded that they seldom visit the library.

PURPOSE OF VISITING THE LIBRARY

Staff

Table 11.11 Purpose of Visiting the Library

Purpose	R1	R2	R3	R4	R5	No. Res.
a.	17	4	4	3	2	
b.	7	9	9	4	1	
c.	6	14	8	1		1
d.		3	7	14	4	2
e.			2	8	8	12

Note: a. To prepare lecture notes,

b. To get information for research work,

c. To enrich subject/ GK,

d. To get current information,

e. For entertainment R—Rank, Res—Response

Regarding the purpose of visiting the library 17 staff have given top priority to prepare lecture notes, 14 members have given second priority to enrich their subject and general knowledge, 9 members have given second and third priority for research purpose and very few have responded for entertainment.

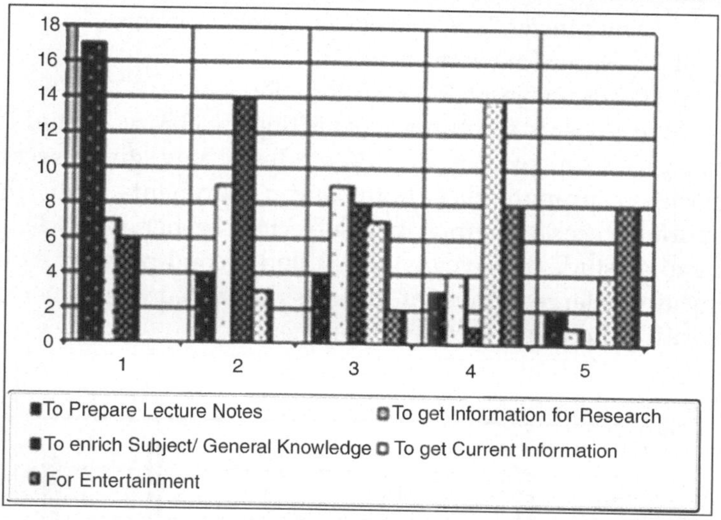

Fig 11.4 Purpose of Visiting the Library by Staff

Students

Since, Sherubtse College is running only undergraduate courses, there is no much scope for research at the student's level. In this group, the students mainly use the library to prepare for their class works, assignments, seminars, competitive examinations for further study and RCSC examinations. Only these criteria vary from the staff on the purpose of visiting the library.

Table 11.12 Purpose of Visiting the Library

Purpose	R1	R2	R3	R4	R5	No. Res
a.	48	36	27	9		
b.	35	41	28	13	3	
c.	18	26	39	31	6	
d.	15	14	22	40	21	8
e.	4	3	4	22	45	42

Note: a. To prepare class notes and assignments

b. To develop subject/GK

c. To prepare for RCSC and other competitive exams

d. To get current information

e. For entertainment, R—Rank, Res—Response

In response to the purpose of visiting the library, 48 students have given top priority and 36 students have given second priority to prepare class notes and assignments. The other important criteria to enrich their subject and general knowledge, 35 and 41 students have given first and second priority. At the same time a large number of students responded with either last priority or no response to entertainments.

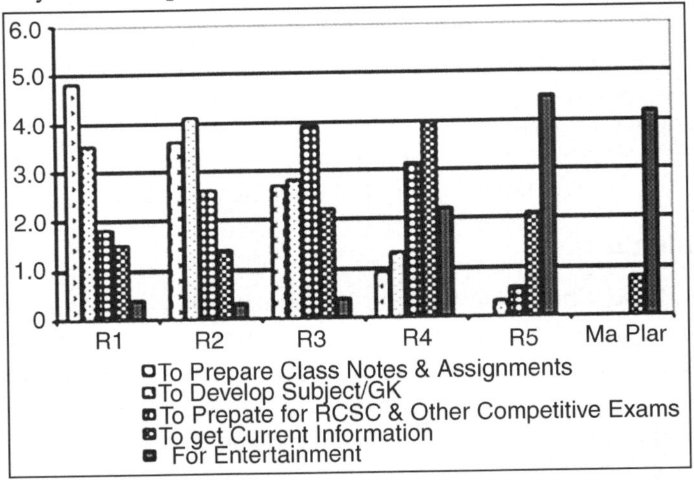

Fig 11.5 Purpose of Visit the Library by Students

EVALUATION OF LIBRARY FACILITIES AND SERVICES

To evaluate the services and facilities of the library, a few questions were framed for both students and staff. This includes the availability of reading materials such as textbooks, reference books, journals, e-books and online journals, also general facilities, library working hours, approach of the library staff, and overall services in the library. In response, about 63 per cent of users told that the library is above normal. However, few members have told that the facilities are very poor, which can't be neglected.

Table. Evaluation of Library by the Users

Lib Facilities and Services	Best	Good	Normal	Poor	Worst
Avail Tbk/Ref	14	71	44	17	4
Access of Jrs	20	75	43	10	5
E-bks and internet	12	53	54	23	8
Library working hrs	41	84	25		
Approach of Lib Staff	20	76	48	4	2
Lib infrastructure and Facilities	23	72	44	6	5
Overall Lib Services	15	84	42	8	1
Total	145	515	300	68	22

Note: Lib: Library

Tbk/Ref: Text books and Reference Materials

Jrs: Jounals

hrs: Hours

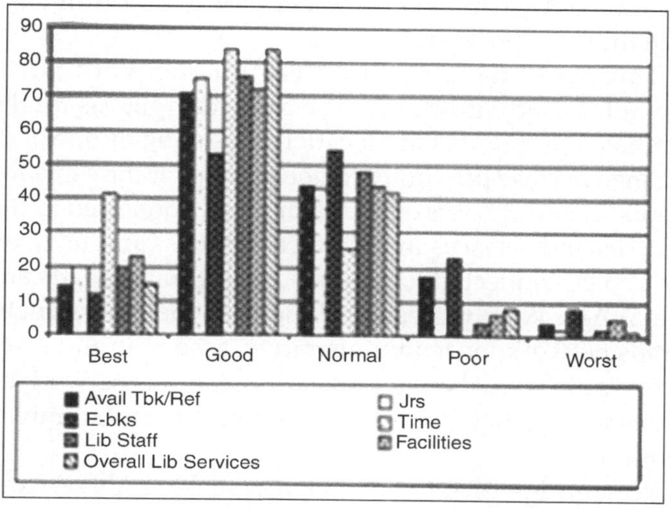

Fig 11.6 Evaluation of Library by the Users

It is easy to understand that the Sherubtse College Library is an ideal place for skill enhancement for both the library staff and the users. In addition, the Royal University of Bhutan Library Task Force Committee has recommended to start the

Library and Information Science Course in the UG level at the earliest possible. This would be an effective solution for the skill enhancement of library professionals for the country in the near future.

CAMPUS NETWORK MANAGEMENT
BEST PRACTICE BY KUVEMPU UNIVERSITY

UGC has launched an ambitious programme to bring about a qualitative change in higher education and research centres. In this direction UGC is extending help to modernise the ICT infrastructure in university campuses with state-of-the-art campus wide networks under UGC-Infonet programme. Under this programme, it is proposed to use Information and Communication Technology and Internet to transform learning environment from a monodimensional one to a multi-dimensional one. Campus wide network is the basic required infrastructure in the universities for the effective utilisation of UGCInfonet Digital library e-consortium as well as the internet e-resources.

Therefore, the structured campus network is a sine quanon for every university. The term 'campus' as used here refers to a main university location consisting of one or more buildings in close proximity to one another at the same locale. All buildings and floors on the campus are connected to shared resources and services in a data centre, the campus network may also be connected to remote location such as Off campus via a WAN. With the establishment of the well structured campus network most administrative, academic and research processes are carried out online, so any campus network down time or inefficiency has a negative impact on the university bottom line.

Secure, high performance, high available LAN services are crucial to ensure that each campus facility is always online, so that administrative, academic, research productivity as well as user satisfaction are maximized. This chapter focuses on the issues and challenges in establishing and maintaining the campus network at Kuvempu University for effective utilisation of the UGC-Infonet e-resource, internet services and for other administrative and academic applications through adopting proper planning and implementation. A campus network design that meets campus security, connectivity, and performance challenges while enabling key IT initiatives is needed. It also must scale, offer operational simplicity and flexibility, accommodate new computing trends without much alterations in the original structure and design.

OBJECTIVES

- To highlight the issues on how the Kuvempu University has planned and established campus network for effective utilisation of UGC-Infonet programme.
- To know the issues and challenges faced in establishing the campus Network.
- To know the issues related to changing campus needs.
- To know how best the UGC-Infonet and internet services reaches the end users of Kuvempu University.
- To know the use of campus network for different administrative and academic services.

UGC-INFONET DIGITAL LIBRARY E-CONSORTIA PROGRAMMES AT KUVEMPU UNIVERSITY

The Kuvempu University was established in year 1987. Till then it was functioning as a post-graduate centre of University of Mysore. The university has started to get the benefits and assistance provided by the UGC through Inflibnet Centre, Ahamadabad for automation of its library as early as 1995. In 1997, the university library has received financial assistance of ₹ 6.50 lakhs from Inflibnet for its automation activity.

The university library has taken a lot of initiatives in automating its library activities by making use of the grants and other assistance of the UGC. Again in 2004 the UGC has sanctioned ₹ 7.14 lakhs and considered the Kuvempu University as one among the 50 universities in the First phase of the UGC-Infonet programme. Under this programme the UGC has initially given 128 kbps BB VSAT for Internet purpose during 2004 and later it was upgraded to 256 kbps BB VSAT. In 2008 the bandwidth was upgraded to 2 MB leased line for better utilisation of UGC-infonet programme and other internet services for the benefit of the administrative, academic and research community.

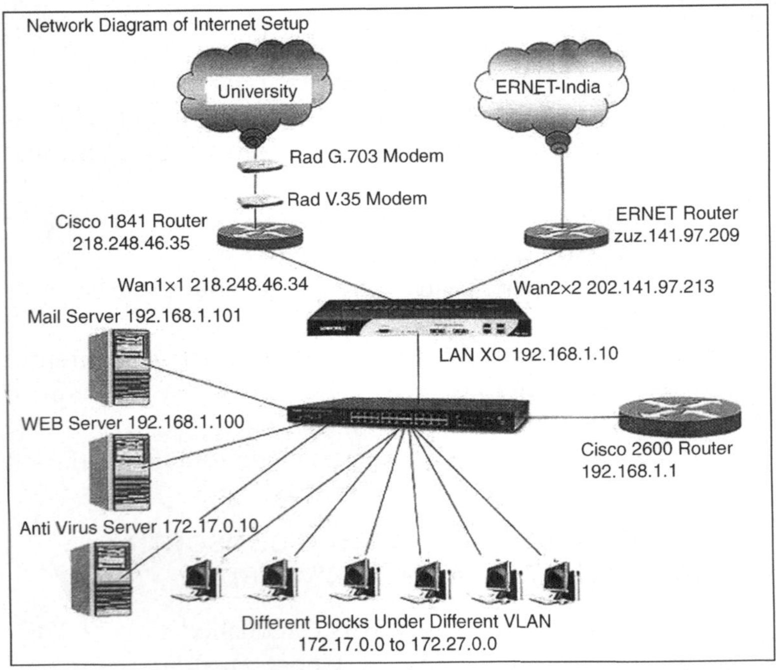

Fig 11.7 Integration of Two 2 MB Leased Line Connectivity

The university library was instrumental to initiate and implement the campus network, establishing Network Operation Centre in library building itself. Initially, the programme was confined to library by creating a LAN with 24 nodes for all its users. Then it was extended by establishing a campus network throughout campus to all the academic and administrative blocks in the campus by creating number of virtual LANs, by laying OFC backbone. Later through different stages the LAN network was extended to the other blocks in the campus including hostels, Guest House and Residence of the Statutory Officers. As for as the bandwidth of the internet is concerned the university on its own has subscribed additional 2 MB BSNL leased line connectivity and integrated the same with the 2 MB of UGCinfonet to meet the speed requirement.

The integrating techniques have been applied to integrate the Two 2 MB leased lines connectivities, by making use of Sonicwall Firewall and is as shown in the figure, for effective utilisation of the UGC-infonet programme and other internet based applications.

SERVICES UNDER CAMPUS NETWORK

Any campus network must provide the following high level services to optimise the administrative, academic and research activity in the university. In this direction the Kuvempu University has taken several measures under campus network.

They are:

- *LAN (Local Area Network) Connectivity*: The entire campus has been covered by extending secured wired and wireless LAN connectivity by creating independent virtual LANs.
- *WAN Connectivity*: The WAN connectivity has been created through reliable, and secured Network Operation Centre for maintaining servers for different application like Web server, Mail server, Proxy server, Antivirus server and Database server.
- *Remote Access Server*: Remote Access Server is also enabled for effective use of the e-resources, and other database service by the remote users.
- Antivirus, Anti-spy ware, Anti spam, Content Filter, and Intrusion Prevention Services: The Kuvempu University has taken much and top priority to protect the network and the data by applying antivirus solution by creating network based antivirus server with a powerfull antivirus as well as the antivirus control at the firewall level to avoid the virus from outside, along with Anti-spyware, Anti-spam,

Content filtering and Instruction prevention facilities also taken at the firewall level.

- *Security*: Security is critical to all campus network services. Access to network and application must be open and pervasive, yet remain secure and controlled. Today's networks not only need to effectively handle unmanaged devices and guest users attempting network access, they also need to address support for unmanageable devices, post admission control, application access control, visibly and monitoring. A high end firewall with antivirus, anti-spyware, anti-spam, content filtering, and intrusion prevention, etc., installed at Network Operation Centre in the library takes care of the security.
- *High Performance*: The higher performance of the speed in the wired and wireless LAN must be provided at all time throughout the campus. Due to the creation of number of VLANs and strong OFC backbone the speed performance in both wired and wireless LANs is good. LANlike speed must also be maintained over the WAN when accessing any centralised applications or resources.
- *High Availability*: Downtime of the internet connectivity either by the services provider side or by the user side is not an option in today's campus network but it must offer at least 99 per cent of reliability with a goal of approaching the level of service. For this the university has taken several measures like opting high end core network devices, Softwares, and redundancy in the network structure, etc.
- *Centralised Management*: The centralised management is very much required to maintain the campus network activity. Kuvempu University has set up main Network Operation Centre at its central library and the library staff with the help of computer programmer is maintaining and controlling the entire campus network at all levels. From this Network Operating Centre all

network switches, firewalls, routers and other security devices and servers are installed and maintained. Centralised management solutions reduce the time and expense required to configure and manage network devices. In addition network traffic can be more easily analysed with such a system facilitating network performance optimisation.

PREREQUISITES FOR CAMPUS NETWORK LAN DESIGN

The following are the minimum basic prerequisites which we have considered under the functionality, scalability, adaptability and manageability issues while designing and establishing the campus network:

- The proposed network should be aimed at the goals of the organisation.
- Set up a technical expert committee chaired by the head of the institution comprising the technical experts from both inside/outside the institution.
- Campus Network must scale and accommodate emerging computing trends and additional network services without an entire redesign of the campus network.
- The adoption of unified communications including voice and data services is on the rise such deployments have a direct impact on the high performance and high availability requirements of a campus network.
- Requirements of suitable bandwidth from the service provider like BSNL in addition to the UGC allotted Bandwidth based on the load and requirement.
- Care should be taken for the network must be leveraged with high end service such as wireless coverage and remote access to maximize productivity by avoiding any LAN downtime or inefficiency that impacts the institution bottom line.
- Security issues to avoid any sort of internal and external attacks.

- *Wireless services*: One of the main drives of better business decisions is access to key information and resources at all times from all location in the campus. Administrators, Faculties, Students and researchers use their laptops, expect wireless access to all of their applications, data stores, resources and services. For this reason the wi-fi provision should be made available throughout the campus with suitable secure to access it. Such wireless services enable users to access whatever materials are needed to support their requirement.
- *Server centralisation or centralised operation*: Is highly opted to centralise and control the server and their operations from a single point. For this there is a need to establish Network Operation Centre to operate, control, maintain the campus network to reduce costs, simplify operations and comply with regulatory guidelines.
- *Upgradation and expansion activity*: The network infrastructure in today's campus is no longer sufficient to satisfy the user requirements. Also due to the fast advancement in the computer and communication technology and in their services inevitably we have to invite and accept for upgrading the existing setup regularly.

Based on the increase in the number of users in the campus and new applications both in administrative and academic environment we have to expand the campus network for effective use of different resources:

- *Survey of the Campus*: Survey of the campus and all building blocks in the campus is very much needed before starting planning and establishing the campus network.
- *Manpower*: Skilled, technically qualified and sufficient number of staff required at different levels to operate and maintain campus network.
- *Budget*: Appropriate budget provision should be made for planning required campus network project.

KUVEMPU UNIVERSITY CAMPUS NETWORK ARCHITECTURE

Three layer approach of campus network at Kuvempu University consists of the following:

Core Layer Level

The Core Layer Level consists of all high end network accessories, Servers, and WAN Connectivity, established and installed in the centralised Network Operation Centre.

The Network Operation Centre of Kuvempu University consists of:

- 2 MB plus 2 MB leased line connectivity from ERNET-BSNL and KU-BSNL respectively.
- Both the connectivities have been integrated by using high end sonicwal Firewall device.
- High End CISCO Routers are used for Leased Line connectivity.
- CISCO-2600 series Router used for routing purpose.
- Sonic-wall Firewall device used as a Gateway and Firewall also used as a Anti-Virus, Anti-Spam, Anti-Spyware and Intrusion Prevention Control tool.
- Cisco L2 Catalyst Manageable Switch is used for maintaining different VLANs.
- Sufficient number of OFCs have been terminated by using appropriate OFC terminating network accessories.
- Proxy server with Linux OS platform is configured and using for campus net maintenance.
- WEB server is configured and hosted with university web site.
- E-mail services is also configured and implemented and maintained for university mail services.
- Importantly Antivirus server is also maintaining by installed 250 users Trend Micro network based antivirus software for taking care of antivirus problem in the campus network.

- Some D-link manageable switches are also used to maintain the Local LAN of the Library.

Aggregation Level Layer

The aggregation level layer sometimes referred to as the distribution layer aggregates connection and traffic flows from multiple access layer switches to provide high density connectivity to the LAN core. Due to their location in the network aggregation layer switches must provide scalability, high-density wirerate ports, and high availability hardware and software features that deliver carrier class, reliability and robustness. OFC-Optical Fibre cable with 4 Core and 6 core used and laid between the different blocks from the main network operation centre with redundancy between some important blocks/ segments.

Access Level Layer

On a campus, the access level layer provides network connectivity to end users by connecting devices such as PC's Printers, IP Phones, etc., via wired and wireless LAN access points. In the access level layer the switches typically reside in the wiring closest of each floor in each campus facility. The access level layer provides connectivity Power over Ethernet (PoE), QoS, and Security with policy services and network access control.

Access Lavel Layer Design Consideration includes:

- Wired port connectivity
- Wireless LAN (WLAN) connectivity
- Power over Ethernet
- Virtual LAN (VLAN)

Campus network use VLANS to logically group sets of users, devices or data regardless of location into logical networks through software configuration instead of physically relocating devices on the LAN. The VLANs help to address issues such as scalability and network management. One such VLAN established in Bioscience block is illustrated.

OPTIMISATION IN UTILISING THE UGC-INFONET PROGRAMME

The university has taken up some of the following initiatives in creating awareness among the academic community as well as administrative staff for effective utilisation of internet based resources and services:

- Training and awareness programme to educate, operate and maintain the campus network for selected technical professionals
- Developing IT culture about the use and awareness of the existing available infrastructure
- Creating awareness about the worthiness of internet as an information source
- Accessibility to Internet Services
- Education and training programme
- Monitoring internet use for academics
- Ensuring the access speed of Internet
- Creation and compilation of web sites

ACTIVITIES UNDER KUVEMPU UNIVERSITY CAMPUS NETWORK

The University has established and utilising the campus network to meet its administrative, academic, research and other activities as mentioned below:

- Establishment of Network Operation Centre to control and maintain the campus network.
- Creation OFC Backbone structured segmentwise Campus LAN.
- Creation of Block-wise LANs and WLANs under different VLANs connecting more than 450 nodes.
- Functioning of Wireless LAN in Dynamic mode.
- Creation of Proxy Server for campus network maintenance on Linux Platform.
- Creation of Web server for hosting Kuvempu University web site and its application.
- Creation of Mail Server for Kuvempu University mail services.

- Creation of Antivirus server with 250 users to maintain the antivirus.
- Creation of database servers on different applications.
- Setup of Tele Medicine service facility at University Health Centre connecting with one of the popular and prestigious cardiology centre in Karnataka, *i.e.*, Narayana Hrudayalaya, Bangalore for the 24 hours online treatment of cardiac diseases for the benefit of the university staff.
- Conducting regular training/awareness programmes to make use of campus network as well as UGC-Infonet programme with the cooperation of Inflibnet Centre, Ahmedabad.
- Arrangement of online demonstration of products/services.

EXPANSION ACTIVITIES

The expansion of the campus network both physically and logically is a continuous process based on the requirements of the future programmes of the university and its Post-Graduate Centres. In this direction we have already planned and initiated the expansion task of campus network to the off campus at Post-Graduate Centre, Davanagere in the coming days. The execution of the task is in progress.

CHALLENGES

Any campus network task that should be in a position to accept the challenges at different levels and in different forms due to the continuous technological changes, environmental changes, financial constraints, human resources, user satisfaction, and for many other reasons as listed below:

- Maintenance of Campus Network by adopting new technologies as and when they available and discard the obsolete one.
- Constant upgradation of the existing setup along with upgradtion of bandwidth.
- Regular training to the technical staff and their retention.

- Recruitment of trained and skilled manpower to handle and maintain the campus network and its applications.
- Expansion activities.
- Effective utilisation of campus network for administrative, academic, research and many other purposes.
- Regular training/awareness programmes to the administrative staff, faculties, researchers and students.
- Provisions for making appropriate budget for maintenance, expansion activities.

FUTURE PLANS

Because of the technological revolution and globalised situation all most all the organisational functionaries are network based online applications. For this there is a need to make use of this campus network to the university's all online and network based applications in the coming days.

They are:

- Further strengthening of the digital library applications.
- Implementation of university e-governance application.
- Addition of different servers for different applications.
- Video-conferencing/Teleconferencing facility between the Main campus to its post-Graduate centres.
- Permanent setup of training/awareness training cell.
- IP based camera services for connecting important areas in the campus.
- On-line registration, examination services.
- Establishing e-learning centre.
- Online distance education mode.

ICT FACILITIES AND SERVICES AT M. K. TATA MEMORIAL LEARNING CENTRE FOR VISUALLY CHALLENGED

Disability can be defined as a physical or mental condition that prohibits an individual from the use of his or her body (either partially, completely and with ease) to perform daily tasks. It can also be defined as meaning that one cannot learn easily. It should be noted that in addition to the physical challenges, visually impaired and physically handicapped people face the ignorance barrier, a major prejudice and most harmful social discrimination.

These difficulties are not compensated for by emotional speeches. Public awareness and equal opportunities are necessary conditions to integrate them into society. It is already established that access to information is one of the most important human rights: it allows the individual to develop himself/herself, and participate actively within a democratic society, fully exercising his/her rights and duties. A badly informed community, or one that restricts information to an elite group, in the long term becomes a non-democratic society in which ignorance and inequality of opportunities will unfailingly lead to intolerance and discrimination among citisens.

All citizens should therefore have access to information that will enable them to be active and equal contributors and participants in society. The World Wide Web provides a great potential to the academic and research community as an instrumental tool that extends the content of the curriculum, enrich class room discourse, remote communication and enhance learning opportunity. It has become possible to connect with learning resources located in libraries and information centres across the globe, and TISS proposes to establish M K Tata Memorial Learning Centre for Visually Challenged students of TISS to access to such learning resources.

EARLY INITIATIVES AT SDTM LIBRARY

The present library, Sir Dorabji Tata Memorial Library, is one of the premier social science libraries in the world established with the support of Sir Dorabji Tata Trust and is used by people from all over the world. Presently the library is in the process of expansion of library facilities by having digital library, cyber library, document delivery system for the

Asian library users. However, some of visually challenged students are at a disadvantage as they will not be able to make use of these facilities.

Since, the institute has admitted several visually challenged students in various programmes and library has only one Galileo Reading machine at present donated by Sir Dorabji Tata Trust in the year 1999 and inaugurated by Shri. Ratan Tata, Chairman, Tata Group. To ensure equality of access to ICT for Lifelong Learning, to Litreature, and for the Information needs for those with a disability, the library had submitted a proposal to M K Tata Trust in September, 2007 for the establishment of "M. K. Tata Memorial Learning Centre for Visually Challenged Students" at TISS Library. Development of M. K. Tata Memorial Learning Centre for Visually Challenged Students therefore bridges the gap between visually challenged and others and give an equal opportunity to access available information sources in the form of book, journal, online databases and electronic journals.

Objective

To establish a learning centre exclusively for the support of visually challenged students which will have computer assisted reading facilities.

Justification and Anticipated Impact

One of the major difficulties faced by visually challenged students is to access learning materials available in print and electronic version. Not all information is available in Braille version.

This learning centre will provide:

- Independent reading of books/journals and library services.
- Computer Training for Independent Access of Computers and other ICT equipments.
- Provision of curriculum in alternative format namely Braille, large print or soft copies on CDs.
- Congenial Classroom environment.

Funding and Sustainability

It is proposed that the M K Tata Trust be approached to support the establishment of the M K Tata Memorial Learning Centre for Visually Challenged. From the current academic year, TISS has started charging the students a small fee as 'Development Fund' to pay maintenance of these new facilities. The centre will cater to the Visually Impaired and Physically handicapped students. A computer reading facility for visually impaired will be provided which reads and stores all printed documents including letters, books, magazines and newspapers in floppy. Even stored information in the floppy can be read through this machine. The user can record it in tape and listen the information at home. This machine is used by the students as well as general public in and around TISS. Library will set up a separate unit for the Visually Impaired students where 10 dedicated computers with JAWS software loaded and Galileo Reading System have been installed.

SALIENT FEATURES OF M K TATA MEMORIAL LEARNING CENTRE

Provision of the following facilities is critical to the quality of teaching and learning experiences in Computer training centres for the visually impaired:

- Computer Training for Independent Access of Computers.
- Independent reading of text books/ library services
- Provision of curriculum in alternative format namely Braille, large print or soft copies on floppies or CDs.
- Congenial Classroom environment.
- Barrier free access to the disabled.

Computer Training for Independent Access of Computers

Today the visually impaired, deaf, deaf blind and physically challenged can also learn computers. JAWS Software for the blind, which converts a normal PC into a talking PC, Magic Magnification Software for low vision persons and speech recognition software like the Qpointer

Hands free, modified keyboards, switches, pointing devices for physically handicapped and Converser FM assistive listening devices for deaf make it possible to train the disabled in computers. Knowing computers would also help them in their education as they can acquire an ocean of knowledge and information from the Internet.

Independent Text Reading

The blind and low vision students today are dependent on voluntarily readers and are able to barely manage to study their textbooks but due to acute shortage of human readers these days, the problems have multiplied. However, with the use of Text Reading machines, like the K1000 OCR reading software, which using a PC and scanner convert any printed text into sound and magnify the text for low vision on a Standard TV/ monitor, or even provide support for reading, writing and studying for dyslexic [learning disabled] they can simply borrow any book from the library and read the same independently and Prisma print magnifier connected to a 21 inch TV or monitor for low vision.

Provision of Curriculum in Alternative Format like Braille Computer Lessons

With the setting up of a high speed computerised mini Braille printer, they can get their lessons of their choice in Braille, even one copy, if so desired on demand as and when needed. They can also carry home notes or a few chapters of a textbook taken from the library duly converted into Braille for studying at their own pace at home. This facility can be extended not only to English language but one can also produce Braille text in Indian languages. Besides, one can also provide Braille print-outs not only in text but also charts, maps, diagrams, pictures incorporated along with the text.

M.K. TATA MEMORIAL LEARNING CENTRE: *STATE OF- THE-ART ICT FACILITIES*

M. K. Tata Memorial Learning Centre has been setup at Sir Dorabji Tata Memorial Library, TISS in 2008 to provide innovative teaching techniques and philosophy that continues to have far-reaching effects on the lives of visually challenged and taking them to new heights of independence. M. K. Tata Trust, Mumbai has funded the project. Ms. Piloo Tata, Chairperson, M. K. Tata Trust was inaugurated the centre on 7th May, 2008 during the Institute Convocation function. The Centre has acquired latest technologies to assist visually impaired readers. For the first time, partially sighted people can now read for long periods of time without tiredness. It is a unique computer reading facility for visually impaired with a congenial classroom environment. The Centre is aimed to provide barrier free access and independent reading of library materials. The Centre believes that with proper training and opportunity, visually challenged people can compete on terms of equality with their sighted peers. Provision of the following latest assistive technologies is critical to the quality of teaching and learning experiences in computer training centres for the visually impaired.

JAWS Pro Talking Software

For conversion of a normal PC into a Talking PC to enable the blind to operate computers independently including Internet Access and also to train blind persons on using the computer.

Kurzweil 1000 OCR Reading Software

An excellent support for blind students to read any printed books from the library to have independent access to not only their text-books but also other general reading. It is used with a combination of a scanner and a PC.

Magic Magnification Software Pro

Useful for enlarging the screen from 2x to 16x enabling Low vision students to view the monitor screen as well as use the add-on support tools for enhancing visibility.

Talking Typing Teacher Pro

Talking Typing tutorials specially designed for the blind with complete guidance and practice lessons for learning keyboarding skills and developing typing speed in a systematic manner. Since, the programme also has a complete display of all lessons, even the low vision students can read and learn to type.

Braille Scanning Software—OBR (Optical Braille Recognition)

Optical Braille Recognition (OBR) is a Windows software programme that allows you to 'read' single and double sided Braille documents on a standard A4 scanner. It scans the Braille document, analyses the dot pattern, and translates it into normal text that it presents on the computer screen.

Prisma Magnification Device for Low Vision

Prisma is a full colour video magnifier with a stylish, adjustable camera stand and integral table that allows a tremendous range of magnification in a convenient size. The simple controls allow you to view in full colour or enhanced reading modes. Magnification is achieved by raising or lowering the camera and re-focussing with the large focus control located on the top. Prisma uses a standard TV for its display, so you can take it just anywhere. The clearance under the camera allows you to write easily and even perform hand tasks such as needlework or carving.

Zoom—Ex Instant Tex]t Reader

Zoom—Ex is a small portable device that uses the new generation Motion Sensor technology in combination with its proprietary Zoom Office software to make scanning and instant reading of text fast and easy. Place a book under the highly sensitive camera and start reading or listening instantly and that too with an Indian Accent Voice! and with every turn of a page, the camera takes a snapshot of the page automatically. It then converts these photographic images to readable text. A book of 200 pages is ready in 8 minutes! Now read it at your own pace for long hours.

Index Basic D Braille Embosser

Index Basic D low cost, High Speed, Double sided Tractor Feed continuous sheet, new generation technology Braille embosser.

Important features are:

- It produces 2 pages, *i.e.*, front and back at the same time; uses Tractor Feed paper which can be spiral bound using plastic wire making it very economical; does not require any special binding equipment; supplied with an acoustic cabinet. The acoustic cabinet is very important for reduction of noise level during printing as well as protection of the printer from heat and dust. It also enables collection of the paper in an orderly manner.

Freedom Scientific's SARA

Freedom Scientific's SARA™ (Scanning and Reading Appliance) is an affordable and easy-to-use solution for reading a wide variety of printed material including books, mail, newspapers, magazines, and so much more. SARA uses the latest in advanced optical character recognition technology to scan text and then read it aloud in crisp, clear speech. SARA automatically stores and remembers the contents of hundreds of thousands of scanned pages.

DSpace Digital Archive

A separate digital archive has been maintained in the DSpace Digital Library portal where all the essential reading materials required by visually challenged students are digitised and maintained in the archive.

Infrastructure Facilities

- *Desktop Computers*: 20 Hp Pentium computers under LAN environment.
- *LAN Connection*: For inter connecting the computers for better management and control by the computer trainer.
- *HP Scanners*: For use with K1000 for reading by blind students.
- *Headphones*: To avoid disturbance and confusion when listening to JAWS by many persons at the same time.

- *UPS units*: For providing stabilised and uninterrupted power supply for at least 10 minutes to prevent loss of data and damage to the equipment caused by frequent power breakdowns.
- *Air-conditioner*: Required to protect the equipment from heat and dust and also to maintain a cool temperature which is important in areas with high temperatures during summers.

Bibliography

Antaki: *Automation Challenges,* London: Open University Press, 2001.

Argyris: *Integrated Library System,* New York: Academic Press, 2002.

Armstrong, J.: *Integrating and Interfacing Library Systems,* New York: Wiley Press, 2000.

Bellenger: *Automating Acquisitions in Libraries,* Chicago: American Marketing Association, 2003.

Brewer: *Emergence of an Electronic Library,* London: Academic Press, 2006.

Brown, A.: *Library: Science and Technology,* Brisbane: Australian Academic Press, 2003.

Bruce, L.: *Automated Circulation Systems for Large Libraries,* England: Allyn & Bacon Press, 2004.

Bryant: *Integrated Online Library Systems,* New York: Cambridge University Press, 2003.

Cameron: *Principles, Planning and Implementation in Libraries,* London: Academic Press, 2004.

Chamala: *Microcomputer Circulation Control Systems: An Assessment,* Brisbane: Australian Academic Press, 2003.

Chambers, R.: *The New Alexandria: CD-ROM in the Library,* London: Intermediate Technology Publications, 2004.

Clark: *How to Evaluate Integrated Library Automation Systems,* New York: Plenum Publication, 2003.

Coulthard: *Characteristics and Experiences of Integrated Library Systems Installations,* London: Longman Press, 2005.

Crabtree: *Availability and Cost of Online Search Services*, Chicago: University of Chicago Press, 2001.

Dorothy: *Introduction to Automation for Librarians*, San Diego: University Associates, 2000.

Elliott: *The Automation Inventory of Research Libraries*, Milton Keynes: Open University Press, 2003.

Fonow: *Planning for Library Automation: Academic Libraries*, Bloomington: Indiana University Press, 2003.

Jackson: *Library Automation: Planning and Implementation*, New York: Cambridge University, 2000.

Kemmis: *Library Automation Using RFID*, Victoria: Deakin University, 2003.

Kuhn: *Library Automation: A Feasibility Study*, Chicago: University of Chicago Press, 2001.

Lakatos: *Standards in Library Automation and Networking*, London: Cambridge University Press, 2003.

McTaggart: *Library Automation and Organizational Changes*, Geelong: Deakin University, 2003.

Robinson: *Intelligent Library Systems*, Oxford: Pergamon Press, 2003.

Senge: *Trends in Library Automation*, San Diego: University Associates, 2000.

Steier: *Selection Criteria for Library Automation Software*, London: Cambridge University Press, 2005.

Winter: *Library Automation Proposal*, London: Falmer Press, 2002.

Index